Intensive Transactional
Analysis Psychothera

Intensive Transactional Analysis Psychotherapy: An Integrated Model (ITAP) introduces a new approach of psychotherapy. Based on psychodynamic foundations, the ITAP integrates the most recent trends in short-term dynamic psychotherapy and Transactional Analysis. This book develops an innovative, clear, and complete clinical model of ITAP and introduces the reader, step-by-step, to the theoretical basis underlying the technique of this intervention.

The authors introduce the therapeutic procedure by bringing together the theory with brief clinical examples, thereby demonstrating the attitude of the intense therapist as well as which theoretical pathways to take to progress with the patient. In addition to the modulation of the technique based on the level of the patient's suffering, there is also a systematic examination of which cases should be treated with ITAP, and in what way.

Intensive Transactional Analysis Psychotherapy is a therapy which can be easily used by all therapists, and this book will be of great interest to Transactional Analysis therapists and other therapists interested in Transactional Analysis and short-term dynamic psychotherapy.

Marco Sambin is a Full Professor of Clinical Psychology at the University of Padua, a CTA-P, and Director of CPD – Centre of Dynamic Psychology, School of Specialisation in Psychotherapy. He is a past Vice-President Research and Innovation ITAA.

Francesco Scottà is a psychologist, a psychotherapist, and a CTA trainee. He is a teacher and a collaborator at CPD – Centre of Dynamic Psychology, School of Specialisation in Psychotherapy. He works privately as a psychotherapist.

"In the sphere of current psychotherapeutic conception, open to an integrated vision, this text offers methodological solidity, geometric rigour and useful clinical references."

Dolores Munari Poda – Eric Berne Memorial Award 2009

"I read Marco and Francesco's book with enthusiasm. A refreshing blast of novelty in the world of modern Transactional Analysis: a manual focused on themes of brief psychotherapy with reference to issues of diagnosis and research. It also constitutes an important alternative to Goulding's redecisional theory."

Michele Novellino – Eric Berne Memorial Award 2003

"Among the main rules of Eric Berne's San Francisco Seminars, since the 1950s, there was one that said: 'Cure patients faster'.

This was an idea that accompanied the founder of Transactional Analysis from the very beginning of his theoretical development until the end of his life. In his last article, published posthumous, he stated: 'There's only one paper to write which is called How To Cure Patients – that's the only paper that's really worth writing if you're really going to do your job.'

This phrase of Berne could legitimately had been the title of this book, which is clearly and firmly devoted to curing the patients as fast as possible, anchored in the pragmatic approach of TA and in its psychodynamic roots. It fully resounds of Eric Berne's legacy: he would probably be proud of it, and I'm personally happy to hear the voice of the master echoing in this new, up-to-date book."

Marco Mazzetti – Eric Berne Memorial Award 2012

"Agile and intensive like the theoretical model it presents, in keeping with the effectiveness endeavours of video-informed psychotherapy. Sambin & Scottà provide a new scientific approach to the anatomy of therapeutic interaction. With an eye to earth and one to the sky, classical and innovative."

Ferruccio Osimo (one of the leading figures in Short-term Psychodynamic Psychotherapy)

Intensive Transactional Analysis Psychotherapy

An Integrated Model

Marco Sambin and Francesco Scottà

With Enrico Benelli, Irene Messina, and Davide Facchin

LONDON AND NEW YORK

First published 2018
by Routledge
2 Park Square, Milton Park, Abingdon, Oxon OX14 4RN

and by Routledge
711 Third Avenue, New York, NY 10017

Routledge is an imprint of the Taylor & Francis Group, an informa business

British Library Cataloguing-in-Publication Data
A catalogue record for this book is available from the British Library

Library of Congress Cataloging-in-Publication Data
Names: Sambin, Marco, author.
Title: Intensive transactional analysis psychotherapy : an integrated model
    / Marco Sambin and Francesco Scottà.
Description: Milton Park, Abingdon, Oxon ; New York, NY : Routledge,
    2018. | Includes bibliographical references.
Identifiers: LCCN 2017060255 | ISBN 9781138303676 (hbk) |
    ISBN 9781138303683 (pbk) | ISBN 9780203730850 (ebk) |
    ISBN 9781351398589 (web) | ISBN 9781351398572 (epub) |
    ISBN 9781351398565 (mobipocket)
Subjects: LCSH: Transactional analysis. | Psychotherapy.
Classification: LCC RC489.T7 S26 2018 | DDC 616.89/145—dc23
LC record available at https://lccn.loc.gov/2017060255

ISBN: 978-1-138-30367-6 (hbk)
ISBN: 978-1-138-30368-3 (pbk)
ISBN: 978-0-203-73085-0 (ebk)

Typeset in Times New Roman
by Apex CoVantage, LLC

Printed and bound by CPI Group (UK) Ltd, Croydon, CR0 4YY

Contents

Preface

Transactional Analysis (TA) is traditionally a humanistic psychotherapy; however, in this volume Marco Sambin and Francesco Scottà present a version of TA which is fiercely psychodynamic and they outline their own creative synthesis of short-term psychodynamic psychotherapy and transactional analysis.

The book begins with a succinct summary of the history of brief psychodynamic therapies, noting key theorists along the way. Sambin and Scottà then outline the central theoretical constructs that underpin their theoretical model. There is an elegance and efficiency in the theories presented, which also allow for working with complexity in the therapeutic arena. The book is liberally illustrated with helpful diagrammatic schema which enable the reader to make sense of the theory and process that the authors present.

Sambin and Scottà explore how to analyze the client's thoughts, feelings, and means of communication and how to approach these as a point of access to the client's unconscious. They present their thoughts on the nature and structure of the therapeutic alliance and provide a detailed exploration of the enormous range of observable cues that may shed light on some of what the client is experiencing on a moment-by-moment basis. The approach of paying attention to bodily indicators of the emergence of unconscious material is grounded in the theory of short-term psychodynamic psychotherapy, but is one which also has a place within TA. Eric Berne, the originator of TA placed great emphasis on the importance of close observation of the client and of noticing physical indicators that may provide a means of exploring the client's internal world. I invite you, the reader, to pay close attention to these, and perhaps they will help you become a more perceptive observer of people and their processes.

The authors propose that the ideal therapist stance is an active one, where the therapist is relentless in their pursuit of the therapeutic aims. The psychodynamic aims of Intensive Transactional Analysis Psychotherapy (ITAP) can perhaps be loosely summarized as: supporting the client to gain insight into their own process and the origins of their distress, and also helping the client in identifying and expressing emotions that have hitherto been buried deep within their psyche. ITAP works with the emotions which may have been buried but which are far from dead and which have exerted a compelling influence over how the client experiences and relates to their self, others, and the world around them.

A very brief introduction to some TA concepts

Transactional Analysis rests on a number of concepts that underpin the entire approach. I have the honour of briefly introducing some of them here for readers who are unfamiliar with TA, in order to make some of the following pages more accessible.

Within TA theory, the human personality is comprised of three categories of experience. These are: Parent, Adult, and Child. The Parent is the part of ourselves which is formed by "taking in" thoughts, feelings, and behaviours from others, most notably, our parents. The Adult is the part of us which is present *here-and-now* and is all of our thoughts, feelings, and behaviours which are linked to and appropriate to the current reality. The Child is made up of all of our thoughts, feelings, and behaviours linked to our past experiences and our history. ITAP works directly with each Ego state and gives the therapist a framework to help the client to access and process emotions which may have been held in their Child Ego state for a considerable amount of time.

When people communicate with each other, they do so from one (or more) of their own Ego states. Their communication is received and responded to by one (or more) of the recipient's Ego states. Each unit of communication – the message that is "sent" and the response to that message – is referred to as a *transaction*. In TA, we pay close attention to how people communicate, not only to improve how we relate to each other but also because we see that a person's transactions can reveal something about their history and their way of experiencing the world. As therapists, we understand that many transactions our clients have experienced in their lives have hurt them or been dissatisfying in some way; also, we understand that our transactions with our clients have the capacity to promote their healing and to support them in moving forward in their lives. ITAP gives the therapist a way of thinking about the transactions that occur between them and their client in the therapy room and a means of reflecting on the dance that is created by them.

The concept of *life script* is also central to TA theory. A life script is a narrative or "story" that an individual develops (primarily in childhood) as a means of making sense of their experiences and of forming their own identity. An individual's life script will have many components, beliefs, and attitudes about one's self, others, how one should relate to others, and what one can expect from interactions with others. Our sense of who we are, what we can expect from life, our hopes, dreams, and deepest fears can all be linked to our life script, which can in turn be clearly related to our life experiences and the many different ways in which we responded to them.

Many readers will already be familiar with some of the psychodynamic concepts in this book – for example, indeed, the concept of the unconscious is so ubiquitous in our modern culture that it needs no introduction.

So, in the spirit of keeping things brief and intense and without further ado, I shall leave you to explore the pages that follow. Tread deftly, purposely, and carefully.

Mark Widdowson, PhD
Teaching and Supervising Transactional Analyst
Manchester, UK. January 2018

Acknowledgements

We want to thank enormously the two colleagues who helped us to write this manual: Enrico Benelli and Irene Messina. Their ideas, and those of another important collaborator, Francesca Bianco, have strongly influenced the thinking underlying the whole book. Special thanks go to Jeremy Kemp who did a splendid job in translating the manual from Italian, displaying courage and resourcefulness, "entering the fray" with us in this new experience. We also thank the whole ITAP group including the various trainees who have helped with the preparation of various material: Virginia, Giulia, Elisabetta (who prepared the figures), Agnese, Francesca. Big thanks also go to Alice Arduin and Michele Mazzocco, treasured colleagues within the CPD (Centro Psicologia Dinamica) in Padua, Italy, who, day after day, drove us to believe in the realization of this project. We also want to thank Joanne Forshaw and Charlotte Taylor for their invaluable support in completing this book; Mark Widdowson for having believed in us from the start and for having supported the publication and dissemination of the ITAP model with priceless energy; Susan Hajkowski, Stephen Buller and Felicitas Rost, who by their example and thanks to their passion, have shown us how to improve the work. We thank the numerous participants who participated in our workshops over the years in various conferences in Italy, Spain, the United Kingdom, Germany, and Israel. Last, but not least, we thank those patients who trusted in the experimental nature of the ITAP therapy model: without them all this would not have been possible at all.

Francesco Scottà would also like to thank personally the following people: Helen, wife and life companion, constant presence, inexhaustible source of support – she has understood how important writing this book has been for me, and has graciously accepted many absent weekends while I worked on it. Alessandro, who with his discrete and sure presence has always accompanied me on this and many other journeys. Marta, who has shared with me the joys and tribulations of growing as a person and as a professional. Riccardo and Mariagiorgia, and my other dear friends, who I never seem to get to see. I also thank my family who have supported me over the many years of my training as a psychotherapist and who continue to believe in me and in my passions.

Finally, I dedicate this book to my nephew Riccardo Scottà. Welcome to the world!

The authors can be reached at itap.workshop@gmail.com

1   A brief and "intense" history of brief psychotherapy models[1]

Introduction

What follows is a brief yet, we believe, sufficiently indicative excursus of brief psychotherapy intervention models. Attention should be paid to the adjective "brief". As we shall see below, there are theorists who place a time limit on the therapy and so, clearly, there is a connection between its duration and the term "brief". However, not all "brief" psychotherapies impose a time limit on the number of sessions; many refer to its "brevity" as being related to its focus, that is, to limit the arguments dealt with thereby concentrating the energy of the therapeutic couple on a well-defined problem in the expectation of finishing the task in less time. All brief psychotherapies, to varying degrees, see the therapist as being "active", as interacting a lot with the patient. Davanloo, one of the most important exponents of brief psychodynamic psychotherapy, would describe the therapist as being "relentless". This type of intervention can be found to be reflected in the adjective "intense". The intensity, much like the focus, is related to its brevity; the expectation is that the intensity of the interventions reduces the time taken and therefore results in brevity.

The model we propose is above all intense and, therefore, it is also brief.

We have used the terms "intense" and "brief" in a generic manner, that is, without taking into consideration a particular context. As we shall see in the theoretical presentation, both the intensity and the brevity are linked to the type of relationship that the couple manages to enact. An interlocutor (we favour this term over "patient" or "client") who is resourceful and has a well-defined focus together with a well-prepared therapist will allow the realization of an intense and brief intervention; in another therapeutic couple where the interlocutor is less resourceful and the therapist less skilled, the therapy will be less brief and probably less intense; in a third couple where the interlocutor is less resourceful but the therapist is skilled, the therapy will be less brief even though there is the possibility of it being very intense. Therefore, intensity and brevity enjoy a certain degree of correlation but they are not rigidly parallel, they depend on the couple engaged in the treatment.

These various properties are more easily indicated by the term "brief" because it is the simplest and easiest concept to measure; however, we prefer the term "intense" because it more faithfully reflects the characteristics of the intervention.

Intensity is related to the degree of activity enacted by the therapist, and this opens up the possibility of examining the following theme. In psychodynamic theories, and more precisely in psychoanalytic theories, an attitude of relative inactivity is often suggested, indeed it is thought of as a distinctive characteristic of psychoanalytic treatment. For example, in the words of Schlesinger, "the whole question of the meaning of activity and passivity (or inactivity), with respect to the analyst's functioning, deserves a careful discussion" and he continues "I think one must distinguish sharply the analyst's relative inactivity, meaning that he does not often say or do very much that could be identified as such by an outsider, from the enormous effect that his judicious abstention from interfering can have" and he concludes with a metaphor, "by way of an extravagant analogy, a person who watches another commit suicide without interfering would not be adjudged to have been 'inactive'" (cited in Menninger, 1958, p. 28).

In reality, the line between actively intervening and assisting without interfering is delicate and depends on various conditions. Discussing them at the outset, without having the direct experience of a therapy, risks triggering a set of inappropriate ideas regarding the modality of intervention.

Instead, let us turn to a less extravagant analogy. Helping an infant while he/she walk requires the intervention of an adult who walks in an upright manner. Human babies raised by quadrupeds (wolves, dogs, and wild cats) not only cannot speak, but they also walk on all fours; children who are blind from birth wave their arms in a way that is different from sighted children. Without resorting to the extremes in which there is no adult to model behaviour, let's try to think about what happens to an infant who wants to learn to walk in a situation in which the adult remains inactive: something is missing, that learning process which should be present in interaction is left to only one of the partners, the neediest one; therefore, learning does not occur with the same natural ease as would be the case when there is interaction with a competent adult. In this case, abstaining borders on culpable indifference or even sadism.

Supporting and encouraging an infant who is learning to walk does not mean detracting from their learning: the muscular effort is theirs, the conquests and failures are theirs, and the new balances are theirs. Theirs is also the desire to move in one direction rather than another. The pleasure of conquest is theirs.

Being active does not mean interfering with the other, replacing them, inhibiting potential learning experiences, undermining their resources.

The same occurs, with careful consideration, in the case of the psychotherapeutic journey.

In this case, we are not contemplating an *a priori* lack of activity since it is part of a theory of technique. Explanations for "abstention", for "the rule of abstention", or for "frustration", are covered by the classic manuals of psychoanalysis, and we know that this theme is periodically addressed and readdressed. This book will not deal with this topic.

We can, however, provide the following momentary conclusion.

In the 1970s Cesare Musatti, an important exponent of Italian psychoanalysis, used to participate in the informal congresses held in Trieste in the late spring. His role there was that of father of perceptual psychology (which he had studied in his formative years) rather than that of psychoanalysis. During the convivial dinners that followed our symposia, he often introduced nuggets from the world of psychoanalysis into our discussions about perceptual psychology. It was always done with good humour and sometimes with a hint of mischief. Once he told us about a particularly verbose patient who made it almost impossible to avoid the temptation to fall asleep during their session. Such was the boring and repetitive dialogue of the interlocutor that Musatti would have been able to continue the session in a perfectly appropriate way even if he had missed some of what was said. What is certain is that the therapy in that moment was neither active nor intense. With all due respect to Musatti, who achieved much in many fields of psychology, we can say that we can "sleep" in the relationship with the other even if we don't actually shut our eyes and have a nap.

From Freud to the present: historical critical analysis of brief psychotherapy models

Within this chapter the reader will find an account of the historical evolution of brief dynamic psychotherapy. It is not possible to provide a complete analysis of all authors. Rather, only the authors of utmost importance will be examined. The analysis will be carried out concisely with the aim of highlighting the noteworthy elements of each model and by following to a greater extent the organization suggested by Flegenheimer (1982).

The dawn of brief psychotherapy

When talking of brief dynamic psychotherapy, we must start with its deepest roots and with the man who laid down the foundations that allowed this form of psychotherapy to develop: Sigmund Freud.

In *Studies on Hysteria* (1895) Freud and Breuer describe elements of the cathartic method that would go on to form the inspiration for future brief therapies. They hypothesized that the symptoms were caused by the traumatic memories and by their related emotions. They posited that if it were possible to bring to consciousness the repressed memories, consequently reliving them and being freed from the related emotions, the symptoms would have disappeared. These aims were to be reached through the use of hypnosis to facilitate regression and to access the repressed material. Alternatively, with other patients who could not be hypnotized, a concentration and suggestion technique was used. This technique entailed the patient lying down on a couch with their eyes closed while the therapist asked them to recall events related to the origin of the symptoms (Flegenheimer, 1982).

This might be defined as the embryonic stage of future psychoanalysis and should be regarded as very different from what was to follow in as much as the technique utilized tools based on suggestion and on other principles which would be modified and refined through subsequent years.

It is important to recall, however, that Freud himself carried out therapies that could be defined as brief. The therapy with the duration that most closely resembles that of the present day is that of Lucy R. who was seen for nine weeks, with a frequency of once a week. Emmy Von N. was seen for seven weeks in the first year of treatment and eight in the second year, with daily sessions. Anna O. was seen for 18 months with daily sessions.

Furthermore, we can add two cases in which the efficacy of Freud's method is reported retrospectively. That of Bruno Walters where, in 1906, resolution of the problem occurred in six sessions, and that of Gustav Mahler who, according to Ernest Jones (1957), was helped with a problem of impotence in only four hours.

Naturally we cannot seek to detect in Freud's brief analyses the beginnings of brief psychotherapy, above all for external reasons but also because it refers to a period before the real start of the psychoanalytic movement. We can, however, take note of the basic and precious contribution to the development of subsequent techniques.

Works by Sandor Ferenczi and Otto Rank were important in beginning to lay the foundations, during the First World War, of the movement towards shortening the time needed for analysis and towards facilitating the therapist in a more active way.

Rank (1924), based on his trauma birth theory, placed much attention on the process of separation and the consequent sense of loss that must be dealt with and resolved during therapy. His idea of therapy was based on this intuition that moved the author towards the use in therapy of a pre-established time limit.

He believed that the end of the therapy represents a particularly delicate moment for the dyad and that such attention should be applied specifically in this delicate period.

Ferenczi (1922), for his part, maintained that alongside the fundamental technique of free association it is necessary to use more active methods of intervention. Furthermore, he emphasizes how within the course of therapy it is not necessary to retrace the patient's whole life; rather we can concentrate solely on those developmental stages in which the Ego becomes blocked.

These statements, which pre-empt the ideas of modern thinkers, were ignored for a long time and, because of the clear opposition of Freud, led Ferenczi to disown his own work and Rank to a break away from the father of psychoanalysis for good (Grasso & Cordella, 1989).

Ferenczi and Rank propose the idea that you can only bring about change if the patient is helped to relive the emotion and if they reach a sufficient intellectual understanding of the original conflict and related transference using the cathartic method that, according to them, should complement free association. At this point it is evident how the active role of the therapist becomes fundamental both to "provoke" the emotions and to interact with the needs of the patient.

The technical innovations introduced by Ferenczi aim to expose, thanks to greater activity by the therapist, latent tendencies that classical analysis would have reached in more time. In particular, he proposes a modification that consists of increasing the frustration of the patient in order to overcome the so-called "dead spots of the analysis" that can only be resolved when patients are exposed to precisely those unpleasant situations that they attempt to avoid. Through the prohibition or the prescription of the pathological behaviour, there is an attempt to increase the state of anxiety and bring the patient to deal with the emotions thereby overcoming the resistance to a part of unconscious material that once more becomes accessible (Ferenczi, 1920). Ferenczi and Rank underline, therefore, the importance of reliving infant conflicts in the situation of transference without waiting for it to come out through associations.

Another fundamental contribution is that of Alexander and French whose research intended to "define those basic principles which make possible a shorter and more efficient means of psychotherapy and, whenever possible, to develop specific techniques of treatment" (Alexander & French, 1946, p. 3). The results of the treatment of more than 600 patients were reported in the book *Psychoanalytic Therapy* where the authors, referring explicitly to Ferenczi and Rank for the theoretical positions, distinguish themselves for their clarity and strength in the clinical documentation presented (Flegenheimer, 1982).

Alexander and French contested Freud's idea that depth and quality of the analysis were proportional to its length. They instead propose more short-term interventions which they are convinced are better than classical psychoanalysis in as much as the latter kept the patient in a regressive, dependent state that encouraged the therapy to be lengthened without reason. Therefore, the regression is not considered to be indicative of the depth of the analysis, but rather a sort of strategic retreat of the Ego, which, unable to face to remands of reality, regresses to phases of greater dependence. A good therapist should favour as much as possible the capacity to adapt to the external world of the patient without excessively rewarding their need for dependence, therefore avoiding leaning on the therapist because they are incapable of dealing with the real world. Standard psychoanalytic procedure, according to the authors, is not always suitable because, as well as causing regression and emotional dependence, it also means that the heightened awareness of the patient precedes the emotional readjustment. On the contrary, they believe that the heightened awareness is only possible if the patient is capable of tolerating it and, consequently, bringing about useful emotional readjustment.

In concordance with Ferenczi and Rank, Alexander and French believe that it is not necessary to analyze all aspects of the patient's life but only the precise point in which the trauma occurred (Flegenheimer, 1982); this idea also forms the basis on which the noted concept of "corrective emotional experience" was developed by the authors.

According to Alexander and French, each therapy should be personalized for each patient by evaluating many elements, including the strength of the Ego, an element that they believe to be fundamental in predicting the length of the therapy. The greater the strength of the Ego, the greater chance the therapist has to proceed quickly to decrease various risks. So, as far as technique is concerned, the interpretations should be commensurate to the psychological capacity of the subject and the strength of their resistance. In this way, the authors pre-empt the intuitions of future authors, particularly when concentrating on interpretations that can be defined as total and as being capable of forming links between the present life situation, past experiences, and transference. Such interpretations, combined with classical techniques such as free association, lapsus, and dream analysis, reinforce the Ego and favour the surfacing of new material.

A fundamental aspect of the technique is the "manipulation" of transference during therapy. The active role of the therapist in managing the transference relationships within the dyad by taking specific positions provokes, according to the authors, corrective emotional experience in the least time possible. The foundational logic of this concept is simple. The adjustment to reality of the subject, transferred within transference, can provide the opportunity to the therapist to react in a way that is different from the expectations of the patient thereby interrupting that relational modality that had been sought, presumably during infancy or a subsequent period, in the neurotic relationship with one or both of the parents/caregivers. If a subject's Ego is met by an unexpected response then they will experience the inadequacy of their own emotional reactions and will be able to correct them (Grasso & Cordella, 1989).

Other technical elements that utilize the manipulation of transference to favour corrective emotional experience, such as trial interruption of the therapy or the variation in the frequency of sessions or using a chair instead of the couch, have proved to be controversial in the historical period in which they were set out. These elements, in contrast to the concept of corrective emotional experience, did not receive the acceptance they deserved.

Despite the huge scale of the discoveries made by these authors, their ideas influenced above all long-term psychoanalytic psychotherapy without impacting on short-term psychotherapy, even if many of the case studies reported could be defined as short-term.

The reasons for this lack of influence remain unclear but, in accordance with Flegenheimer (1982), we can presume that the divide between psychoanalysis and short-term psychotherapy was too great to be bridged in such little time. It was perhaps necessary for long-term analytical psychotherapy to be legitimized as an effective treatment before professionals would be able to take into consideration further technical modifications.

Regarding modifications of the technique and setting brought about by the authors, it is worth underlining what Ferenczi writes concerning combatting the efforts of the patient infinitely to protract that therapy thereby latching on to the treatment rather than on to reality (Ferenczi, 1920). He had already acutely observed how great the risk of dependence was and consequently the great importance of clearly identifying a conclusion to the therapy. Rank himself had tried to find a solution to this by scheduling the end of therapy in advance and communicating this end to the patient in order to facilitate the process of dealing with anxiety and conflict concerning the separation.

Naturally, limiting the length of the therapy in this way, also subsequently sustained by Mann (see the paragraph dedicated to him), presents some limits that Ferenczi noticed. The main risk is that the patient might interrupt the therapy before it has had any effect where the therapist is not able to go back on his or her decision to limit the number of sessions. Furthermore, the problem of resistance, Ferenczi always noted, should be seriously considered because determining the end of the therapy in advanced helped to diminish this phenomenon.

Alexander and French also reported the same two problems, observing how the excessive dependence on the treatment and the resultant difficulties in relating normally to the demands of reality, were either the cause of premature abandonment of the therapy by the patient or cause of the lengthening of the therapy itself.

Alexander and French did not give precise instructions concerning the duration of therapy but, in line with their general style and bringing forward considerably the determined end point, they assert that therapy should last as long as is needed for the patient to get better (Grasso & Cordella, 1989).

Balint's focal psychotherapy

From the 1960s onwards, Michael Balint began to work together with other colleagues on the creation of a psychotherapeutic technique with the aim of identifying processes underlying brief psychotherapy. Revisiting the idea of focal conflict espoused by French (1958), the authors identified as a defining factor of their therapeutic model the identification of a "focus [which] must be specific (not a general idea like 'homosexuality' or the 'Oedipus complex'), sharply delineated . . . and unambiguous" (Balint et al., 1972, p. 152). Therefore, the focal point, once it has been identified, should be kept under constant consideration and the material that surfaces must be selected on the basis of its pertinence to the previously chosen area of work. Once the focus has been chosen, the work must proceed through the use of attunement with the patient and through the tool of conflict interpretation, leaving aside material that is not relevant. The interpretative intervention, thought to be central and fundamental in the idea of the authors, should be prepared through opportune verifications in the course of the therapy which are then formulated in the final phase of the therapy.

As far as the selection of the patients is concerned, a first attempt was made by Alexander and French (1946) through the identification of characteristics that are fundamental for treatment such as the strength of the Ego and a good level of motivation. Subsequently, Balint and colleagues (Balint et al., 1972) specify some precise criteria to apply when selecting suitable patients: (a) a good initial therapeutic alliance, (b) good motivation to deal with the problems identified, (c) the capacity to accept the trial interpretations, (d) the capacity of the patient to have a consistent self-image, (e) the possibility to identify a focus in the first four to five sessions.

The focal therapy had a duration of 40 meetings during which transference was precociously interpreted (Balint et al., 1972). As we can observe, the work proposed is strictly psychoanalytical with a strong predominance on the use of interpretation. The attention on one conflict differentiates this methodology from subsequent ones in which there is an approach which is principally defined as being multi-focal.

David Malan's brief psychotherapy technique

Like Balint, Malan also began his research career in psychotherapy in the Tavistock Clinic where, at the beginning of the 1960s, he conducted a first careful study of 21 cases treated with a brief dynamic methodology. Subsequently, he conducted a second study, reported in various works (1976a, 1976b), that involved

30 patients. This research helped considerably in the validation and study of his treatment methodology.

Malan attributes much significance to the selection of the patients, applying specific criteria such as: good motivation for change, the capacity to establish a relationship with the clinician that includes an emotional involvement, the capacity to sustain and draw benefits from interpretation. Furthermore, he identifies categories of patients who are not suited to such a method and for whom the treatment is contraindicated. These categories include: patients who have previously attempted suicide, patients with a history of drug addiction, patients who have spent long periods of time in hospital, chronic alcoholics, patients with serious obsessive symptoms, and people with serious destructive behavioural problems directed at themselves or others. Within his methodology, Malan identifies in its initial phase a specific focus and conducts, right from the first session, trial interpretative interventions with the aim of "trying out" the patient's response. The interpretative technique is considered to be central to the successful outcome of the therapy. The number of meetings per treatment is, in the first place, determined to be between 20 or 30 sessions according to the experience of the therapist; this practice is then modified to allow a final date to be scheduled, although some elasticity is left for the therapist to decide how many sessions to conduct and within what date (Fossi, 1988). The principal tools in this therapy are the triangle of conflict (Ezriel, 1952) and the triangle of persons as conceptualized by Menninger (1958). The former has at its three corners Impulse (I), Defence (D), and Anxiety (A). The latter has the significant relationships of the subject in their present lives (C = Current), the significant figures of the Past (P), and the relationship within the transference relationship (T = Therapist). Intense activity by the therapist in leading the sessions is encouraged in order to make the patient aware of the impulses involved in their relationships. The continuous attention to the unexpressed emotions inevitably leads the dyad to have to deal with the defensive system activated unconsciously by the patient and the anxiety that such a challenge inevitably provokes. The primary aim of the therapist remains that of linking present figures (C) or past figures (P) with the transference relationship (T). Indeed, the results of the research confirm that the interpretation of the transference bond – attachment figure (T–P) are the most important factors in terms of the efficacy of therapy (Flegenheimer, 1982). When there has been a good selection of the patient and the central topic has been properly formulated by the therapist, the therapeutic procedure should be quite standard and involve a first phase of work in the triangle of conflict, followed by the triangle of persons, and then the interpretation of transference – parental figures – retracing the vertices, above all P and T.

The interesting research conducted by Malan at the Tavistock Clinic and the psychotherapy technique using the triangles remain fundamental elements for whoever wishes to explore further the world of brief dynamic psychotherapy. The ITAP (Intensive Transactional Analysis Psychotherapy), our proposed methodology of intensive therapy is, on the theoretical level, a development of the initial intuitions of Malan.

James Mann: time-limited psychotherapy

In 1964, James Mann worked in the psychiatric ward of Boston Hospital and in the same period he started to reflect on the utility of psychotherapeutic treatment in public structures and on the need to find a methodology that works in an effective and time-limited way.

The central aspect of the work of Mann resides in his conception of time in relationship to psychotherapy which, he believes, has not sufficiently been examined and discussed. Mann, therefore, turns his attention to this factor and in the book *Time-Limited Psychotherapy* (1973) he analyzes this dimension with particular reference to the therapeutic journey.

Mann believes that time can be experienced by humans from two contrasting perspectives: one sees time as eternal and the other sees it as finite. In early childhood, the total fusion with the mother and the consequent sense of omnipotence mean that the child lives in a sort of atemporal stage, indefinite and infinite.

The child, if accompanied by a "good enough" mother (Winnicott, 1965) who is able to "integrate" him/her physically and psychologically, will be able to start to relate to the objects of the external and internal world. Once more, through the primary object the child will be able to understand that internal needs are satisfied by the mother and so will be able to create the mnemic connections in order to self-gratify while waiting for external satisfaction.

This process of nurturing leads the child to undertake a pathway towards the separation of time into past–present–future. The period of growth known as separation-individuation is formed in this way in the normal process of development (Mahler, 1968) and leads the child to differentiate himself/herself from the fusional object and, simultaneously, to integrate the variable of time, no longer infinite and unlimited but real, finite, and mortal.

Mann identifies four basic universal conflicts: dependence/independence, passivity/activity, adequate self-esteem/diminished or lost self-esteem, grief/unresolved or deferred pain. He maintains that the way in which someone overcomes the phase of separation/individuation described earlier determines how the subject deals with such conflicts and overcomes them positively. The author proposes a therapy that has a fixed end point agreed previously with the patient precisely with the aim of dealing with such conflicts by working on the concept of time. The work, therefore, concentrates on the ability to separate from figures of support by overcoming the separation anxiety and developing an internal positive image that is less ambivalent compared to the parental figure (Fossi, 1988).

Mann divides his treatment into three principal phases: the return to atemporality, the emergence of reality, the conclusion (Mann, 1973).

The first phase takes us back to the previously described stage of separation-individuation in which the individual deals with the conflict between total primary well-being and the necessity, with time, to become independent from maternal gratification. In this phase, the sense of omnipotence and the illusion that any change is possible prevails. We can normally observe a rapid symptomatic improvement and a concurrent increase in the production of meaningful material.

The second, closely linked to the first, defines the degree of activity in the individual when seeking out their independence and the passivity from which they have to separate in order to relinquish the total dependence on the mother. Adequate self-esteem allows the individual to believe in the competences they acquire and, capitalizing on their own experiential and learning baggage, to deal with the surrounding reality with the capacity to love and to be loved freely.

In the last fundamental phase, there is a necessary integration of the two previous phases through the presentation of the problem related to the end of the therapy. This problem necessarily needs to be dealt with by the 10th session. Mann underlines:

> [A]ctive and appropriate management of the termination will allow the patient to internalize the therapist as a replacement or substitute for the earlier ambivalent object. This time the internalization will be more positive (never totally so), less anger-laden, and less guilt-laden, thereby making separation a genuine maturational event.
>
> (Mann, 1973, p. 36)

It is for these reasons that Mann decides to limit the therapy to 12 sessions not including the initial evaluation meetings, which should number no more than four.

Similar to most other authors on brief psychotherapy, Mann, before beginning the treatment proper, conducts some diagnostic meetings. The areas of inquiry that are most important in the diagnostic stage include the motivation that has brought the patient to undertake the treatment, the patient history, the psychodynamic hypothesis, and the defences utilized. Mann states that certain types of patients are not suited to the treatment he describes. Patients who are not suitable include those with psychotic reactions, those with a deep depression, those who did not demonstrate a predisposition to therapeutic work, and those who do not possess a strong enough Ego and an adequate motivation to be able to face the therapy.

Once the initial process of evaluation has been completed, the therapy progresses to the definition of a central focus which should be the expression of a theme that links the symptoms of the patient with other past difficulties, and with childhood problems which, according to the therapist, can be dynamically correlated with present problems (Flegenheimer, 1982). Linking past difficulties with a present emotion, which is comprehensible to the patient, instils in them faith in the therapist and pushes them to "let go" in an omnipotent relationship that characterizes all of the first phase of the therapy. According to Mann, the formulation of the central focus should be chosen with extreme care. It should link defensive emotions with present problems in a way that the patient sees as being comprehensible and empathetic. The central focus characterizes the whole course of the therapy by constituting the basic structure. As far as the evolution of the therapy is concerned, you can see, in the first part of the therapy, the patient's surrender to dependence on the basis of the expectation that the relationship will have an unlimited duration. As the sessions follow, they begin to become aware of the temporal finiteness of the relationship and begin to accept, with the help of empathetic interventions by the therapist, that there will be an inevitable conclusion.

Mann utilizes various tools and techniques in different ways during the therapy. Those of greatest importance include suggestion, abreaction, clarification, and interpretation. It is worth noting that patients are not selected for their capacity in accepting interpretations and therefore these interpretations will never reach a deep level (Grasso & Cordella, 1989).

Peter Sifneos: Short-Term Anxiety-Provoking Psychotherapy (STAPP)

Peter Sifneos was a psychiatrist and psychotherapist with the Department of Psychiatry at Beth Israel Hospital, Harvard Medical School, when he became interested in brief dynamic therapies. The model he created is called STAPP (Short-Term Anxiety-Provoking Psychotherapy) and it refers to a particular type of therapy that centres on the provocation of anxiety as a way of reaching the goals. One of the characteristics of this methodology is a rigorous selection of the patients on the basis of the following characteristics (Sifneos, 1972, 1992): to be capable of limiting the symptoms present; to have had at least one significant relationship of an altruistic give-and-take nature during childhood; to possess the capacity of relating flexibly with the evaluator demonstrating the capacity to experience and express both positive and negative emotions in an appropriate way; to be intelligent and psychologically-oriented enough to understand the psychotherapeutic interactions; to be motivated for change and to not expect purely symptomatic relief through psychotherapy. It can be noted that these characteristics might lead to people being included in treatment who are relatively healthy, motivated, and have the intention to commit to their course of treatment. Such people would represent only a small minority of those who access a public service seeking help (in Sifneos's experience, approximately 25%).

During the first evaluation meeting, the therapist should formulate a history of the patient that is as complete as possible, consider whether the inclusion criteria have been met, and identify the psychodynamic focus on the basis of an Oedipal-level conflict. This conflict will constitute the neural centre of therapy and is defined by the author as an index of the capacity of the evaluator to bring together, in a global overview, information on the patient that are apparently not correlated, they might regard past events, fantasies, memories, behaviours, actions, and so on (Sifneos, 1992).

The principal technique of STAPP consists in intense activity by the therapist with the aim of provoking anxiety in the patient in order to activate defence mechanisms. Once the defence mechanism has surfaced, it is systematically confronted through interventions that are active rather than interpretative. Concurrently and in addition to anxiety-provoking techniques, there are also measures intended to support the patient's resources and frequent summaries that afford the patient a constant intellectual reference point (Flegenheimer, 1982).

The principal aim of the therapy is to help the patient to relate their difficulties in the context of the therapist relationship and with current figures, comparing them with past experiences and with the parental figures (vertices T and C linked to P in the triangle of persons, as envisaged by Malan). No precise time limit is specified by Sifneos but it is merely specified that therapy will be of a brief duration.

Habib Davanloo: Intensive Short-Term Dynamic Psychotherapy (ISTDP)

Habib Davanloo became interested in brief therapy in 1962 at Montreal General Hospital. In the field of brief psychotherapies, the name of Davanloo is certainly among the most important and, regarding his technique, Malan writes that if Freud discovered the unconscious, Davanloo capitalized on using it for therapeutic aims (Malan, 1979).

Davanloo himself describes his approach in the following way:

> [L]ike the workers before me, but quite independently, I began to reverse the tendency toward passivity, becoming more and more active in my technique, yet adhering strictly to three fundamental psychoanalytic principles: releasing hidden feelings by actively working on interpreting resistance or defences; paying strict attention to the transference relationship; and making links between the transference and significant people in the patient's current life and in the past.
>
> (Davanloo, 1980, p. 40)

In addition to being a brilliant and innovative clinician, he is also a scrupulous researcher who back in 1963 began research on the outcome of his therapies. Between 1963 and 1974 he evaluated 575 patients, of which 23% (130) he considered to be suitable to embark on a therapeutic course. The results that the author reports are considerable: 115 out of 130 were considered to have a positive outcome and the average duration was of 20 sessions. In 40% of cases follow-up interviews were conducted after a period of time that ranged from two to seven years; the improvements that were noted at the end of the therapy were maintained for the whole period of the follow-up (Flegenheimer, 1982).

Naturally, we cannot but help noting the narrow selection of patients that Davanloo applied: he included less than a quarter of the subjects evaluated. The conclusion that we can draw from his technique and from his writings is quite clear: it is a very active and confrontational therapy which requires a stable patient with enough resources to deal with it. In reality, the author extended his technique to various pathologies including those not of an Oedipal or loss origin, those with neurotic or personality disorders, and those with multifocal pathologies. Therefore, the careful selection is discernible in the type of structure or pathology that the patient presents with and in the capacity of the patient to cope with strong pressures from the therapist. How can these elements of the patient be tested? By conducting what Davanloo calls trial therapy.

Davanloo explains how it is fundamental during the initial interview to not only collect information on the medical, psychological, psychiatric history of the patient but also to verify directly whether the individual is suited to this type of therapy. Trial therapy is conducted in one or two hours during which the therapist, after having gathered the general information necessary, invites the patient to tell their story and the reason why they have requested therapy. The therapist listens and in a systematic, polite, and firm manner starts to analyze the feelings that surfaced during the trial therapy. The strong attention placed on the feelings experienced invokes in the patient defensive movements expressed through escape, passivity, evasiveness. Naturally this does not stop the evaluator who, on the contrary, compares and calls into question the defensive modalities to a great extent. The patient's reactions at this point, in general, inevitably involve anger which can be manifested in a direct way or through non-verbal or paraverbal body language. An important aspect for the therapist at this stage is seeing what relationships the patient has and to be ready, in any moment, to not confront patients who do not demonstrate enough strength of the Ego. If the patient recognizes their own state of mind an important objective has been reached: the creation of a part of the therapeutic relationship.

In this way we have seen that

> the insurgent anger in the face of the therapist can be linked to analogous emotions experienced in the past but not expressed, directed towards other significant figures which, on the other hand, can explain why in the present moment the patient is incapable of managing their own anger in an adaptive way.
>
> (Grasso & Cordella, 1989, p. 74)

In the trial therapy, initial interpretations are provided of the patient's reactions to this first contact with the process, which will possibly be extended to the entire therapy. These reactions will determine the decision of the therapist as to whether to consider the patient as suitable to progress.

Alongside this fundamental selection criterion, Davanloo (1980) identifies a further seven functions of the Ego that the subject should have: sufficient quality in meaningful relationships, capacity for emotional functioning, treatment motivation, capacity for psychological processing, responses to interpretations, intelligence, organization of defences with limited use of primary defences. The therapy devised by Davanloo is considered to be suitable for patients who present depression, somatization, phobias, panic attacks, obsessive disorders, and neurotic personality.

In practically all of the patients considered, Davanloo identifies an unconscious, murderous rage directed towards the significant primary figures responsible for having caused the childhood trauma. Murderous rage that is accompanied by a sense of guilt and pain which are responsible for the activation of the defences that characterize the subject.

Naturally, the earlier the trauma, the more difficult the therapist's job is to deal with a demanding and punitive Superego which blocks potential and increases suffering.

A fundamental role of the analysis is that of provoking insight and linking such conflicts within transference.

Finally, the author proposes a formulation of discharge patterns of unconscious anxiety which will be explored further in Chapter 6 and which posits a difference between a more aware way of controlling anxiety and a more primitive one which is less influenced by the functions of the Ego.

Furthermore, Davanloo makes diagnoses on the basis of the defences utilized (see Chapter 12). The author distinguishes between:

- Tactical defences
- Major defences
- Regressive defences
- Primitive defences

A technical aspect that characterizes the interventions of Davanloo (1990, 1994) is the use of energetic confrontations of the defences deployed by the patient. During the therapy sessions, he focuses his own interventions on unexpressed past feelings in social situations of present life and, above all, within the trans-ference that is considered their true vehicle of change. The feeling of rage and its expression in the therapeutic context become objectives of a circular process of confrontation of defences and the regulation of anxiety. Through the concept of relentlessness, Davanloo tries to interact in an extremely active way as if to invite the patient to do the same during the process of change, thereby discourag-ing any symbiosis or passivity. The task of the therapist consists of exploration and encouraging in the patient the recognition of how they defend themselves (D) from feelings or conflicting impulses (I), which generate anxiety (A) in the relationships of the present life (C) and in the relationship with the therapist (T), until finally finding the origin of the relationship with the past parental figures (P). The transference resistances are dealt with in a direct way and are confronted relentlessly above all if they concern unexpressed emotions of rage. In this way, the patient experiences the expression of emotions that have been "prohibited" in a context of containment and acceptance.

Davanloo is one of the most important exponents of brief dynamic psychother-apy and has given birth to a whole new generation of researchers who continue to develop and modify his model. The most important thinkers include: A. Abbass (2015), J. ten Have-de Labije and R. Neborsky (2012), F. Osimo (2003), D. Fosha (2000).

We will deal with the views of Abbass and ten Have-de Labije in Chapter 6 concerning the management of anxiety.

Note

1 This chapter was written by Francesco Scottà. The introduction was written by Marco Sambin.

References

Abbass, A. (2015). *Reaching Through Resistance: Advanced Psychotherapy Techniques.* Kansas City: Seven Leaves Press.

Alexander, F., & French, T. M. (1946). *Psychoanalytic Therapy: Principles and Application.* New York: Ronald Press.

Balint, M., Balint, E., & Ornstein, P. H. (1972). *Focal Psychotherapy, an Example of Applied Psychoanalysis.* London: Tavistock.

Davanloo, H. (1980). *Short-Term Dynamic Psychotherapy.* New York: Jason Aronson.

Davanloo, H. (1990). *Unlocking the Unconscious: Selected Papers of Habib Davanloo, MD.* New York: Wiley.

Davanloo, H. (1994). *Basic Principles and Techniques in Short-Term Dynamic Psychotherapy.* New York: Jason Aronson.

Ezriel, H. (1952). Notes on psycho-analytic group therapy: Interpretation and research. *Psychiatry,* 15(2): 119–126.

Ferenczi, S. (1920). *Further Contributions to the Theory and Technique of Psycho-Analysis,* 2 vol. New York: The Hogart Press.

Ferenczi, S., & Rank, O. (1922). *The Development of Psychoanalysis.* New York: Nervous & Mental Disease Publishing Company.

Flegenheimer, W. V. (1982). *Techniques of Brief Psychotherapy.* Lahman: Jason Aronson Inc. Publishers.

Fosha, D. (2000). *The Transforming Power of Affect: A Model of Accelerated Change.* New York: Basic Books.

Fossi, G. (1988). *Psicoanalisi e psicoterapie dinamiche [Psychoanalisys and Brief Psychotherapies].* Torino: Bollati Boringhieri.

French, T. M. (1958). *The Interpretation of Behaviour,* vol. 3. Chicago: University of Chicago Press.

Freud, S., & Breuer, J. (1895). Studies on hysteria. In J. Strachey (Ed. & Trans.) (1958). *The Standard Edition of the Complete Psychological Works of Sigmund Freud,* vol. XII (pp. 145–156). London: The Hogarth Press and the Institute of Psychoanalysis.

Grasso, M., & Cordella, B. (1989). *Psicoterapie dinamiche brevi [Brief Dynamic Psychotherapies].* Roma: NIS.

Jones, E. (1957). *The Life and Work of Sigmund Freud.* New York: Basic Books.

Mahler, M. (1968). *Infantile Psychosis.* New York: International University Press.

Malan, D. H. (1976a). *The Frontier of Brief Psychotherapy.* New York: Plenum.

Malan, D. H. (1976b). *Towards the Validation of Dynamic Psychotherapy.* New York: Plenum.

Malan, D. H. (1979). *Individual Psychotherapy and the Science of Psychodynamic.* London: Butterworth & Co. Publishers.

Mann, J. (1973). *Time-limited Psychotherapy.* Cambridge, MA: Harvard University Press.

Menninger, K. (1958). *Theory of Psychoanalytic Technique.* New York: Basic Books.

Osimo, F. (2003). *Experiential Short-Term Dynamic Psychotherapy, a Manual.* Bloomington, IN: Authorhouse.

Rank, O. (1924). *Das Trauma des Geburt und Seine Bedeutung für die Psychoanalyse.* Wien: Leipzig. Zurich Internazionaler Psychoanalytischer Verlag. (Trad. It. Il trauma della nascita e il suo significato psicoanalitico, Guaraldi, Firenze, 1972).

Sifneos, P. (1972). *Short-Term Psychotherapy and Emotional Crisis.* Cambridge, MA: Harvard University Press.

Sifneos, P. (1992). *Short Term Anxiety-Provoking Psychotherapy.* New York: Basic Books.

Ten Have-de Labije, J., & Neborsky, R. J. (2012). *Mastering Intensive Short-term Dynamic Psychotherapy: A Roadmap to the Unconscious.* London: Karnac.

Winnicott, D. (1965). *Maturational Processes and the Facilitating Environment.* London: Hogart Press.

2 ITAP

A psychotherapy technique
open to integration[1]

Intensive Transactional Analysis Psychotherapy (ITAP) is a theory and a technique of intervention that utilizes psychodynamic language while making reference to metapsychology (an idiosyncratic way in which psychoanalysis refers to the theory) and to Transactional Analysis (a psychodynamic model with clear psychoanalytical heritage).

Despite the strong influence of the psychodynamic model, ITAP can also be used by therapists from other theoretical traditions.

As we shall see, ITAP is based on the observation of a basic structure of psychic functioning: the fact that impulse, anxiety, and defence are interconnected. Furthermore, this functioning can be enacted in the current life situation of the patient (C), it has been enacted in the past (P), and it reappears and renews itself in the therapeutic relationship (T).

It is a rather simple structure and, therefore, not very conceptually demanding. In contrast, the technical application is a little more complex and involves various modalities of intervention in order to make it as effective as the theoretical conceptualization promises.

The conceptual instruments of ITAP can be easily mastered by referring to this manual regardless of models utilized by the therapist in the past. The most demanding aspect, while still not being influenced by the model used in the past, is learning the intervention techniques that are outlined in this manual in their basic form. A future volume will include extended examples and cases treated with the ITAP technique, together with a presentation of their results.

Functioning of the person: the intrapsychic triangle

The psychic functioning of ITAP is based on three fundamental pillars: impulse, anxiety, and defence. This triad is already present in Menninger (1962) and is adopted by Malan (1979), and to a great extent by Davanloo (1990).

By impulse, we mean any spontaneous manifestation of the functioning of the person. In terms of psychoanalysis, it corresponds to the manifestations of the Id, whereas in Transactional Analysis it would be described as a Child Ego state (see Chapter 12). In more general terms, we can categorize impulses as emotions, feelings, needs, and aspirations. Therefore, impulses include anger, disgust, fear, happiness, sadness, surprise, as per the classification of Ekman and Friesen (1971), but also all emotional manifestations towards people, animals, things, places, and memories. We can also include the need for heat, nutrition, contact, recognition, sex, success (see Berne's psychological hungers). In addition, we can consider the fulfilment of people's potential: skills, life plans, profession, and creativity. Creativity is taken to mean both simple, everyday manifestions and sublime art.

We can summarize all of these manifestations with the term "driving force". Indeed, they are vectors that set in motion people's existence. It is no accident that the corresponding term in psychoanalysis is Trieb (Freud, 1915a), which has the etymological root meaning driving force. We will continue to use "impulse" to mean this collection of forces so as to be consistent with the historical terminology used in brief psychotherapy.

As we know from our own personal history and from the observation of others, the fulfilment of impulses is by no means as simple as we would like it to be. The obstacles that stand in the way of our impulses being satisfied are so varied and scattered in our history that we can create sense in our lives through the fulfilment of our driving forces. Our life plan requires continuous investment: we learn, we improve, we encounter new experiences throughout our lives – death included. The obstacle to the satisfaction of our impulses manifests itself in the form of anxiety. We could see anxiety as being the psychological and somatic reaction (see Chapter 6) to the lack of satisfaction of the life drive that guides our existence. We have, therefore, manifestations of anxiety that vary in degree, in terms of subtlety, violence, and intensity, as a result of the way in which our driving force and our personal creative force (I) have been obstructed. Given that the obstacle (A) to our vitality (I) is painful, in the various ways in which psychic pain manifests itself, we react by defending ourselves (D). This defence consists in all of the ways in which we try to avoid the suffering that derives from the obstruction of our vitality. And so, we act in order to keep the suffering away (defence mechanisms, which aim to deny, to scotomize, to exclude), or we act in such a way as to get rid of the suffering we already feel inside (the various ways in which we project or we hallucinate), or, as happens in most situations, we defend ourselves by distorting reality (all of the ways in which we alter reality to make it less burdensome).

We have not made reference to the technical names of the defence mechanisms as laid down by psychoanalysis (see, for example, McWilliams, 1994) or as classified for the purposes of research (Perry, 1990) to demonstrate that defensive actions can certainly be identified, as labelled conventionally by psychoanalysts, but that at their root is a way of experiencing life that can also be described through different conceptual tools that come from other models. On this note, see Chapter 12 dedicated to the comparison between metapsychology and Transactional Analysis. The latter model describes the defence phenomenon in a very different way from classical accounts of defence mechanisms.

The three modalities of impulse, anxiety, and defence are therefore a continuum of strongly interdependent psychic processes that acquire the denomination I A D for the purposes of conceptual simplification and in order to provide a technical point of reference that facilitates the work of the therapist.

The interdependence of I A D is envisaged through their placement at the three vertices of a triangle, as can be seen in Figure 2.1. This graphical representation indicates an interdependence of the following form: each modification of each of the vertices has, as a consequence, variations in the other two. For example, a therapist intervention on the impulse vertex will bring about variations in anxiety and defence. Likewise, confronting defence has the effect of increasing anxiety, but also the possible recovery of impulse. Making contact with anxiety might provide more room to impulse but will also have repercussions for defence. A large part of the ITAP technique is founded on the operations concerning the intrapsychic I A D triangle, thereby clearly remaining within the tradition of brief psychotherapies (Davanloo, 1990).

The interpersonal triangle

The second triangle on which much of the work of the "brief" psychotherapist is based concerns the patient's significant others. Menninger, in his manual of psychoanalytic technique (1958), dedicates a substantial chapter of some 30 pages to interpretation and to other interventions, and it is here that he introduces a connection between past experience, present life, and the therapeutic relationship, as seen through a triangle that he calls the triangle of insight.

> I define insight as the recognition by the patient (1) that this or that aspect of his feelings and attitudes, this or that technique of behaviour, this or that role in which he casts other people, is of a pattern; (2) that this pattern, like the foot print of a bear which has lost certain toes in a trap, originated long ago and stamps itself on every step of his life journey; it is present in his contemporary reality situation relationships, and it is present in his analytic relationships; (3) that this pattern originated for a reason which was valid at the time,

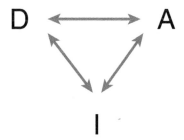

Figure 2.1 The conflict, or intrapsychic, triangle

and persisted despite changes in some of the circumstances which originally determined it; (4) that this pattern contains elements which are offensive and injurious to others as well as expensive and troublesome to the patient.

(Menninger, 1958, pp. 147–148)

Therefore, as he confirms a few lines later: "insight is the simultaneous identification of the characteristic behaviour pattern in all three of these situations, together with an understanding of why they were and are used as they were and are" (Menninger, 1958, p. 148).

For this reason, the three areas can be connected in a triangular manner, which Menninger defines as the triangle of insight. The graphical representation proposed by Menninger is less schematic than that which the literature subsequently adopted and which we also follow. In Figure 2.2 we can see a representation of the triangle of insight:

The term "P" stands for the past of our interlocutor and concerns the significant relationships that have contributed to forming their history. The term "C" refers to present relationships, those which our subject has in their present life: life partner, family, colleagues, friends, social relationships. The term "T" means the relationships that are established within the therapeutic couple. "C" and "T" refer to present aspects of the interpersonal life of the patient, therefore they take place in the "here and now". "P" represents past relationships and therefore the "there and then".

The insight that is asked of the patient in the Menninger's formulation is the optimal objective, in which the awareness of the patient manages to connect together the three vertices of the triangle with great lucidity.

Nevertheless, it is not always possible to obtain such a full and definitive result. In order to reach such a result, it is necessary to take progressive steps, which we can refer to as partial insights. While not being extraordinary, these progressive steps are nonetheless indispensable. Partial is a qualifier that we can attribute after the fact, i.e., when we already have an idea of what final result the person might obtain. In reality, while the therapy is in progress, partial insights do not have this quality of incompleteness. Rather, they are the indication of the journey that the patient is making, of the steps of awareness they are taking. We might presume

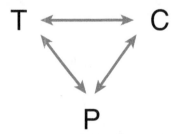

Figure 2.2 The triangle of persons or triangle of insight

that the true insight is the one indicated by Menninger; in reality, we have an approximate vision of the destination point that our subject might reach. Therefore, each insight, or reorganization of the field, is a step forward in which the adjective "partial" simply indicates the degree to which the journey undertaken can be further perfected.

We can also quickly examine another aspect of insight that, in the words of Menninger, is overshadowed. The reorganization of the field, which we call insight, occurs when we live our experience in all of its various aspects. We can therefore witness cognitive, emotional, corporeal, and behavioural insights where the reorganization of the field leads to the "solution" of a problem. From a clinical point of view, we can refer to the moment in which the patient realizes something that was not previously clear. Examples of this are as numerous as our problems: "Ah, but that friend of mine really did betray me . . ., he was close to me . . ., he got it before I did that . . ." Or "only now can I see that the way my mother nurtured me was . . . adequate, excessive, cold, invasive, etc." or "without realizing it I have chosen a job as a way of . . . breaking free, being a slave, resisting, competing, honoring, etc. the figure of my father". These are all partial insights (because they do not take into consideration all the vertices of CPT), and are substantially cognitive in nature, or at least they are expressed here in cognitive terms.

There are also insights of an emotional order. For example, it is easy to intuit that the cognitive insights referred to earlier are accompanied by differing degrees of reorganization of the emotional field. Discovering that my mother nurtured me inadequately because she was a mean (both with emotions and with money) will have repercussions on my emotional state. I might be sad because of the suffering experienced or happy because I have finally understood why I always deny myself the occasional treat in an expensive restaurant.

However, there are also reorganizations of the field that are more clearly emotional, where the cognitive portion is merely instrumental. Feeling that I have chosen a partner to show myself, and maybe directly show my father, how I would have liked him to treat my mother, can doubtless be described verbally, but it has much more to do with emotional movements. Again, in this case I might be disappointed and dejected after discovering that I had not been free in my choices or I might feel satisfied with myself for having been creative in a way my father could not manage.

Finally, there are insights of a non-verbal order that are reflected in the behaviour of the person. A non-clinical example of this can be found in specific moments of learning a new motor skill: the execution of a topspin backhand in tennis, the sound in wind instruments generated by the reed vibration set off by a stroke of the tongue against the reed, the repetitive and smoothening movement needed with the trowel in order to create Venetian plaster, and so on.

Other examples are more relevant to clinical situations: I might notice something in my body, beyond words or feelings, indicating that I am carrying a burden that I should let go of and I probably have a "weighed down" posture with little elasticity, closed shoulders, a downcast look, slowed down metabolism, etc. (Lowen, 1975). When I am able to offload the weight that I was carrying then my non-verbal experience, my body, my behaviour, and my attitudes change. I am not always able to verbalize these results, even if they represent a powerful indicator of a reorganization of the field. Often a friend or acquaintance who sees us after a while tells us something that we are not aware of "you're looking really well" or "you've really changed" (for better . . . for worse . . .). Or maybe it is something that even they are not aware of but, in the end, they offer you a drink or invite you to some sort of event. Reorganization of behavioural, corporeal, and expressive fields can come about even in the absence of a corresponding verbal aspect.

The distinction between three types of insight is a bit academic and serves the purpose of facilitating didactic objectives. It also basically has the purpose of focusing attention not only on the verbal indicators of change but also on emotional, corporeal, behavioural, expressive, metabolic, aesthetic, economic, and value-based indicators. There are countless points of view we can take in order to observe the changes in our patient. In the reality of the flow of experiences that characterize our life, insights do not come about in scholastically classified, watertight compartments. Rather, they are reorganizations of a field formed by a multitude of conditions that continuously create and destroy equilibria of varying degrees of permanency. Insight, therefore, is the experiential peak in which we witness a dramatic mutation of the field conditions, however we try to describe them: cognitive, emotional, corporeal, etc.

In Wertheimerian thinking, insight involves a change of the field, having as result a new more stable, simpler, more "economical" organization (Wertheimer, 1945).

Therefore, its distinctive character can be found in the effects to which this reorganization gives rise (we will take up this topic again in Chapter 4).

The first effect is that of a solution being created that was not present before. Whereas in the beginning the field was characterized by tension, by the necessity of something that was missing, nostalgia, now it possesses a different quality. After the insight, the object becomes more solid, free of tensions, with greater balance and stability.

The second effect is that of constituting energy saving. The "solution" no longer requires the workings we were exposed to in its absence; the realization now allows forces to be put aside for other tasks. In this sense, the insight, the reorganization of the field, is a doubly creative operation: it introduces something new where there was not anything before, and furthermore it allows energies to be deployed for other tasks.

The structure of change that we denominate as insight can be traced in forms of our experience – from everyday experiences, such as not being able to remember a person's name, to more intensely clinical ones, like finding an equilibrium in our emotional life that was missing before.

In a clinical setting, as in others, the first effect of insight is there for all to see. The solution is so evident, to the subject and those around them (not least of all the therapist), that it cannot pass unobserved. It constitutes a meaningful point of anchorage for the therapeutic course. A resource to dip into in times of scarcity.

The second effect, which is a secondary indicator of insight, can help us to obtain information on the reorganization of the field, even in those situations in which there has not been verbalization, nor an evident corrective emotional experience, nor a tangible corporeal experience. For reasons that we need not explore now (fear of change, intrapsyhic envy towards our own "rebirth", competition with our own therapist, inability to recognize ourselves), a patient, and at times their therapist, might not become aware of the reorganization that they have enacted. But if something has been achieved, then the functional effects will be seen on other fronts. Energy saving pervades experience, and the ways in which it manifests itself are countless: the subject will dress more appropriately (smarter in some situations, less so in others); they will be more punctual (for the sessions, in life, with their deadlines); they will have news to share about something (of any nature, significance, mode); they will have a lighter verbal, facial, and kinetic expression. In short they will be "lighter" in the many ways us humans can achieve lightness.

This secondary effect can also be a significant, almost instant, indicator of the fact that reorganization of the field has been achieved. Let us take a hypothetical intervention by the therapist (and we hope that every single intervention is a facilitator of the reorganization of the field because it is at the heart of the intensity of the therapy) and observe what happens in the interlocutor. It might or might not reorganize the field (an epic insight is not needed, even a small breakthrough in equilibrium is enough). If the field is not reorganized, then we do not have any signal (be it explicit or implicit) of change, and subsequently our interlocutor is, on the contrary, sending us an evident signal of no change: this is important information, we must change something. Alternatively, if, because of our intervention, the field is reorganized, even in a small way, then an explicit signal might be sent: a phrase, an emotion, an expression, even of a corporeal nature. This, for us, represents a strong indicator of the progression of our transactions. However, it could be that for various reasons that they do not send an explicit signal that is directly connected to the evidently partial or minimal insight. Therefore, we have to be sensitive to the indications of energy saving that our interlocutor might show us. There are many "places" where we can find this information. Let us look at some examples here: ideation is either slower or faster, moments of silence, responses are quicker, topic is changed; the interlocutor speaks figuratively, eccentrically, metaphorically; they become imperceptibly colder emotionally, they become imperceptibly warmer emotionally, they close up, they open up, they are evasive, they linger; on the verbal front they change the intensity of their voice or the place in which the voice resonates in the body, they accentuate or diminish paraverbal utterances (for example, "eh", "mmm"); in terms of eye movements, they narrow or widen their gaze, they move their eyes in a way that is not usual, they throw a glace up, down, or to the side, they open wide or close shut their eyes; in terms of facial expressions there are many examples, they open up, they close down, they come closer, they move away, they are interested, frightened, perplexed, safe; in terms of lip movements, they purse them or release them, they smile, they curl them, they accept or they refuse; in terms of body movements, various "stations" can be observed; in the case of a face-to-face therapy (as it must be when the therapy is "brief"), the observations of posture, of the movements of their head, of their arms and their hands, are indicators of available energy, they emit a message that says "yes, I'm here, let's move forward" or "no, I can't make it, something is missing" (see Chapter 5).

All these secondary signals of insight can be instantly picked up on, much more and with greater "truth" than that of "verbalization". Therefore, equally instantaneously, and perhaps beyond the "verbalization" of the therapist themself, they inform and give shape to subsequent operations.

Naturally, what is proposed here is a classification that should only act as a guide. Indeed, using this list and other helpful resources as a starting point, each therapist should hone their own way of observation. The indications in this work are only a canvas on which to "improvise", exactly as baroque music scores gave approximate instructions and left a lot of space to the creativity of the artist, not to mention modern jazz.

Note

1 This chapter was written by Marco Sambin.

References

Davanloo, H. (1990). *Unlocking the Unconscious: Selected Papers of Habib Davanloo, MD*. New York: Wiley.

Ekman, P., & Freisen, W. V. (1971). Constants across cultures in the face and emotions. *Journal of Personality and Social Psychology*, 17(2): 124–129.

Freud, S. (1915a). *Triebe und Triebschicksale*, Gesammelte Werke, Chronologisch Geordnet, Book. X, 1946 (pp. 210–232). A. Freud et al. London: Imago Publishing Co.

Freud, S. (1915b). *Instincts and their Vicissitudes*. Standard edition of the complete Psychological Works of Sigmund Freud. Vol. 14, 1967 (pp. 110–140). J. Strachey (Ed. and Trans.). London: Hogarth Press.

Lowen, A. (1975). *Bioenergetics*. New York: Coward, McCarin & Georgen.

Malan, D. H. (1979). *Individual Psychotherapy and the Science of Psychodynamic*. London: Butterworth & Co. Publishers.

Mc Williams, N. (1994). *Psychoanalytic Diagnosis Understanding Personality Structure in the Clinical Process*. New York–London: Guilford Press.

Menninger, K. (1958). *Theory of Psychoanalytic Technique*. New York: Basic Books.

Perry, J. C. (1990). *The Defence Mechanism Rating Scales Manual* (5th edn.). Copyright by J. C. Perry, M.D., Cambridge: Cambridge Hospital.

Rogers, C. (1951). *Client-Centered Therapy: Its Current Practice, Implications and Theory*. London: Constable.

Weiss, E. (1960). *The Structure and Dynamics of the Human Mind*. New York – London: Grune & Stratton.

Wertheimer, M. (1945). *Productive Thinking*. Oxford: Harper.

3 ITAP

The theoretical model[1]

The ITAP model of intervention is characterized by a framework in which the interaction between the intrapsychic triangle (Ezriel, 1952) and the interpersonal triangle (Menninger, 1962) is highlighted. In the literature on brief psychotherapy it is Malan (1979) who addresses the two triangles together even though they had been devised separately by Ezriel and Menninger. It is Davanloo, however, who makes joint use of them.

The two triangles graphically represent, in various ways, that which the therapist and the interlocutor enact: creating reorganizations of field; which comes about through an interaction between a persons's internal movements (triangle of conflict or intrapsychic triangle) and movements between people (interpersonal triangle or triangle of insight).

The more complete graphical formulation appears in a work by Angela Molnos (1983), but as far as we know it has not been followed up.

ITAP proposes a graphical representation (Figures 3.3 and 3.4) which highlights the ample possibilities offered by the interaction between the two triangles. A dynamic presentation that progressively moves the IAD triangles towards the CPT one makes evident how this sort of diagram enables various passages. Indeed, even a static representation on a page can also give the same idea.

Let us hypothesize the application of an intrapsychic triangle to each of the vertices of the interpersonal triangle. We would obtain a diagram like Figure 3.1 that shows how the conflictual aspects that link IAD are applicable to all areas of the patient's experience.

Given that the structure of constructing experiences has the tendency to repeat itself (repetitive coercion of varying degrees), it is likely that the impulses, of the defence and the anxiety, are transferable, and de facto trasferred, from the patient's formative experience (his Past, P) to his present experience (his Current, C), and then to the relationship they have with the therapist (Transference or Therapist, T). The transition, transference, from one area to another is not so mechanical as to involve the same rigid structure of I A D in the three CPT areas. Indeed, it is precisely the comparability and the differences observed that give origin to such significant possibilities for change (insight) in the experiences of the therapeutic couple.

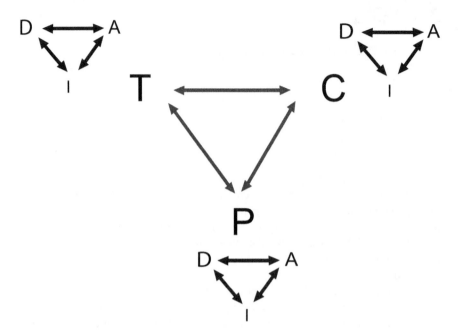

Figure 3.1 Relationships between the interpersonal triangle and the intrapsychic triangles

For example, a person with anxiety problems (let us assume of a generic nature without referring to a classification system) might have the tendency to inhabit the A–C zone, espressing their anxiety concerning their present life. It will be difficult for them to move from A–C to D–C; or, in other words, the suffering that they experience is an obstacle that stops them from seeing its defensive aspects. It will be even more difficult to access I–C given that they cannot manage to contact the need, the emotion, and the motivation that lead to the feelings of anxiety. The beginning of therapeutic success consists in managing to "dislodge" this person from the position they find themself in. And perhaps it will not be so simple. Any movement that takes the structure I A D into the P zone will be difficult, even more so than taking it into zone T. The presence of A–C is so dominant that it drains much of the energy of the Ego and therefore makes it difficult for an insight to reorganize the field.

Another person, who we can generically define as depressed (again without referring to a classification system), will be placed in the stations of Figure 3.1 in a different way. It might be linked to their past through reference to a happy moment that can no longer be experienced, something they have lost and that they miss. In this case we can place them in P, probably between I and D. The potential that this person has to change can be indicated from his or her capacity to move across the T and C side, above all T. This would cause them to stop living with an attitude of "paradise lost", but it woud open up the possibility of instigating positive aspects of impulse in the here and now.

The synthetic descriptions, of the various ways in which "the anxious subject" and the "the depressed subject" can be placed on Figure 3.1, are defined with reference to the position, even if they are generic. Each has different ways of experiencing A, of manifesting D, and of having access to I. Also, the interaction of I A D varies according to the person it refers to: CPT. The following manual leads us towards understanding these differences.

We can, therefore, note some lines in Figure 3.1 that graphically demonstrate the possible pathways, like a sort of map with all of the possibilities that the couple can travel along. It is a diagram and therefore represents opportunities that are frozen in time, as if all of the possible connections have been represented together. The journey of the therapeutic couple favours certain pathways compared to others according to the resources available, the therapeutic project, and the structure of the patient.

The representation then becomes as per Figure 3.2.

The dotted lines indicate the comparison pathways possible. In terms of a simple list, there are 18 arrows that represent the possible movements in the transactions of the therapeutic couple. A bit of obsessiveness: 18 comprises nine dotted arrows together with the nine small arrows, the big arrows are not counted because they summarize the dotted arrows. Without further calculating the various ways these 18 options could be summed (and there would be many such combinations), it is evident that once the experience of the couple has been read by using such a diagram it is difficult to countenance that there are not options for transactions to be enacted. The concept of activity and intensity of brief therapy is based on

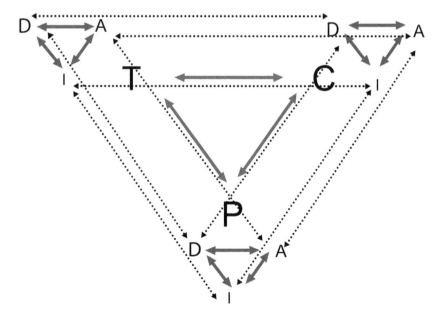

Figure 3.2 The ITAP Triangle: the interaction between IAD and CPT with suggestions of possible comparisons

the continual possibility of making a movement that brings about change. Such a diagram offers the therapist a guide and a stimulus to not lose themself in their passivity or in the passivity of the subject.

Clinical practice, and the examples that we propose, will demonstrate that some options indicated in the diagram with dotted arrows vary in their productivity. Some are not practical in certain moments; others are so obvious as to involve little creativity; others are travelled along again and again for the sake of a sense of security. Given there are 18 possible pathways that a couple might move along, we can assume that they might favour some and neglect others. So, if we imagine graphically underlining each pathway that has been taken at the end of the therapy, we would be left with a more pronounced line for some journeys and a less pronounced or even absent line for others. We would therefore have, for fans of formality, constructed a "trianglegram" or more elegantly "the diagram of insight" that has come out of that specific therapeutic couple – a sort of snapshot that can summarize the most favoured movements. Malan (1979) would suggest that we can expect that most successes will come from couples where it was possible to positively compare what happens in therapy with what happens outside (interpretations on transference, to use psychoanalytic langage). Whereas with reference to Menninger (1962, pp. 150–154), we can say that therapies where the patients (and with them the therapist) limit themselves to only two vertices of the interpersonal triangle are not as productive as those therapies where all three vertices are moved through.

For example, the diagram of the insight of the "anxious patient" mentioned earlier could be the one indicated in Figure 3.3. The circles that surround D and A in C are a graphical representation of that which remains anchored to anxiety and to their defences.

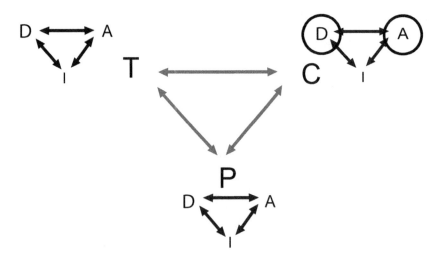

Figure 3.3 The trianglegram of an "anxious patient"

In the case of the "depressed subject" the diagram of insights might be like Figure 3.4 where the circles show investment that favours aspects of impulse and of defence in relation to events of the past.

At the end of the therapy we expect that the diagrams will be different. In Figure 3.5, a possible change is indicated for the "anxious subject" who has managed to contact his or her impulse on the present by decreasing their anxiety and their defence and who has been able to see a connection to significant figures from their past. For now, we do not ask the anxious subject to create a connection with T, a step that would probably not be easy for them.

In the case of our "depressed subject", a situation of change might be represented by Figure 3.6 where the recovery of impulse is evident, both in the present situation and in the relationship with the therapist, as well as the consequent lowering of defence.

The diagrams of insights presented here are a graphical way of showing which operations have been enacted by the therapeutic couple.

The diagram of insights

We can come up with various methodologies for creating the diagram of insights. What follows does not constitute the construction of an evaluation tool with the necessary associated methodological considerations. Such an operation is possible but is not contemplated given the scope of this volume. Rather it deals with general observations concerning how an evaluation of the therapeutic process based on the diagram of insights might be used.

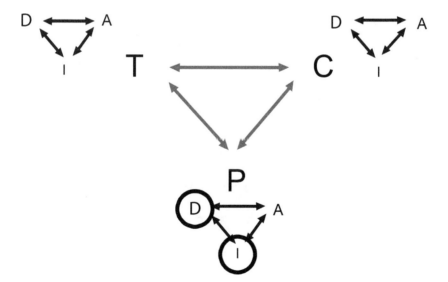

Figure 3.4 The trianglegram of a "depressed patient"

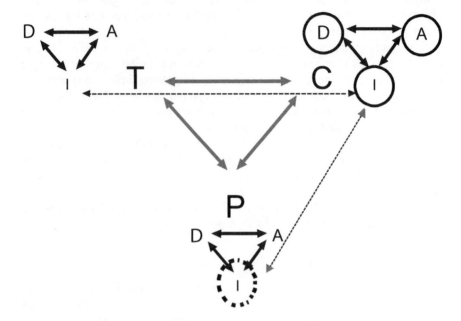

Figure 3.5 Changes in an "anxious patient"

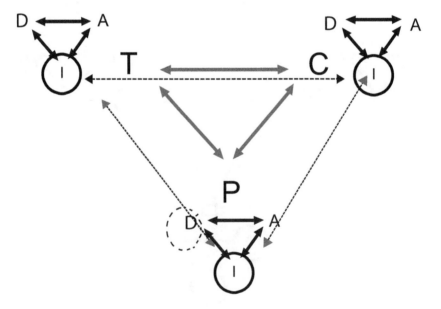

Figure 3.6 Changes in a "depressed patient"

One first dimension on how to operate might derive from the modality of data collection: intuitively or according to codified rules.

The intuitive modality involves the construction of the diagram without using codified procedures and by simply making use of what we see without turning to other forms of reasoning. This very immediate modality might seem compromised by subjectivity, but it has the advantage of a global vision that appeals to clinical intuition and of not being expensive: onerous procedures are not required whereas it is a general synthetic impression, free from excessive cognitive elaboration.

The second modality, the more codified one, relies on standard methods used in psychotherapy research and involves a schema to be applied to the pertinent topic using opportune methods. The evaluation grid is based on the components in Figure 3.4. The phenomenon is the unraveling of the transactions in the course of the psychotherapy. And, finally, the best methods might include the evaluation by external raters of which portion of the diagram is activated in any given moment. The data collected are the frequency of activation for each of the diagram components from Figure 3.4.

A second dimension on which to base the achievement of the diagram of insights is due to data from the temporal extension. We can apply the diagram to a very short segment of the therapy, extend it to a longer time period, or cover the entire psychotherapy.

Is an interaction between these two dimensions conceivable? Certainly. By crossing the two dimensions we can, on the one hand, construct intuitive insight diagrams referring to time-limited periods and more extended periods; on the other hand, we can envisage more methodologically consolidated insight diagrams that refer to narrower temporal periods or to much longer moments.

None of the possibilities contemplated above, with the necessary methodological considerations, will be developed here. Nonetheless, having proposed the various types of diagrams of insights can help us to understand how the therapist uses them.

We can help ourselves by revisiting the musical analogy mentioned at the end of the previous chapter. Figure 3.4 can be seen to represent a musical score that is open to creative interpretation. Baroque music, contemporary music, and further still jazz music make use of the stave in a creative way, utilizing it as a canvas that has core principles while at the same time allowing the artist the freedom of certain creative choices. There are themes that can be defined and repeated, transposed and developed, ad libitum. Ad libitum sometimes even appears in rigid romantic scores. Each execution is therefore different from the others, not only in its interpretation but also in the structure and duration.

The same thing happens in clinical performance. Themes that come up are developed, transposed, repeated, explored, taken up again. And the execution of a therapeutic dyad is different each time, even more so than in the example of musical works.

Therefore, Figure 3.4 is a guide that establishes some basic modalities that then liberate the creativity of the therapist. There are therapists who prefer to utilize certain pathways that other colleagues move along less, just as the same therapist utilizes different modalities according to the patient they are dealing with.

As you will see in the next chapter regarding the psychic equations, the therapeutic couple draws great advantage from the mobility that it manages to achieve within the various possibilities contemplated in Figure 3.4. The availability of a schema that contemplates and distinguishes among all of the various possibilities might suggest to the therapist a range of options that sessions not guided by the schema might ignore.

Note

1 This chapter was written by Marco Sambin.

References

Ezriel, H. (1952). Notes on psycho-analytic group therapy: Interpretation and research. *Psychiatry*, 15(2): 119–126.
Malan, D. H. (1979). *Individual Psychotherapy and the Science of Psychodynamic*. London: Butterworth & Co. Publishers.
Menninger, K. (1958). *Theory of Psychoanalytic Technique*. New York: Basic Books.
Molnos, A. (1983). *The Diagram of the Four Triangles*. Copyright © 1983 by Angela Molnos. London, June 1983. Available at: http://fox.klte.hu/~keresofi/psyth/a-to-z-entries/bk43four.html

4   Intervention technique[1]

In order to have a conceptual guide concerning the implementation of ITAP interventions, we can examine the idea of the problem. In our everyday experience, when we think of a problem, we associate with it another idea for which a solution might exist, and subsequently another thought comes to us: that in order to get to the solution it is necessary to take certain steps. These steps are what unites–separates the problem from the solution. In a very general manner the conceptual schema, when we are confronted with a problem, envisages: (1) a reality that requires a change because it is not balanced enough, it lacks something, needy of intervention; (2) stages of variation with characteristics of connection with the problem, even if they aim to move away from it, organized in an order sequence of operations that realize progressive and interconnected evolutions of these stages; and finally (3) the achievement of a state of balance, of completeness, of levelling that was missing in the initial situation. Indeed: from the problem by way of steps to its resolution.

Sometimes we have the pleasant impression that a problem can find a rapid solution and that the steps to reach it present themselves with pleasing naturalness; at times, the pathway is less smooth and we get trapped in the intermediate steps, stumbling around in the dark of uncertain choices; other times the solution appears as if by miracle like a happy change of scene that moments before was devoid of exits.

The productive thinking of Wertheimer (1945) admirably describes the problem-solving processes in which there is a big difference between a laborious process for successive steps imposed externally (a procedure, a calculation, previous techniques) compared to a "bright" solution by means of insight in which the inadequacy of the field, its need for a solution, transforms itself instantly into a new, more solid and more efficient organization.

Wertheimer highlights these processes of the reorganization of the field through examples of mathematical and geometric problems. In order to underline the various experiential processes that the individual follows to reach a solution, he refers to simple facts such as the demonstration of the similarity of angles, the calculation of surfaces, or modest arithmetic problems. In the case of processes without insight, the solution is more external to the person's experience – it is a procedure that is learnt but not lived so much, that which links one step to the next is not of an intimate nature but it is a learnt "calculation". This type of solution is costlier because it is based on the recall of a procedure and it is less permanent because the procedure does not always retain all of its steps and their correct sequence. The parts are not interconnected in an organized structure, rather they are held together by a "blind" external sequence which requires effort in order to be remembered.

On the contrary, the solution by insight flows from the field conditions and moves towards a new organization with admirable ease and rapidity. The effort "saved" means that the new solution is energetically efficient because it can better balance all the conditions that were previously less well connected. These characteristics make the solution stable through its intrinsic, strong organization and through the release from the solution-achieving procedure that in this case is self-generating. It is as if the problem resolves itself, which leaves us feeling satisfied. The goodness of the solution releases effort that was previously dedicated to keeping together the pieces of the puzzle. Thus, in addition to the unpleasant feelings, we can deal with new tasks. A gestalt has closed, others can be opened.

It should be highlighted that the insight-based solution is not the experiential micro-miracle that it first appears to be; it also requires "work", albeit of a very different type. The preparation of the terrain where insight flows involves a type of shrewd attention, although not of the type which has been codified in a consolidated procedure. It is a creative process that is sustained by patience, openness, and curiosity. It must leave aside previous ways of connecting events: it is an expectation that is not forcedly correlated with the change it tends to produce, but that is its precondition.

Wertheimer tells us all of this, albeit in his own characteristic words and in light of his cultural climate, using simple problems as examples; we use an analogous structure in order to deal with more complicated processes of change in which, at times, the quantity of variables and of equilibria at stake might overshadow the realization of the experiential structures that bring about the solution to the problems.

In therapy, as in the examples of Wertheimer, change can occur with codified steps that are "imposed" on the experience and in which the result is obtained by successive, small changes that are not at all dramatic; or, it might also happen because we obtain results that are impressively unexpected and that have, nonetheless, originated in a less evident "underground" work. The therapist must be able to prepare for, accompany, and highlight each form of change and therefore there must be flexibility at the service of the various modalities with which the interlocutor changes their mode of experience, i.e., resolves their problems. A therapist's own personal ideas in change might constitute an obstacle. They might be indisposed to rapid changes, believing that they should not be trusted. They might be bored by procedures that require patience and prudence, believing that they are a waste of time. They might expect something that is coherent with their own understanding of change and so do not let themselves be guided by the demands of the interlocutor's, mostly non-verbal, modes of change. The therapist would therefore find himself or herself not being open to the modalities with which the field is being reorganized.

At this point, we can ask ourselves which form to give to complex modalities of change. Once more, our recourse to simple entities helps us to understand the underlying structure, even if in practice it is concealed by the quantity of variable at play. For this reason, we have described the problem in the form an equation. The x is an unknown to which we have to add normally successive steps that can be simple or complex which might or might not lead to a solution.

Let us look at some basic examples.

The formulas

$x = 10$ or $x = a$

are of such simplicity that no step-by-step explanation is needed. The solution is indicated explicitly in the text. We know that x is equivalent to 10 units, whatever their nature is. If we have a problem knowing when a certain event occurs, x tells us that it will occur in 10 days or 10 months or 10 seconds. If x represents the number of tons that a cart can transport then we know that it is 10, and so on.

The formula $x = a$ is also simple. It stands for the size of x indicated by a, and we can attribute various means to a: x weighs a kilogram, is a metre high, is rich, is stupid, and so on.

Let us see what happens if we make the situation more complex.

For example

$x = ka + hb + jc$

It is a formula with more elements than previously but which does not require multiple steps to solve it. It could be the schematic representation of a situation in which x is equivalent to the combined presence of a certain weight a, a certain volume b, and a certain temperature c; attributing defined values to the coefficients h, k, j we could discover, for instance, that x weighs 1200 grams, has the volume of one decimeter squared and has a temperature of 20° Celsius. x cannot be an elephant, nor my uncle Ernest, nor the Ebola virus, nor can it be an infinite quantity of other objects and situations. Rather, it could be a bottle of mineral water, a sample of plastic, a Chinese Ming vase, a hook and moor (a hooked pole that facilitates mooring), and so on.

We can make the example more complex still.

$x = ka + (hb/jc)$

This could be a way of identifying a series of situations in which, given a certain weight of an object, as the density increases, the temperature decreases proportionately.

It could be a bubble of any sort of expandable material that is so well thermically sealed that as the temperature decreases, the volume increases.

What is the point of saying all of this? Certainly not to engage in abstruse exercises of chemistry, physics, or any other form of technical knowledge. The aim is to become sensitive to the connections there are between phenomena and their modality of being treated by using formulas. The equations are a schematic and efficient way of managing those portions of the world that are of interest to us, normally because they are the cause of problems or because they facilitate understanding (in short, the two statements clearly go hand in hand).

We can therefore translate the phenomenon that interest us into equations, not so much to find a "scientific" solution, but rather to highlight, using this structure, a clinician's way of proceeding that would otherwise pass unobserved. The clinician works "scientifically" without allowing the underlying methodologies that have been adopted to come out.

Let us consider an interlocutor who presents a problem such as: "I am angry with my wife". We have before us our x "I am angry" and its equivalent "the wife" and we translate it, if necessary, in the simplest form: $x = a$. We could even invert the terms and attribute "the wife" to the x and "the anger" to the a and we would have a similar "equation". In this case, there would be little to do except note it.

The therapist and most probably the patient themself, are not satisfied with such a simple "equation" but rather start to look for the value of the "coefficients", they "break down the determinants" into simpler elements, they "multiply", "sum", "divide", and "subtract" for opportune values so as to obtain more information and move in the direction of the "solution" to the problem. The modality of proceeding of the two camps is characterized by similar structures applied to very different contents. On the one hand, we have mathematics with simple elements that have been reduced to pure syntax (or at least this is the illusion) and only scarce connections to semantic aspects, generally reduced to the role of defining, after the syntactic steps have been completed, "what meaning" the symbols have. And these are the most controversial aspects among mathematicians themselves. In any case, the syntactic part is most important, while the semantic part is often almost reduced to a "nuisance" that cannot be eliminated. On the other hand, the clinical work has strong semantic elements to the extent that we can be of opinion that the syntactic dimension has been lost, that is, the clinician is not guided by procedures of "calculation". Putting together two such extreme fields can help us to understand better how a clinician operates. Undoubtedly, they manage variables connotated by the significant presence of semantic aspects. The things that the two interlocutors say to each other are, or should be, full of "sense", refer to phenomena, be connected to aspects of life, and not depend on abstract symbols. It is true that this dominant presence of semantic aspects means relegating the "algorithm" to a less conspicuous role in the clinician's work. However, we must not be misled so easily. As we will see more clearly with the aid of some examples, the clinician is continually "calculating", following certain "algorithms" that guide his or her work. Often these operations are silent to the clinicians themselves, just as the solution to a square binomial expression is "silent" to a secondary school pupil who then applies the solution successfully in any case. "Silent" does not mean absent. What we do in this part of the book is reveal that the clinician has very evident and very complex rules of calculation (see the following paragraph) and that these rules are left "silent" because semantic aspects are held to be more interesting than syntactic ones. In terms of the objectives of the therapeutic couple, the meanings that are exchanged carry much more value than the rules according to which the exchange occurs. Therefore, given that energy is a finite resource, clinicians concentrate their attention on what is most important, meanings, neglecting the modalities utilized to obtain them. To take an example from another world, a builder who builds a wall, brick by brick, is interested in how the wall is shaping up, if it is "plumb line" straight, as demanded by the project. They are much less likely to concentrate their attention on the codification of the gestures with which they lift the brick, they put on the mortar with the trowel, they rotate it by 180° and place it, they tap it with the trowel handle to settle it, and with the blade of the trowel they get rid of the excess mortar to obtain the right esthetic. Building the wall is the semantics, describing the steps to do it is the syntax: there is no semantics without syntax (and vice versa). In the example of the wall, we are interested in the result and not the algorithms needed to build it. There are special cases when we are interested in the "syntax" of the wall. For example, the result is not what we want, and therefore we have to ask which operations of the builder might have contributed, something that wouldn't happen if the result has been as expected. Alternatively, if we are interested in the ergonomics of building a wall and therefore we want to highlight the operations necessary to build it, then in this case our attention will intentionally shift on the "syntactic" aspects which in other situations would remain in the background, present but in the shadows, not absent.

The same thing happens in a clinical setting: that which we are building is so interesting for us that we leave aside the modalities followed to obtain it. Therefore, attention is shifted to the meanings and not to the "calculations" undergone to get them. In the lines that follow, we direct our attention to the algorithms that characterize clinical work. At least three reasons drive us.

The first is to highlight the work that needs to be done and therefore bring to the fore the operations that are necessary so that they can be learnt. The first few times that the builder built walls they spent a lot of time concentrating on managing the bricks, mortar, and trowel; with time, these operations were sidelined and left instead a prominence of the completion of the work. Therefore, there is a didactic intent in underlining the syntactic movements enacted with the therapeutic couple.

The second reason is to bring awareness not only to the results but also to the operations conducted: this allows greater creativity. Let us return to the example of the builder. During the training of a builder there are moments where conditions are non-standard. The scaffolding is hard to use, the mortar is hardening, the sun dries out the bricks too much, and so on. The knowledge of the operational modalities allows modifications to be carried out when non-standard conditions require it. In clinical work, standard conditions are only present in the manuals. In practice, every case is non-standard and it is precisely this that is of interest in clinical work. Therefore, it is even more so the case that competence on the "algorithms" allows the application of creativity that each case requires.

The third reason is to highlight that the operations of knowledge enacted by a "scientist" and those enacted by a "clinician" take account of the same structure and that what separates them is the degree of complexity, not the diversity in their proceedings. We do not want to make clinical work too scientific, that would mean it losing its intrinsic nature. And we do not want to make science too clinical, although it would not hurt. Both such attempts would be destined to failure. Through this comparison we wish to highlight that the learning structure, which can be easily identified in terms of very abstract knowledge, can also be identified in more complex and vital forms (Sambin et al., 2015).

The theory of psychic equations

Up until this point we have constructed the idea, more in an analogue than a "digital" way, concerning how a clinical problem can be described in terms of an equation. We have not pursued this analogy in a detailed way in order to avoid unnecessary meticulousness. However, we have developed the idea that the complexity of a problem could, if we were pushed in this direction by some unusual necessity, be traced back to formal determinants. The procedure would probably be complex and laborious, certainly inefficient; however, it would be possible, at least theoretically.

Operating on an equation, however, offers fewer possibilities compared to those offered by a simple two-equation system. Clinical situations are generally complex and therefore difficult to reduce to a simple equation.

In order to prepare ourselves for this complexity, we can briefly see what the structure is of the operations adopted to resolve a system of equations. Therefore, we are not resolving anything but we are highlighting the passages adopted to reach the solution.

In a system of equations, it is generally the case that when two equations meet, each is characterized by two unknowns and are therefore irresolvable if taken singularly. However, this problem is overcome by referring to the system, not to the single equation. The first equation of the system can be solved through the unknown x, and therefore the second unknown y is contained in the solution; now in the second equation the first unknown x is substituted with its solution, therefore the second equation will remain with only one unknown, the y; the second equation is resolved by obtaining an expression free of unknowns; in the first equation there is the substitution of the second unknown, the y, with this solution, thereby obtaining an equation with only one unknown, the x, and therefore it can be resolved; then, in the second equation the x is substituted with the solution of the first equation, thereby obtaining an equation with only one unknown, the y; the second equation is solved by obtaining the value of the second unknown, the y. The procedure is more difficult to describe than to resolve through its steps.

By using the system both the first and the second unknowns could be resolved, while using only the single equations would not have allowed such a resolution.

The same procedure happens in the case of clinical problems. We might encounter a problem that can be traced back to a single equation; if it is simple and does not contain too many unknowns then it can be solved without resorting to other means. Very often, however, the problem we have to deal with is not so easy to deal with. In more fortunate cases there are at least "two unknowns", therefore, it is not resolvable on its own. We therefore resort to a "system of equations"; we place another equation alongside it, generally with the same "unknowns", thus allowing a "solution". We have thus realized that which we call a system of psychic equations.

Let us consider an example. Our interlocutor comes to us with a problem: "I am angry with my wife because she neglects me". It is an equation with three potential unknowns: anger, wife, neglects me (let us leave aside the connector "why", which could itself be treated as an unknown). It could be that with opportune operations within the clinical couple we manage to "resolve" one of more of the unknowns. This solution would satisfy the two interlocutors and there would not be any need for further operations.

Simple systems of psychic equations

However, "psychic equations" are not always so easy to resolve. Often, the operations conducted on the declarations of the interlocutor are not sufficient or they fail to produce the desired solution. The clinician consequently resorts to a system of equations. That is, they will construct equations to place alongside those proposed by the patient. A system of psychic equations will therefore develop in order to guarantee a solution that a single solution does not allow for. For example, new equations can be constructed with a request along the lines of: "Are you ever angry with other people?" Or perhaps the following: "Do you feel neglected in other situations as well? But other "equations" are also possible, such as: "Are you angry with me?" or "Am I neglecting you?"

With the clinician's questions, another simpler front is opened where it is more probable that the equation will have a solution. Indeed, the new equations are constructed by the clinician so as to have two simple solutions: yes or no. Then, based on the solution to the second equation (the one provided by the clinician), various "solutions" can be derived in the first equation (the one provided by the patient).

Later, displayed in a pedantic (mathematical?) way, are the developments of the "calculations" of the system of psychic equations. Explaining the theory is much "colder" than "applying" it in the clinical reality. Watching a video recording of ITAP in progress is an opportunity to watch how the clinician manages the systems of psychic equations. Nonetheless, our aim now is to highlight the structure of the calculation method thereby becoming more "syntactic" and less "semantic" than what would normally be expected from a therapeutic session.

Let us see the eight possible developments, two for each of the four second equations.

First system

First equation: I am angry with my wife because she neglects me.
Second equation: Are you often angry with other people?
Solution one of the second equation: No.

Transport in the first equation → the clinician, and probably their interlocutor as well with greater awareness, understand that the term "wife" is linked exclusively (at least for now) to the anger.

Solution two of the second equation: Yes.

Transport in the first equation → the clinician, and probably their interlocutor as well with greater awareness, exclude the possibility that the term "wife" is linked exclusively to the anger.

**Second system

First equation: I am angry with my wife because she neglects me.

Second equation: Do you feel neglected in other situations?

Solution to the second equation: No → The couple must investigate the joint variables neglect and wife.

Solution to the second equation: Yes → The couple must exclude the variable wife from the variable neglect.

***Third system

First equation: I am angry because my wife neglects me.

Second equation: Do you feel angry with me as well?

Solution to the second equation: No → The couple creates a difference between wife and therapist with respect to being angry. New field to investigate. For example: "How come you are not angry with me?"

Solution to the second equation: Yes → The phenomenon can be directly observed: "We have the occasion to see your anger here and now"

****Fourth system

First equation: I am angry with my wife because she neglects me.

Second equation: Am I neglecting you?

Solution to the second equation: No → The couple has created a difference between wife and therapist with respect to being neglected. "What do I do differently from your wife so as not to neglect you?"

Solution to the second equation: Yes → The phenomenon can be observed live. "What is happening now to make you feel neglected?"

These are simple systems because the second equation foresees a dichotomous response with two clear solutions: yes or no. In the therapeutic couple, sufficient strength is necessary in order to create such a structure. This means that the sum of the energies present in the couple has to be capable of sustaining the sequence of the operations. The sum of the energies can be obtained from various distributions of the two sources: the clinician and their interlocutor. The results are the resolution of at least one of the three variables from the first equation.

We have espoused the structure of the operations in a schematic way in order to demonstrate the syntax: the rules with which the semantics are dealt. The lines of speech reported are only general indicators that represent families of statements that specifically embody that particular step.

A clinical example would demonstrate in a much more meaningful way, precisely because it would introduce the semantic sphere, which results can be produced by following this syntax.

Systems of complex psychic equations

It is not always possible to produce sufficient energy in the therapeutic couple to obtain the reorganization of the field by resorting to a simple system of equations, such as those demonstrated in the previous paragraphs.

In such a case, it is worth turning to more complex systems. The conditions that give rise to the necessity of a more complex system reside in the lack of resources in order to have dichotic responses to the second equation of the system. For various reasons, it is not possible to have a definitive response: yes or no. It could be due to the defences of the interlocutor, the lack of structure imposed by the clinician, or the complexity of the topic. Often the clinical work, like life, leads us to fundamental questions to which we need to provide a simple answer, while at the same time requiring many resources. When the therapeutic couple does not have these resources, the system of psychic equations becomes more complex. The complexity derives from the operations necessary to compensate for the lack of a clear response to the second equation.

Example of a complex system.

P1 – I am angry with my wife because she neglects me.
T2 – Am I neglecting you?
P3 – I feel confused.

At this point, the response of the interlocutor has not generated information for the solution of the second equation, it also contains an unknown and cannot be resolved. Indeed, it is characterized by a defence that could, in a schematic way, be traced back to two forms: a tactical defence with the aim of stopping the clinician from proceeding with their operations and consequently will generate the transaction T4a, or a structural defence derived from the fact that the interlocutor is actually confused when in contact with the feeling of being neglected and consequently will generate the T4b transaction (the letters and the numbers are represented in Figure 4.1).

Let us look at the possible developments. Following the statement in P3, the therapist can be disoriented in two ways.

In the first case, the defence is considered to be a diversion and therefore the next step can occur.

T4a – How is the confusion linked to being neglected?

The possible responses are of two classes: the interlocutor comes out of the tactical defence (P5a1), or alternatively the interlocutor remains in the tactical defence (P5a2).

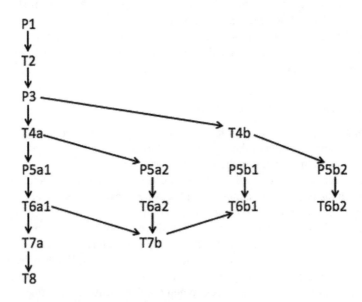

Figure 4.1 Graphical representation of the options in a complex system. P represents the patient, T represents the therapist. The numbers indicate the progression of the transactions of the therapeutic couple.

In the second case, where the therapist believes that the defence is structural, there will be a transaction as indicated in T4b that originates in turn from two reactions: P5b1 or P5b2.

In order to have a schematic vision of the options that present themselves, we can refer to the following figure that synthesizes the complex of sequences mentioned here.

In only a few lines of speech the therapist is facing at least four operative options, which are those transactions generated from the patient at level 5: P5a1, P5a2, P5b1, and P5b2.

Let us look at them not only graphically but also with the whole sequence.

First option, characterized by the pathway that contains P5a1.

P1 – I am angry with my wife because she neglects me.
T2 – Am I neglecting you?
P3 – I feel confused.
T4a – In what way is your confusion linked to feeling neglected?

The therapist hypothesizes that the confusion is a tactical defence and is not structural.

P5a1 – If I am neglected, I get confused.
T6a1 – Are you confused now?

P7a – No.

T8a – Good. How come you're not confused now?

The patient has resolved the tactical defence and has enough resources (the Adult Ego state) to verify the onset of their confusion in relation to the therapist and its connection to feeling neglected. The couple is producing new material. We will not report here further possible developments.

However, the patient in P7 might respond differently:

T6a – Are you confused now?

P7b – Yes.

Following this transaction, the therapist can hypothesize that the tactical defence also has structural aspects, or that it was a structural defence; in any case, the sequence for proceeding might become that of T4b reported below.

Let us return to level T4a where we can see the other possibility, that characterized by P5a2.

T4a – How is your confusion connected to feeling neglected?

P5a2 – I don't know.

T6a2 – What are you feeling in this moment?

The therapist determines that there is a primary persistence of the defensive aspect and that this fact gives them the information that the patient does not have a sufficiently strong Ego concerning this theme, the Adult Ego state is contaminated. The focus is consequently shifted onto the defensive aspect. The system of equations does not have enough resources to be resolved and there the therapist must open another equation in order to increase the chances of finding a solution.

The couple does not produce new material but is committed to process the defence, that is they are aiming to overcome the difficulties that obstruct the "solution".

Figure 4.1 also showed us a third possible sequence, that which is characterized by P5b1. Let us look at it verbally.

T2 – Am I neglecting you?

P3 – I feel confused.

T4b – Are you confused now?

P5b1 – Yes

T6b1 – Let's stay with this confusion. What is it? What's happening to you? What do you feel?

The therapist, in replying to P3, has made the judgement that the defence was structural and therefore he takes the perspective of the patient and "regressively" accompanies them through their confused state, helping them to pursue this line without making requests of the Adult part.

As we indicated in the schema, an alternative sequence might occur.

P3 – I feel confused.
T4b – Do you feel confused now?
P5b2 – No.
T6b2 – Interesting. Before you were confused but you aren't anymore. What does this suggest to us?

The therapist judges that the patient is making some progress regarding the confusion and therefore tests which resources are available concerning this issue. The patient will be able to prove that they have a vision of their movements regarding confusion, or alternatively they will not be able to resolve it and show that they do not have sufficient resources regarding the issue. Depending on the responses, the therapist will proceed in a different way.

At this point, however, we will cease to explore the possible developments so as not to overburden the "tree" of dialogue too much; in other words, we do not wish to make the system of equations too complicated even if in therapeutic practice it is possible to deal with greater complexity.

We can already draw some conclusions.

The graphical description of the sequence of transactions is much more difficult to manage mentally compared to the same sequence described with the verbal contents. In therapy, the complexity is much higher and is also manageable. Indeed, the clinician can do without keeping track explicitly of the syntactic aspect, rather allowing themself to be guided by semantic aspects. In such a case, the complexity pays off because it acts as a guide, precisely the opposite of what happens with a scientific attitude which, aiming for simplification, impoverishes the object thus depriving it of resources that might serve the resolution; the formalization helps only for certain aspects but loses others. If we look at the level proposed by the tree of options in Figure 4.1, we have an overall view, and rather than understanding what the contents are, we can extract some guidelines concerning how we can proceed; at the same time, we lose the vivacity of the facts, the contact with reality. If, on the other hand, we place ourselves at the levels of the contents, rather than being guides by symbols we are guided by the expressed sense of the phrases and therefore, the sequence has a logic that means it is connected, easier to remember, well-organized; like the other side of a coin, the global vision of all the possible options is lost.

The schematic description is close to a "scientific" attitude, a way of giving form in a controlled way to a phenomenon that in this way is greatly reduced if not distorted. The clinical attitude preserves the sense of the phenomenon and is less interested in its formalization. Moreover, the work of the clinician is guided by the syntactic procedures represented in Figure 4.1. The formal description is more burdensome than its execution. The clinician completes these steps without having to think about it; this happens precisely because they are guided by complexity without neglecting semantics. It is as if they are able to undertake the calculations required intuitively, without bringing them to a conscious level.

From the sequences depicted in Figure 4.1 it possible to infer another fact that is representative of intense therapies: the reactions of the therapist are guided by the responses of the patient, as it obviously would be for any therapy; moreover, in the case of intense therapy this occurs with a flexibility and variability which is so heightened as to introduce changes, even line by line. This range of different options, and of various, consequent, technical choices, is enacted by the therapist on the basis of the evaluation that they are conducting. In the next chapter, the modulation of the technique that guides the interventions of the therapist will be outlined in detail. Here we can say what the general rule which the therapist follows is: the enhancement of the conflict-free Ego (the Adult Ego state), and the continuing evaluation of whether the answers of the patient originated from a conflict-free Ego or not. We can approximately subdivide the patient's answers into three large categories: free from conflict, marked by a relatively "treatable" defence, derived from a defence so engrained that a special alliance without too much pressure is applied. According to the type of responses, the clinician adopts various intervention modalities. If it is the Adult state that responds then the therapist can proceed, if a defensive response is obtained then the defence is confronted, if an archaic defensive aspect responds then the therapist does not confront the defence but puts themself at the service of the patient's weak Ego.

In any case, the overarching objective is to energize the healthy parts of the Ego. Therefore, even if various modalities are used, the therapist turns to the functioning part of the Ego: directly where possible, or "clearing out the weeds" in the situations in which the Ego is "contaminated" by other instances, or, finally, substituting itself for the functions of the missing Ego in situations where it is necessary. The attitude is that of entering into alliance with the Ego or, failing this possibility, being ready to do it as soon as it is necessary. Sometimes, this attitude might seem forced to an external observer, but also to parts of the patient's own Ego; as if it were a request for something that is not yet part of the possible functioning of the person. In reality, this attitude of the therapist is a strong inducer of the functions of the Ego, allowing it to avoid regression and/or avoid resorting to defence.

Here we have merely given a general idea on how to act in the face of the patient's responses. We are interested in highlighting the syntactic procedure, showing the sequence of the possible operations.

The following chapters of the book display in greater detail how to proceed while taking account of the semantic aspects.

The presentation of this syntactic structure happened through sequences of transactions between the components of the couple of interlocutors. We have seen that these transactions are not mere symbols (pure syntax) but that they are also bearers of elements of meaning (semantic aspects). In order to keep our exposition as simple as possible we have used simple phrases, perhaps in an overly schematic manner, to embody the content that each interlocutor wanted to relay, choosing only one of the many possible phrases. In the practical clinical setting, the dialogue could be that listed in the examples or it could take many other analogous forms. The variations are determined by a vast complex of variables:

communicative "style" of the therapist, communicative "style" of the interlocutor, strength of the alliance, intensity of the defence, resources present in the patient, resources present in the therapist. We can only imagine the vast variety of transactions that can be enacted while remaining guided by the operations indicated in Figure 4.1.

It is precisely this large variety, together with a generally well-defined syntax, that might represent a warning sign. How is it possible to make sense of such a large quantity of possible interventions, especially when it is necessary to respect the sequences proposed? It can seem difficult to master such a method.

We can deal with such a problem with an analogy. Imagine that you want to learn to play a musical instrument. Rather than mastering the basics of the instrument, you want to set out to do advanced techniques. Not the simple execution of notes but also embellishments such as trills, appoggiaturas, and ornaments. For example, in order to execute a trill the instrumentalist has to alternate as fast as possible between two neighbouring notes. The first time this is executed it requires great concentration and constant cognitive monitoring. The player reads the notes and says to themselves that they are playing a C and a D in close succession: C D C D C D C D, and so on. With practice, the cognitive control necessary in the initial phases is progressively set apart and with it the "wooden" quality of its execution, eventually giving way to a more fluid procedure, which is freed from its syntax and open to semantics: the trill is therefore able to be sweet, strong, dampened, defined etc., just as is required by the score.

The same thing happens in the clinical setting; becoming "virtuous executors" requires a study of the syntax in order to reach meaningful aspects, the difficulty that seems insurmountable in the beginning reveals itself to be anything but impossible.

Continuing with the musical analogy: certain trills are easier than others. For example, the clarinet has complex fingering because it does not proceed by octaves but by thirteenths. An F-G trill is very easy to execute because it simply involves the rhythmic raising and lowering of the index finger of the right hand (I am referring to music set in B flat rather than music transposed in C). On the contrary, a C-D trill is an almost insurmountably difficult, as it involves balancing the clarinet on the right thumb and raising all fingers to uncover the holes and play a C, followed by the position for playing a D, which involves closing all of the fingers on the open holes including the register key commanded by the left thumb. This is such an endeavour that the clarinettist tries to avoid it by resorting to alternative positions, or so-called unnatural positions, which are simpler physically but do not always have the correct intonation. Even this simple description shows the difference between the two operations both defined as a trill.

In the same way, in the clinical setting some "trills" are easy to execute, others require much more difficult "unnatural positions" that involve more energy with fewer automatisms on the part of the therapist. In general, we start with the simplest operations, after these have been consolidated you can move on to more complicated ones. When we say, "in general", we do not mean to exclude "innate clinical virtuosos" who immediately attempt the most difficult sequence. In any case, even a "virtuoso" is helped by knowledge of the procedure to be surer on the choices that they are adopting.

Another impression that might arise from this exposition concerns the fear of forcing the interlocutor into a psychological Procrustean bed designed by the clinician. The structure is so defined that it seems obligatory to force the interlocutor into the modalities chosen by the clinician. The apparent harshness is, in reality, enacted in certain situations where the defensive aspect is so "hard" as to necessitate a similarly firm intervention, and only then with the necessary awareness, skill, and adeptness that will be addressed in the chapter regarding the alliance. The most conspicuous situations are those in which the therapeutic couple "fight" the saboteur within the interlocutor. The "internal saboteur" is a term derived from Fairbairn (1954), used here for its evocative capacity, which has parallels within various clinical models. In any case, the actions of the clinician are always supported by an attitude of cooperation based on the interlocutor's consent to the work undertaken. Even in the most codified and confrontational phases, the activities of the clinician occur through contractual agreement between the two parts (Menninger, 1962; Berne, 1961).

The concept of therapy intensity

At this point of our exposition it is possible to get a more consolidate idea of what an intense form of therapy means. The intensity is due to the fact that each line the therapist utters introduces some sort of variation in the experiential asset of their interlocutor. Therefore, every transaction is utilized to work towards the agreed change. Secondly, the intensity derives from the fact that the therapist tends not to leave their interlocutor alone to contend with their anxiety and their defensive aspect. The therapist is therefore active in taking care of that which weighs down the process of change in their interlocutor. The psychoanalytical rule of abstention, a modality of silent control, does not hold; rather a certain "interventionism" is called for which serves the interlocutor and not the objectives of the therapist. In this sense, the contract between the two parts authorizes the active intervention of the therapist because the therapist acts *in loco patientis*. Imagine if, as my doctor, I have charged you with the task of carrying out an appendectomy, which we have agreed is necessary. I would not be very happy if you operate slowly on me in order to observe the natural course of the ailment, or if you wait for my own natural healing to resolve the problem, just so that I will be responsible for my own state of health. I would much prefer it if you operate with a sharp scalpel, excise with precision, and sow the wound with skill (assuming, of course, that surgical operations are still undertaken in such a way); you are, in fact, operating in my place (*in loco patientis*) because that is what we agreed on.

This type of activity contributes to the intensity of the therapy and avoids the passivization of the interlocutor, who actively continues to be a holder of the contractual agreement. The various forms of abstention or of passivity on the part of the clinician are a sort of theft of the patient's contractual power. It is a way in which the clinician does not honour the contract that binds them to the patient.

We can see how the variable of time intervenes. Some of the operations outlined here come about at lightning speed, in moments, others can take hours. From this perspective, time is not perfectly correlated with intensity, as we have seen in the preface to Chapter 1. With certain therapeutic couples, the resources available do not allow sequences that are too fast; in others, slow sequences represented wasted potential. Therefore, intensity does not always mean brevity; rather, it is correlated with how much each intervention by the therapist advances the journey towards change. The term "relentless", adopted by Davanloo (1980), indicates that each line of dialogue by the therapist should give rise to something without allowing the defensive modalities of the interlocutor to put a brake on things, indeed the patient should be actively helped to overcome their own defences.

The idea of brevity arises in relation to the achievement of results. The more results there are in as little time as possible, the greater the efficiency of the therapy. In this sense, brevity and intensity go hand in hand: in most cases, an intense therapy is also brief. However, as we have seen, this correlation is not perfect. We tend to prioritize intensity rather than brevity and we believe that brevity is a secondary product of the intensity, welcome but not necessary. On the other hand, it is much easier to measure brevity as opposed to intensity and this might explain why there is a tendency to underline the brevity.

Furthermore, prioritizing the intensity side helps us to understand the ITAP method and is applicable even to patients with "severe" issues. Such patients have fewer resources, greater difficulty in obtaining the desired changes, and, therefore, longer courses of therapy. The therapy remains intense but it is not as brief as we would like it to be.

Note

1 This chapter was written by Marco Sambin.

References

Berne, E. (1961). *Transactional Analysis in Psychotherapy*. New York: Grove Press.
Davanloo, H. (1980). *Short-Term Dynamic Psychotherapy*. New York: Jason Aronson.
Fairbairn, R. (1954). *An Object-relations Theory of the Personality*. New York: Basic Books.
Menninger, K. (1958). *Theory of Psychoanalytic Technique*. New York: Basic Books.
Sambin, M., Palmieri, A., & Messina, I. (2015). *Psiconeurodinamica [Psychoneurodynamic]*. Milano: Cortina Editore.
Wertheimer, M. (1945). *Productive Thinking*. Oxford: Harper.

5 Modulation of the intervention[1]

The procedure espoused in the previous chapter is not applied abstractly but must be modulated considering the resources available in the therapeutic couple. The procedure is a syntactic fact that has to generate meanings; if it is applied blindly it will not produce the results that we suggest are possible. In this chapter, we propose some ways to evaluate the resources present so as to modulate the application of the procedure. In this exposition, we take for granted the fact that the therapist has basic skills in using the technique and, therefore, we turn our attention to how to evaluate the interlocutor's resources. The knowledge and the experience concerning the approach outlined in this book represent the resources of the therapist.

In order to apply the technique, constant evaluation of the resources made available by the interlocutor is required. Each diagnosis is also an evaluation of resources, so we might think that we are required to make a diagnosis concerning our interlocutor. This is true in the sense that we cannot refrain from a constructing a diagnostic overview; however, it is not enough, and while useful, it is not indispensable. What we need is an immediate and ongoing way to evaluate whether our next comment can or cannot not be received by the interlocutor. It is, therefore, a very different sort of attitude as compared to traditional diagnosis, which aims to place the clinical phenomena, reported by the patient, in a well codified classification system. In this case, the cost necessary for bringing about this operation means we are reluctant to concede any flexibility, we have invested so much knowledge and we have integrated so much information, that the final result, that is the diagnosis, seems to be a sort of stable project, consequently, we have little incentive to leave this construction; our interlocutor, not to be outdone, remains on the same wavelength and confirms the clinical picture. The type of diagnosis that ITAP utilizes is completely different: it is much less onerous, more flexible, open to the large changes that the technique entails, it is continuous and dynamic.

We propose two modalities of resource evaluation. One derives from the analysis of the transactions espoused in this chapter, while the other from the observation of the body, which we will present in the following chapter. These two modalities, as will be evident from their practical application, are certainly synergistic and, indeed, can even be utilized separately.

The contract: the evaluation of the transactions in the definition of change

The first exchanges in which the two interlocutors share information refer to the object of change. The therapist asks their interlocutor why they are in therapy, what the problem is, and what they want to change. It is the moment in which the interlocutors of the couple construct their contract (Menninger, 1962; Berne, 1961). This phase is crucial because it represents the first interactions between the two and, therefore, immediately highlights both the ways in which topics are dealt with by the interlocutor but also the way in which they relate to the therapist, another important source of information.

The evaluation of the resources occurs through the type of transactions that are exchanged in the couple. In the following account, we make a distinction between the three principal modalities of transactions. These transactions differ among each other because they are indicative of different psychic structures of the patient.

On the left of Figure 5.1, the letter T indicates the therapist, on the left the patient is indicated by the letter P.

The initial question of T, "What is your problem?", can be graphically represented with an arrow pointing towards P.

It is P's turn that will give a response (Figure 5.2), also represented by an arrow, this time towards T.

The first family of transactions: the force of the Ego

To T's question, P has given a reply. We can represent it in the following way in Figure 5.3.

The family of these transactions is characterized by the fact that P responds with sufficient resources; it is not impeded by the internal movements nor by external conditioning. In psychoanalytic terms, we would say that it is a sufficiently strong Ego and that it is responding based on reality testing, it is using a part of the Ego

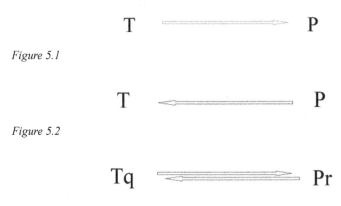

T ————————⟶ P

Figure 5.1

T ⟵———————— P

Figure 5.2

Tq ⟸————————⟹ Pr

Figure 5.3

that is free from conflict. In Transactional Analysis terms, we would say that they are responding based on the Adult Ego state.

If the exchanges of transactions between T and P were to proceed on this modality, we could conclude that P is in complete possession of all of their resources. There are no intrapsychic nor interpersonal instances that limit self-expression. Therefore, we could infer that the problem does not derive from the way in which P structures their experience, but from an "objective" difficulty that is independent from the functioning of P.

The second family of transactions: defence

However, normally the exchanges do not stop at this level but, sooner or later, P will cease to respond with all their resources, and this is an important indicator. Their reality testing will be less clear, they will respond from a conflicted part of the Ego; in terms of Transactional Analysis, their responses originate from contaminations and not from the Adult Ego state. In other terms, we can say that P is defending themselves. We can represent this family of transactions in a diagram (Figure 5.4).

This diagram represents P responding by adopting defensive aspects. It is no longer at the previous level. Now their responses are not dictated by the here and now and, therefore, they are not able to call on all of their resources to resolve the problem, rather they are weakened (the idea of contamination in Transactional Analysis) by other instances. In this case, psychoanalysts can utilize the constructs of the Id and the Superego. Transactional analysts would refer to other constructs: the Child Ego state, and the Parent Ego state. More generally, we can say that P is defending themselves and, therefore, a part of their energy focused on defence is drained from the functions of the Ego that are no longer fully resourced. Reality testing is reduced to varying degrees according to the severity of the defence.

In the face of this type of transactions T has a different task. They can no longer ask questions because the responses would come from a contamination zone, they would not be dealing with the Ego but with its defence. To use a biblical reference, it would be like building in sand instead of on rock. At this level of transactions, the task of T is confronting the defence, acting to separate the functioning part of the Ego from its contaminations. In the following diagram (Figure 5.5) we indicate the ways this happens.

Following the operations that engage with the defence, it might be that P recovers a greater strength of their Ego and manages to respond from their conflict-free

Figure 5.4

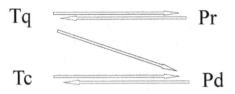

Figure 5.5

Ego. Using language from Transactional Analysis: the Adult Ego state has been decontaminated. If this occurs, the therapist can stop confronting the defence and start to interrogate again, as is indicated in the diagram (Figure 5.6):

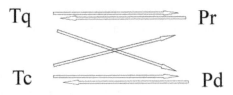

Figure 5.6

The third family of transactions: the regression

However, the communication exchanges between the two can have other modalities that belong in the third family of transactions. In answer to T's question, P's response is particularly regressive, with even less access to resources as compared to the already insufficient presence of resources in the case of the defence. We can say that it is a response of avoidance, of strong passivity in which the functions of the Ego are practically diminished altogether, the reality testing is almost completely lost; in terms of Transactional Analysis, we would say that the Adult Ego state is excluded, overpowered by the Child or by the Parent or by both.

We can represent this family of transactions in the following diagram (Figure 5.7).

The tasks of the therapist in this case are different. The confrontation of the defence is not possible due to the almost complete absence of the Ego. Asking questions is especially unproductive because on the other side there is no Adult Ego state to answer. The resources are reduced to such a low level that the requests of the therapist drain the little residual strength necessary for maintaining the precarious equilibrium. The task then becomes that of reconstruction, of placing oneself in the place of the P and helping them without requiring any performance on their behalf. We represent this in the following diagram (Figure 5.8).

Following the reconstruction interventions of T, it is possible that P will recover their capacity for defence (Pd), or even acceptable reality testing (Pr). In the diagram that follows (Figure 5.9) the upward arrows show the realization of these results within the couple.

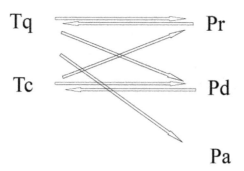

Figure 5.7

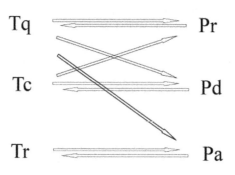

Figure 5.8

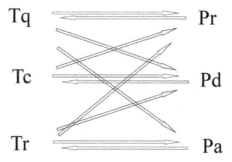

Figure 5.9

The evaluation of resources

The distribution of the transactions in the three families, indicated here and represented in the three levels of communication modalities, constitutes a means of evaluating the resources of the patient.

We can hypothesize a trend of transactions in which there is a distribution with some transactions from the first family (Adult Ego state, strength of the Ego), some from the defensive level, and none from the regressive order. We can say that we are dealing with a case that, while displaying some defences, has resources to manage change. The task of the couple varies in difficulty according to the proportions of Adult transactions as compared to defensive ones; an imbalance in favour of the latter will make the therapy more difficult and probably less brief, even if its intensity is preserved. For therapy in which, in addition to the aforementioned transactions, there are significant instances of regressive transactions, the task of the couple will be more arduous and, therefore, we cannot expect a therapy to be especially brief.

Variations of distribution are connected to variations of the technique adopted by the therapist and the length of the therapy. It now seems clear how brief therapy models characterized by a careful selection of patients can boast of such short times.

It is the resources of the patient that means the length of the therapy is short, as well as the technical ability of the therapist.

The evaluation of the resources of the patient does not only concern the whole course of the therapy but also each moment, transaction by transaction. The therapist can, and on most occasions must continuously, evaluate the type of response that they receive from their interlocutor. It is as if the therapist, while monitoring the level of transactions that they receive moment by moment, is able to graduate the operations of pressure within the intrapsychic triangle on the basis of the resources that are gradually revealed.

Evaluation of the resources through observation of the patient's body language

The "diagnosis" of the resources employed by the patient is not only based on the type of transactions but also on the observation of the body language, movements, and gestures that the patient produces during the conversation.

The diagnosis in this case is made through the evaluation of anxiety. As we know, anxiety (A) is linked both to defence (D) and to impulse (I). Therefore, the ways in which the patient manages anxiety affects the patient's observable defensive asset. A more developed capacity of management will be an indicator of a structure with more resources. Inversely, a clinical picture in which the management of anxiety is less developed is indicative of a structure with fewer resources.

Patients' mimicking, expressive, and motor behaviour represents the most immediate way to observe how the patient manages anxiety. In the next chapter, we examine in detail the different modalities for anxiety management and, so, we will be able to construct a more accurate evaluation of the patient's resources.

Note

1 This chapter was written by Marco Sambin.

References

Berne, E. (1961). *Transactional Analysis in Psychotherapy*. New York: Grove Press.
Menninger, K. (1958). *Theory of Psychoanalytic Technique*. New York: Basic Books.

6 The evaluation of anxiety using ITAP[1]

Introduction

Anxiety can be defined as a basic emotion, directly associated with the perception of danger, which can impair the health or survival of the person. In this form, anxiety represents an adaptive and protective response that favours survival, leads to the adaptation of the human species, and constitutes the basis for the avoidance of danger.

Anxiety can, however, at the same time constitute a pathological condition; no longer a functional human adaptation for avoidance of danger, but rather it develops as a response to situations that are not threatening at all. In such cases, the loss of its functional protection is observed, with all the consequent suffering perceived at the individual level and an increase in dysfunctional somatic reactions, often with an ongoing cyclical reaction.

In this chapter, we concentrate on a fundamental aspect of the diagnostic and therapeutic process: the evaluation of anxiety (vertex A of the triangle of conflict) in the moment in which it presents itself in a session as a dysfunctional pattern correlated with a specific psychological or medical disorder.

Before embarking on this journey, it is worth noting that the information reported represents a reasoned integration of various authors, including: J. ten Have-de Labije (2006, 2012), A. Abbass (2015), Doidge (2007), LeDoux (2015), Goleman (1995), Fosha et al. (2009), Davanloo (1978, 1990, 2005), Siegel (2005), Kandel and Kupfermann (1995).

Taking basic neurobiological formulations as a starting point, we will proceed to describe the physiological manifestations of anxiety in the process of evaluation of the patient, then to a description of the common associated medical consequences, as well as an in-depth look at these aspects in the light of their implications for clinical work.

The process of anxiety: a general overview

As far back as the 1920s, the attention of academics concentrated on the comprehension of physiological mechanisms connected with anxiety. W.B. Cannon (1927) and P. Bard (1928) were the first to understand and describe emotional processes by referring, specifically, to two subcortical structures, the thalamus and the hypothalamus. These structures generate the coordinated control responsible for the regulation of the peripheric manifestation of emotions, and they transmit to the cortex all of the information necessary for the conscious perception of emotional phenomena. In the following decades, the process connected to the regulation of emotions in general, and of anxiety specifically, gradually became better understood and it is currently possible to represent neurobiological regulation of anxiety through the pathway we are about to describe. Our experience in the world mainly occurs through the five senses and proprioception. When we sense a threat from our environment, the information is first processed through sensorial pathways, from the spinal cord through the brainstem, to the thalamus, from which two canals of transmission branch out, one to the amygdala and one to the cortex. The information is sent to the amygdala in a matter of 12 milliseconds, allowing a short latency primitive response on one hand and, on the other, prepares the cortex for more sophisticated information that will arrive at a later point from the cortex. The thalamus sends more sophisticated signals to the cortex, taking about 30 to 40 milliseconds, so as to provide more accurate data concerning what is happening.

We hypothesize that the cortex and the amygdala (in collaboration with the hippocampus) interpret the aforementioned information as being real sources of danger – the amygdala sends signals to the hypothalamus via the locus coeruleus, situated in the brainstem, as well as sending signals to associated cortical areas.

The locus coeruleus coordinates the so-called short pathway of the stress system as well as linking the regions of the brain that produce the hormone CRH (corticotropin-releasing hormone), which releases corticotropin, together with the autonomic nervous system.

Let us now return to the description of the short and the long pathways, as described by ten Have-de Labije (2006).

The short pathway: the amygdala sends signals to the hypothalamus and the regions of the brainstem that regulate the automatic responses to the perceived threat. The hypothalamus then combines information arriving from the cerebral cortex, the amygdala, and the brainstem into a coherent response. It also acts on the autonomic nervous system through the modulation of feedback originating from the internal organs.

The long pathway: the locus coeruleus sends signals to the hypothalamus, which then goes on to trigger the long pathway of the stress system, also known as the hypothalamic–pituitary–adrenal (HPA) axis. The CRH, the most important stress hormone, is produced by the hypothalamus and, via the bloodstream (the hypothalamic-hypophyseal portal circulation), reaches the pituitary gland, which, in turn, releases adrenocorticotropic hormone (ACTH) into the blood. The ACTH stimulates the adrenal glands to produce glucocorticoid hormones, which place the body in a state of alert and increase the levels of blood glucose thereby providing energy to the muscles and nerves. In the case of acute stress, the hypothalamus also secretes vasopressin to further activate the adrenal glands. When the threat is perceived to be no longer present, the system is deactivated through a negative feedback mechanism that allows the hypothalamus to suppress the secretion of CRH, and the pituitary gland to stop the release of ACTH.

Once the threat has passed, the system tends to stabilize again in the shortest time possible to bring the organism back to normal functioning, without there being any consequences for the organs involved. However, when the anxiety is chronic these organs risk being damaged in the long-term.

Discharge pathways of anxiety and associated defensive patterns

Let us now examine how the organism discharges anxiety. There are three discharge pathways (Abbass, 2015) to be monitored during the clinical process, taking into consideration the most common medical manifestations and the associated defensive modalities. The perspective of Transactional Analysis will be gradually introduced through a process of comparison and systemic integration. The various modalities adopted by the patient in the discharge of anxiety provide us with information concerning the capacity of management, they are also linked with specific defensive patterns.

Discharge of anxiety through striated muscle (voluntary)

Striated muscles are those that we can move intentionally. Anxiety at this level manifests itself initially as tension in the muscles of the hands, starting in the thumbs, from the mouth or the periorbital zone (for example, a tic of the eyelids). Subsequently, the anxiety tends to permeate the forearms and then the length of the arms before reaching the shoulders, the neck, the muscles of the face, the abdominal muscles, and, finally, the back and the legs (ten Have-de Labije, 2006). Furthermore, the activation of this pathway is characterized by sighing and the contraction of the diaphragm.

Comment

In the presence of this activated pathway, the associated defence is the isolation of affect (Abbass, 2015); the patient is able to name the emotion but has no direct bodily experience of the impulse. Novellino (2010, p. 52) defines this type of defence as: "a mechanism through which the person quarantines affective content, thought to be dangerous, without feeling the emotional resonance: for example, our patient's friend or relative dies, but even in the knowledge that they have died the patient does not experience any pain". Simply talking about the emotion (for example, in the phrase, "I recognize that there is anger") does not cause the patient to really get in touch with the emotional and somatic side of the Child Ego state, rather it tends to keep the experience at a mainly cognitive level.

In terms of Transactional Analysis, we might be dealing with an injunction, "Don't express yourself" and/or "Don't feel", at varying levels of intensity, which it is possible to observe when the description of the emotion is only made of the Adult Ego state (looking once more at the phrase "I recognize that there is anger") without a sufficient contact with the Child Ego state (in our example, "I'm really angry!", with consequent bodily and emotional activation reactions). When we observe this type of discharge pathway in the patient, we can hypothesize that their Adult Ego state has sufficient strength and structure. Their capacity to tolerate the emergence of anxiety-invoking contents should be considered strong enough to make an intervention possible with the aim of increasing awareness concerning, above all, what is happening at the emotional level.

We can see how this discharge pathway might be associated with particular medical symptoms, such as: tension headaches, chest pain, jaw pain, teeth grinding, shortness of breath, choking sensations, abdominal wall pain, vocal and other tics, leg pain, neck pain, cramps, fibromyalgia, tremors, back pain (Abbass, 2015, p. 12).

What do we observe?

Let us now describe which body signals we should be aware of when we observe the patient. Typical manifestations of anxiety at the level of the striated muscle:

- Feet: repeated movement of the tip of the foot, or the whole foot, in an upwards motion, as if they were small kicks in the air or oscillations, or alternatively, tips of the feet firmly placed on the ground.
- Legs: oscillations or repeated tensing, contraction of the calves or of the quadriceps.
- Stomach: sunken as a possible consequence of contracted abdominal muscles, tensed.
- Back: straight as if it were blocked by a plank of wood, or excessively curved as if folding in on itself.
- Chest: strong prominence towards the frontal part of the body and, probably, consequent tension in pectoral muscles and in the trapezius muscle, or repeated movements of the rib cage because of "short" breaths with possible pain in the intercostal muscles.
- Shoulders: pushed down or contracted towards the neck. Repetitive micro-movements can be observed involving tension in the trapezius and/or deltoid muscles.
- Arms: tense, rigid, "wooden", not fluid at all, or restless, tremoring, jerky.
- Hands: clenched in a fist, contracted, or constantly fidgeting with fingers, nails, knuckles, thumbs. The person might drum their fingers on the arm of the chair, or grip it strongly, their hands might be crossed, and the person can continue to "crack" them.
- Face: tense jaw that frequently contracts, frequent movement of the lips (biting their lip, biting their fingernails or the skin on their fingers), frequent closing of the eyelids (to be investigated, possible eye dryness as a symptom of the sympathetic nervous system), tension in the forehead and eyebrows (frowning).

Discharge of anxiety through smooth muscles (involuntary)

The second discharge pathway of unconscious anxiety involves the smooth muscles of the internal organs, which are not under intentional control. The dysfunctional patterns can manifest themselves in the sympathetic and parasympathetic nervous system (ten Have-de Labije and Neborsky, 2012, p. 49).

What do we observe?

- Sympathetic: dry mouth, dryness of the eyes (see the previous section on striated muscle), vaginal dryness, sweating of armpits, sweating of hands, cold hands, blushing, variations in the acceleration and strength of heart contractions, shivers.
- Parasympathetic: light-headedness and/or dizziness (the patient's eyes wander looking for a spot to fix their gaze in), weakness, constipation, diarrhea, sensation of needing to urgently urinate, nausea, excessive secretion of hydrochloric acid in stomach (frequent rumbling of stomach to be investigated).

Abbass associates this discharge pathway in smooth muscle with the defence of repression. According to the author, the patient might, in the face of the request to get in touch with their emotion, seem calm and apparently at ease, without any sign of discharge in the striated muscle. Such a reaction should be investigated further by looking for signals that might suggest involvement of the smooth muscle. In this second case, the defence involved is the instant repression of the impulse or feeling in the body, and it can, if maintained over time, bring about the medical problems previously described.

We can see that this discharge pathway can also be associated with certain medical symptomologies, such as (Abbass, 2015, p. 14): hypertension, coronary spasms, flushing, hypotension with loss of consciousness, asthma, coughing, choking symptoms, irritable bowel syndrome, gastroesophageal reflux disease, functional vomiting, unexplained abdominal pain, bladder dysfunctional, interstitial cystitis, migraine.

Comment

In terms of Transactional Analysis, the defence of repression can be read as a contamination of the Child with respect to the Adult, who is stripped of the ability to attribute meaning to that which is happening. The aim is to keep away from the sphere of awareness any material, principally of an emotional nature, that could upset established schemas and equilibria. Underlying this is a critical Parent who acts by "squashing" the authentic impulses that manifest themselves through compromise solutions.

Discharge of anxiety through the cognitive-perceptual pathway

The third type of disorder related to anxiety mainly relates to thought, which can become, at various times, incoherent, accelerated, or slow, with the possible occurrence of hallucinations in the most extreme cases. We subsequently report medical conditions associated with this pathway of anxiety discharge.

What do we observe?

During the session there are various indicators that might suggest the involvement of this discharge pathway: visual blurring, visual loss, tunnel vision, hearing impairment or loss, memory loss, mental confusion, loss of consciousness, pseudoseizure, dissociation, hallucination in all five senses (Abbass, 2015, p. 17).

According to the author, the patients who utilize this unconscious pathway of anxiety discharge defend themselves through projection, projective identification, and splitting.

Comment

The emergence of this typology of primitive defence leads us to consider how there can be a structural fragility in a patient with little investment of energy in the Adult Ego state, which has weak boundaries and is excessively permeable. The distortion of reality or, indeed, the loss of contact with reality, can lead in the direction that Transactional Analysis defines as an exclusion of the Adult.

Furthermore, the defences associated with this discharge of anxiety pathway suggest a borderline (or even psychotic) personality structure. They are also indicative of a primitive level of functioning in which split, primitive, internal regulators act, like the fairy and the ogre (Haykin, 1980). We can therefore affirm that, in the presence of these manifestations, there is not a solid structure, and the therapeutic plan will have to take account of this, adapting in light of the consequent decreased intensity.

Patterns of motor conversion

Another somatic pattern can be found in motor conversion. In this case, the patient does not show any sign of tension in the striated muscle; rather, they appear flat, in the sense that they lose energy in one or more muscle areas. Here, the anxiety is completely displaced onto the body in a state of weakness and muscle block. This can lead to the phenomenon known as "belle indifference", in which the person appears to be relaxed despite the muscular paralysis (Abbass, 2015). The reader who is interested in psychosomatic themes can refer to Abbass's detailed treatment.

As far as the defensive patterns are concerned, there is another dimension in the resistance of the guilt that Davanloo calls "perpetrator of unconscious" (internal persecutor) (Davanloo, 1987). This defence can be seen in patients who are very resistant and fragile and who tend to sabotage the therapy process so as not to come into contact with the guilt due to the unconscious anger directed at the caregivers. The intimacy with the therapy is forbidden by the resistances of the

Superego, which tend to interrupt the process, putting the therapeutic alliance at risk (Abbass, 2015).

Evaluation of manifestations of anxiety according to distribution, speed of onset, and duration of disorder

In her interesting work, J. ten Have-de Labije (2006) considers not only the specific pathway but also how much each is used in the various moments of the therapy. If we consider, for example, a hypothetical patient who mostly utilizes the striated pathway and only rarely uses the sympathetic system, we could envisage a person with good ability for managing anxiety and strength of the Ego that is strong enough to manage a particularly intensive process of change in a "safe" way. In terms of Transactional Analysis, we are dealing with a person with an Adult Ego state that is sufficiently energized to be able to react effectively to the somatic reactions of the Adapted Child (anxious manifestations). Conversely, if this hypothetical patient, at the first hint of getting near to their world of emotional experience (Child), were to start to experience diarrhea and nausea and difficulty in thought processing (strong contamination of the Adult by the Child), we would be able to conclude that they have little ability to manage anxiety, and the process would necessarily have to slow down. Moreover, in the extreme case that the symptoms concerning the cognitive-perceptive sphere are more prominent than the symptoms concerning the motor system and the autonomic system, we will know that the patient suffers from fragility of the Ego (Adult strongly contaminated and excluded), and probably they should not be considered as being suitable for this type of intensive treatment.

Furthermore, it is possible, again referring to the work of ten Have-de Labije, to evaluate the patient's capacity to regulate their anxiety, taking account of the speed of onset, the duration of the disorder, and the speed with which the manifestation is resolved. A patient whose anxiety emerges rapidly, lasts a long time, and does not resolve easily will be much more difficult to treat. In this case, the Adult of the patient does not seem able to manage the somatic reactions of the Child, thus supplying us with a clear instruction: to work on the reinforcement of their limits by referring to the unveiling of the material about the Child Ego state. In psychodynamic terms: access to the impulse (I), to a subsequent phase. Conversely, a person whose anxiety appears and resolves quickly during the clinical work will be more capable of regulating it (Adult with a greater ability to keep boundaries) and will be able to, in time, work on emotional aspects with the appearance of ever fewer anxious symptoms.

The breakdown of the pathways of anxiety discharge into three exists simultaneously with the division into three of the different types of psychic functioning, indicated in Chapter 5, which concerns the therapeutic contract. Through observing how anxiety manifests itself in the body, we can obtain an immediate view of the patient's structure and, therefore, we can regulate the degree of pressure we enact during the therapeutic process. The evaluation of the anxiety is a dynamic process that is not limited by the static boundaries of the categories indicated here. Rather, it evolves throughout the course of the therapist's interventions.

Conclusion

The ITAP technique foresees, similarly to other intervention techniques involving rapid mobilization of the unconscious, to keep under careful consideration the anxiety-related reactions of the patient during the course of a session. Depending on the intervention, various anxious reactions can emerge, including strong ones (as we have observed in this chapter), and it is necessary to consider these aspects with regard to the sufficient protection (Berne, 1972) of the patient. Excessive pressure on the defences (for example, drive or incapacitation) of a patient with an Adult structure that is not very solid might lead to contact with sudden, anxiety-provoking contents that are intense and, at times, momentarily incapacitating. Calibration of the interventions, whilst taking into consideration the anxious reactions, results in clinical activity that is more respectful and, at the same time, more effective.

Note

1 This chapter was written by Francesco Scottà.

References

Abbass, A. (2015). *Reaching Through Resistance – Advanced Psychotherapy Techniques*. Kansas City, MO: Seven Leaves Press.

Bard, P. (1928). A diencephalic mechanism for the expression of rage with special reference to the sympathetic nervous system. *American Journal of Physiology*, 84: 490–516.

Berne, E. (1972). *What Do You Say After You Say Hello? The Psychology of Human Destiny*. New York: Grove Press.

Cannon, W. B. (1927). The James-Lange theory of emotions: A critical examination and an alternative theory. *The American Journal of Psychology*, 39: 106–124.

Davanloo, H. (1978). *Basic Principles and Techniques in Short-term Dynamic Psychotherapy*. Northvale, NJ: J. Aronson inc.

Davanloo, H. (1987). Clinical manifestations of superego pathology. *International Journal of Short-Term Psychotherapy*, 2(4): 225–254.

Davanloo, H. (1990). *Unlocking the Unconscious: Selected Papers of Habib Davanloo, MD*. Chichester: John Wiley and Sons, Ltd.

Davanloo, H. (2005). Intensive short-term dynamic psychotherapy. In B. J. Sadock & V. A. Sadock (Eds.), *Kaplan & Sadock's Comprehensive Textbook of Psychiatry* (pp. 2628–2652). Philadelphia: Lippincott Williams & Wilkins.

Doidge, N. (2007). *The Brain that Changes Itself*. New York: Viking Press.

Fosha, D., Siegel, D. J., & Solomon, M. (2009). *The Healing Power of Emotion: Affective Neuroscience, Development & Clinical Practice*. New York: W. W. Norton & Company.

Goleman, D. (1995). *Emotional Intelligence*. New York: Bantam Books.

Haykin, M. D. (1980). Type casting: The influence of early childhood experience upon the structure of the ego state. *Transacional Analysis Journal*, 10: 354–364.

Kandel, E. R., & Kupfermann, I. (1995). Emotional states. In J. H. Schwartz & T. M. Jessell (Eds.), *Essential of Neural Science and Behaviour* (pp. 595–613). New Jersey: Prentice Hall International, Inc.

LeDoux, J. (2015). *Anxious: Using the Brain to Understand and Treat Fear and Anxiety*. London: Penguin Books.

Novellino, M. (2010). *Seminari clinici [Clinical Seminars]*. Milano: Franco Angeli.

Siegel, M. (2005). Can we cure fear? *Scientific American Mind*, Special edit., 16(4): 44–58.

ten Have-de Labije, J. (2006). When patients enter with anxiety on the forefront. *Ad Hoc Bulletin of Short-Term Dynamic Psychotherapy*, 10: 36–69.

ten Have-de Labije, J., & Neborsky, R. J. (2012). *Mastering Intensive Short-term Dynamic Psychotherapy – A Roadmap to the Unconscious*. London: Karnac.

7 The alliance[1]

The term "alliance" is intended to describe a broad phenomenon that, in many ways, remains outside of awareness. This phenomenon extends to various levels of the field that is established when two people meet in an intense manner, as occurs in a therapeutic situation.

It is difficult to account for all of the movements that the interaction between two people involves. Many of them are efficacious independently from theorization, many are so subtle as to make it difficult to theorize.

For this reason, we can make a distinction (while acknowledging that it is reductive and overly schematic) among three types of alliance. These will be described briefly here. The quality that they have in common is the aim of helping the therapist to be present for the patient's problem, leaving aside their more personal reactions. One of the most significant factors of change in psychotherapy is precisely this capacity to be present, to be with the patient and their problem. These are simple words, but they require a discipline on the part of the therapist to relate to what the interlocutor is presenting and to set aside their own expectations, thoughts, and feelings. It is easy to say, but it is much more difficult to put into practice. It is a quality of presence in the couple that, to use a currently fashionable term, is called mindfulness (obviously not the mindfulness of glossy magazines). This concept was already well developed in the work of Rogers (1951), without the need to resort to a sort of transplanted orient (nothing against the thinking and practices of the East). Well-cultivated empathy leads the therapist to think the thoughts of their interlocutor, to experience their emotions, to feel their sensations, while still maintaining an appropriate distance. In short, it is the main instrument with which to construct the alliance and, at the same time, a fundamental technical aspect to bring about change.

In the following, we make some suggestions for each of the three types of alliance. They should be taken as introductory indications and not as an exhaustive and systematic account. The aim is to propose to the therapist a "wave length" that helps them to attune to the patient.

Cognitive alliance

We can summarize the ways of increasing the cognitive alliance through a couple of little rules so simple that they seem trivial: "Think their thoughts and not your own" and "express yourself with thoughts structured in a similar way to theirs, rather than to yours".

They are practical suggestions to get away from the usual way of using our minds.

In the everyday construction of our experience, the objects that we form – from the simplest, such as the book that you're reading, to one of the most complicated, such as the state of mind that accompanies the act of reading – are all "objects" that are formed through the organization of conditions. Even our thoughts are not exceptions to this general rule, they are ways of organizing our experience. Many of our thoughts are so much "ours", and so little "costly" in their formation, that they seem natural, obvious, and we marvel at the idea that others, given the same conditions, might formulate different thoughts. Prejudices are the clearest manifestation of the "naturalness" of some of our ways of thinking. As well as prejudices, there are other less evident forms with which we crystalize our way of thinking and take it for granted. For example, these different ways of thinking can be highlighted by the wonder we experience when we realize that others do something in a completely different way from what we expect. "Ah, so you . . . make mayonnaise, . . . complete your tax return, . . . do a seed stitch, . . . make love, . . . do a backhand in tennis, in this strange way?" The wonder arises from realizing that the way we make mayonnaise, complete our tax return, and so on, does not go without saying.

In a clinical situation, our thinking might take up a lot of our energy. We must take account of so many variables that it is only natural to be in a state of cognitive overload. Furthermore, if we have not yet assimilated our clinical model, a good part of our mind is occupied by browsing the manual that we have in our heads and/or trying to gain the approval of our supervisor, real or imaginary as it may be.

Putting all this aside, now that I am in front of you I can think like you, within the couple our thoughts develop together, in meeting you I can free myself from my everyday mental organization.

To reiterate in a more scholarly fashion, you act so that countertransference does not collude with your transferential needs. All of our activity contains a dose of transference; there is no act or thought or feeling that is objective. Therefore, in the face of the patient, we have to pay much attention to what happens to our thoughts in a session: they form with greater difficulty, they could be faster, more cheerful, heavier, they might worry us, and so on. What other qualities might they have?

So, once we have managed to realize the state of our thoughts, for example "they find it difficult to come", we have to make a distinction. "They find it diffi-cult to come" because normally thoughts come to me with difficulty regarding the topic proposed by my interlocutor (perhaps there is something to resolve here). Or "they find it difficult to come" because my interlocutor manages to impede my thoughts? The first is a transference need of mine and it is an issue that I have to deal with on my own, and, if for nothing else, for the fact that they are paying me to be treated, not so that I can treat myself. The second represents an aspect that is called, with an imprecise term, "countertransferential", that is, it is something that my interlocutor induces in me and, therefore, it is a precious indicator as to how the therapy proceeds. In this second case, it would be good practice to keep account of the information that I get from the countertransference. If the thoughts "come to me with difficulty" because of countertransference issues, I will have to remain attentive both to avoid everything coming to a stop and to not enter reactively into a windmill of cognitive activity. The information supplied by countertransference allows me to attune my way of producing thoughts to that of my interlocutor.

In light of what we have said so far, the second rule is justified: the therapist, in order to attune to the patient, expresses thoughts that, in terms of their intensity, speed, depth, and style, are similar to those of the interlocutor.

The aim of this suggestion is to enable the therapist to attune to the patient even in their own modalities of expression. This will mean that the patient feels "near" to the therapist because they are "similar". The induction of this state in the patient results in a lowering of defensive aspects. The psychic system of the patient does not have feelings of rejection because they perceive that the therapist's interventions can be experienced more as originating from the self, than from the non-self, and therefore, they evaluate that it is not necessary to protect themself with defensive reactions.

All of this is described as an alliance; it is the similarity between the modalities of cognitive functioning of the two interlocutors.

Emotional alliance

In the case of the emotional alliance we can also hazard to propose a couple of "little rules" that are just as simple in their formulation. They are as follows: "Listen to their emotions, not yours" and "Express emotions that mirror theirs".

As far as emotions are concerned, the separation between the countertransferential part and the transferential part of the therapist is more delicate and difficult. In general, we are more able to master our thoughts than our emotions, our learning is more cognitive than emotional, greater efforts are dedicated to thinking than to feeling. On the other hand, emotions are warning bells for a situation that does not have optimal balance, and, therefore, we move closer to defensive functioning, which is accompanied by less awareness and by an Ego that has had to give up on part of its capacity for management. We are, therefore, less "trained" in reading what is happening, and this inevitably brings with it greater difficulty in understanding if what I am feeling as a therapist is my own personal reaction to my interlocutor (the therapist's emotional transference), or it is perceiving, through what I am feeling, what my interlocutor is presenting (emotional countertransference).

When another person expresses themself, I can feel attracted, repulsed, curious, bored; I can feel like "taking them in my arms" or "throwing them out of the window"; I can experience anger, happiness, interest, disgust, and so on, an endless range with multiple nuances. Let us hypothesize that my interlocutor, in this moment, provokes in me feelings of happiness. (Let's talk about something other than problems and heavy topics for once!) What I am feeling could be a self-generated emotion. For example, I could be pleased with myself because, as a skilled therapist, I am applying the ITAP technique with unexpected results, precisely that which I am learning. In this case it would almost be right for me to pay you for the session because I am giving therapy to my narcissistic trait. Alternatively, I am able to make the distinction and understand that, aside from my personal emotions, the happiness that I feel is something that you are placing in my capacity for feeling; this allows me to evaluate with greater attention what you are presenting to me, and to do it in such an intense manner as to feel it myself as well. Indeed, you could be happy because you have obtained a desired result, and therefore I evaluate how to resonate with your expression. Alternatively, you might be pleased with yourself because you have just concocted a way of cheating your brother out of his inheritance, and therefore I have to find a way of making you aware of how I can distance myself from your state of mind.

Naturally, my personal emotional experiences are very important in order to understand yours, and I will be able to understand you better the more I am able to live those experiences. Moreover, in this moment, all of my personal emotions remain in the background, well separated from those that originate within the therapeutic couple. Only in this way am I able to manage the emotions and work towards our objective: your change, not mine.

The separation between the therapist's own emotions and the emotions that originate in the therapeutic couple is not as clear-cut as this passage appears to suggest. There is a continuous osmosis between what I have learnt to feel and experience as a person and what, as a therapist, I am feeling and experiencing. This often represents a rich resource for the interaction between the two, as well as being a secondary benefit for the personal development of the therapist. The discriminating criterion lies in the use that is made of it; the therapist's emotional participation is welcome in as much as it is synergistic to the therapeutic project agreed between the two. If you say to me that you are happy and I feel that it is countertransferential, I will modulate the expression of my happiness so as to remain within our contract. If I express my happiness excessively, it will detract from yours; too little and it might dampen this appropriate emotion. It is precisely for this reason that I will have to examine whether I feel happy on a personal level, I might further burden you or hold you back with my reaction.

What we have said so far regarding the emotional reaction of the therapist helps us to highlight the second "little rule": express emotions that mirror those of the interlocutor. We will never be a perfect mirror and, probably, it is not even required or useful. In any case, mirroring the emotions of the patient helps them to feel understood and to see in the other that which he or she is feeling and, therefore, it offers them the opportunity to engage with the issues.

On this issue, as in the case of the cognitive alliance, the responses, which are synchronized in terms of their closeness and similarity, make the experiences of the patient and the therapist similar, thereby facilitating openings and cooperation. Also on the emotional level, as we have already seen for the cognitive level, the therapist can elicit, or not elicit, movements of rejection in the patient.

Non-verbal alliance

The non-verbal alliance has an enormous quantity of observation stations that provide information regarding what is happening in the therapeutic couple.

When we talked about non-verbal insight (Chapter 4), we drew up a list of possible observations that we can now look at in more detail. The aim is to become aware, as therapists, of the rich nature of information, which is literally astonishing, that our interlocutor offers us without even considering the content of their verbal expressions. To be aware of this richness helps us to attune ourselves to what is often communicated without intention and awareness. It allows us to be fully present for the verbal and non-verbal communication offered in the relationship. This awareness has some significant consequences for the development of the psychotherapy. On the one hand, it guides our full presence, and therefore favours the subtle, beneath-the-surface aspect of the alliance. On the other hand, it is a reliable indicator for us to produce "responses" to what the interlocutor is proposing, thus an alliance is built that is explicit and observable, and it "suggests" to the therapist suitable interventions for the evolution of the therapy (see Chapter 9).

We can organize the quantity of observable material in a "scholastic" yet useful way by referring to a classification that uses the five senses. We will use hearing, sight, smell, and touch, but not taste. Of the remaining senses, we will use proprioception, balance, and pain, but not thermoception.

The observations that follow do not have the intention of being a systematic exposition, therefore our account will not be exhaustive. The aim is to legitimize the therapist's capacity to gather expressive qualities produced by the patient, to give ourselves permission to value intuition, the vague sensation that something is taking form. The expressive qualities that our interlocutor enacts are an important direct indicator and are not mediated by the structure of their experience. For example, the constantly sustained tone of voice, which presses and does not leave space for the other, with which a young female patient talked to me of our meetings – it was the vengeful tone that she would have liked to use with her "mother-witch" who had "poisoned" her. This style of communication was in use right from the start of the therapy, long before mention of the mother, object of so much animosity, and even once the mother appeared it was not until later that the "daughter-Cinderella" became aware of the poison in their relationship. All of this could be revealed, and much earlier, but only in an unaware communication.

Hearing

Let us address, first, our interlocutor's way of speaking. The ideation, the concatenation of thoughts, the syntax of meaning, the use of words, can all be part of the cognitive alliance. Here, we turn our attention to something that is more basic: the type of sound that our interlocutor emits. Basing ourselves on the emission of the voice, we can form diagnoses on the state of health, not only of the organism but also of the psychic state. This awareness is not asked of the psychotherapist, just as other competencies are not required; however, they are required to be open to the communication underlying different uses of the voice. For example, a "head" voice, a "throat" voice, a "belly" voice, send different messages concerning the interlocutor's use of the body, and concerning the degree of involvement, or exclusion, of various parts of the body in the act of communication. We can put it schematically: if I am talking from the "head", I am excluding most of my body as a source of resonance for my expression, and this is certainly meaningful; if I talk mainly using my "belly" as a zone of resonance, I am placing aspects of "primordial" vitality in my communication. What the weight of these modalities is can be deduced from other contextual information. In any case, the message is that between me and you, I also want to place my belly.

Besides its localization, the voice possesses an astonishing quantity of qualities. We can use the voice to transmit any expressive pattern, regardless of the meanings of the words. This type of communication is "true" because, generally speaking, it is outside of the control of the interlocutor.

We can now shift our attention to the paravebal aspects of voice emissions ("eee", "hmm", and other sounds), to the rhythm of the emission (slow, quick, broken), to the tone (high, low), to the musical phrasing of the voice (pressing, smooth, complaining, aggressive, impotent, penetrating, fleeting, commanding, welcoming, seductive. . .). We will realize that the communicative patterns transmitted represent an almost infinite array and that they give us important information regarding our interlocutor.

Sight

The observations that we can undertake as therapists are so many that we can divide them into at least two categories: observations of the face – and here we pay attention both to the face in general as well as to the eyes, the forehead, the eyebrows, the lips – and observations of the body.

It should be noted that we are making these distinctions only for teaching reasons. In reality, the process is much more fluid and less structured. It is like playing a score. To learn it, it is necessary to repeat the same passage, that arpeggio, that slightly more difficult phrase; in the end, these instances of learning fall into the background and leave space for the quality of the whole.

The expressions of the face represent a very rich collection of information that the other person provides us with. They constitute a fundamental guide for our relational behaviour. Before the Superego was formed, and before the Psychic Presence emerged, our behaviour as infants was regulated by the capacity to pick up on the expressions of the faces of our significant figures (Weiss, 1960). A frowning face immediately meant "stay away", while a relaxed, open face meant "you are very welcome", and all of this before the Ego was fully formed.

Therefore, the capacity to pick up on the expressions is at the heart of our survival, and we use it continuously, even in our everyday lives as adults. It constitutes an indispensable guide for our behaviour. Indeed, in therapy all of the expressive information that the patient's face transmits to us are precious and not to be neglected. It is all the more precious due to fact that, while it is not particularly structured information nor very "rational", it does have the advantage of being genuine, regardless of the intentions of the patient themself.

There is no sense in wanting to summarize the quantity of expressive qualities in a face. It would be necessary to compose a list of countless qualifiers. Art, in all its forms, is based on expressive qualities: images, sounds, forms, written words, spoken words; and, therefore, we can only imagine how many nuances can be picked up on through careful observation of expressive qualities.

A particular point of observation are the eyes. It is no accident that they have been called "mirror of the soul". We observe them because of their intrinsic expressive qualities: smiling, fleeting, stunned, intense, bold, cheerful, bewitching, vivacious, immobile, scowling, thoughtful, open, intelligent, staring, blocked, seductive, sad, and so on. But we also observe them because of the power of the relationship that they embody. Eye contact is a strong means for establishing and maintaining a relationship: from Stern and the mother-child relationship, to the seductive eyes of a partner, to the "loss" of the gaze during a psychotic crisis, but also in the process of dying. Therefore, it is an important indicator of how our interlocutor relates with us: can they handle our being or not, are they cooperative in the exchange of gazes or not, or are they avoiding our gaze or staring too much? All of this concerns, albeit synthetically, the relationship within the therapeutic couple.

In addition, the eyes "bring" other figures into the relationship other than the therapeutic couple. Often, our interlocutors, in significant moments, throw glances that are not directed at any of the objects present on the scene, but they are only momentary connections, or episodes populated by people who, consciously or otherwise, they are directing their gaze at. What's more, the gaze is not generic, but takes on the exact expression that they are transmitting in that moment.

The presence of the gaze in the therapeutic couple also have another side: the way in which the interlocutor looks at the therapist. Given that the interaction also occurs through the gaze directed at the therapist, it is necessary that the therapist uses their own way of looking in a knowing way. For example, we can look at two attitudes that are absolute opposites. One use of the gaze is to investigate, to penetrate, to enter the world of the other, while another use is to be receptive and provide space. The first is a gaze that stares, that gathers what there is to see, it is closed, definitive, focused, it has a viewing angle that is acute, it perceives shapes to a less extent, in nature it is the gaze of the predator; schematically we can define it as being "Western". The second is a gaze that blurs, that takes in what there is to see, a peripheral vision, it has an ample viewing angle, it sees movements well, in nature it is the gaze of the prey. Just as synthetically, we can define it as "Eastern". A patient who is looked at with the first type of gaze is induced to activate their defences. While a patient who is looked at with the second type of gaze is led to not be alarmed and to place their trust.

The therapist's observational skills must make it possible to use different ways of gazing in different moments of their relationship with the other.

So far we have explored the eyes, the same structure can be utilized for all the other "stations" in which we exercise, as therapists as well as in everyday life, the use of the gaze. We can look to pick up on things or to welcome.

The whole face is also a bearer of much non-verbal information. We can make a distinction between the parts that are more mobile, and those that are less mobile. As we have seen, the eyes are particularly mobile, another zone is the mouth, and above all the lips. With the mouth we conduct many operations, such as speaking, making sounds, eating, sucking, kissing, spitting, licking, biting; it is a font of much information for us (taste, smell, touch), and it is through our lips that we show so much more than the words we express. Also in this case, the expressions that we place on our lips can be described with an almost infinite list of adjectives.

The therapist is not required to engage in a literary exercise on the linguistic qualifiers of the expressions uttered by the patient's mouth, rather we ask them to be receptive and curious regarding the messages that will arrive.

The mouth, but also the eyes, can react instantly to that which the therapist expresses, sometimes clearly and at other times in an almost imperceptible manner. They are, in any case, an important station of observation of the reactions in the here and now of the patient and, therefore, can provide precious indications concerning the communication process in the relationship. It is worth highlighting the fact that, as well as this expressive function that we can label as transitory, they also have a communicative power linked to more permanent functions.

The scornful, depressed, neutral, serene, friendly character of the mouth can sometimes be a permanent trait (often correlated with the curve of the shape of the lips), which does not necessarily exclude the possibility of there being transitory traits as well. A mouth with a "permanent" scornful expression might also be coloured, "temporarily", by expressions of curiosity, pleasure, cheerfulness. There are many possibilities – so many, in fact, that language might not be able describe all of them without resorting to pedantry. Yet again, the therapist does not have to be aware of a catalogue of expressions, rather they should be open to receive the large quantity of diverse messages from the experience of our interlocutor, and consequently the ability to use them in the experiential process that is ongoing.

Other parts of the face have more permanent expressive qualities. The nose, the cheekbones, the forehead; they are not as mobile as the lips and the eyes. These more permanent qualities of the face derive, not so much from the anatomical conformation, but rather from expressive attitudes that have solidified over time and become stable. A face that is fleeting, open, suffering, pug-faced, serene, and so on, are brought to our glance not so much by bodily dimensions or forms but rather by their expressions.

Despite these more permanent characteristics, even these expressive qualities can change. They also tell us about experiential variations that, perhaps, do not occur in the here and now of the therapy but that need a longer time span to develop. For example, the evident discharge of existential burdens that occur during the session has visible momentary repercussions during the process in the most mobile parts of the face, and at the beginning of the next session will be confirmed, or disconfirmed, in the general expression of the face. There are various linguistic indicators with which we can notice these changes in the face: luminous versus dark, open versus closed, serene versus frowning, light versus heavy, happy versus unhappy. Once more, these many modalities are not an obvious and explicit verbal message, but they occur in an almost subliminal way. They require the application of an "oriental" vision, or perception, open, not defining, capable to welcome and embrace.

In addition, the body in general, and not only the face, sends non-verbal messages of great riches, which we can place on a momentary-transient continuum.

Someone who is burdened by life will have a body and a way of using it that reflects this, and it tends to be permanent. Someone who is not weighed down by life might display these qualities in a transitory manner in response to a momentary stimulus. The latter person will be more resilient compared to someone who is burdened by life, they will also recover a "normal" expression more easily.

In the same way, a person who is happy in life and feels "light" will have this same quality in a "permanent" way, and only momentarily will they have other expressive qualities, such as being "burdened" or any other expressive qualities that their circumstances dictate.

Even in this case, the messages should be read in light of the general pattern presented by the person, rather than in terms of single elements, less in material, physical, or biological forms, and more in the ways in which they express themselves.

Once more, the therapist is not necessarily required to have specific competence concerning the reading of messages transmitted by the body as is; for example, envisaged within some other clinical models (see, for example, the classic account of bioenergetic, Lowen, 1975, or according to methods anchored in the reading of the bioenergetic body, Dychtwald, 1977) but rather a general sensibility for the reception of the message sent by the body and the application in the relationship of the impressions that emerge regarding the body.

Smell

Smell also has a role, albeit to a lesser extent, in the therapeutic relationship. It is significant only in extreme cases. In most cases, people normally emit smell without arousing attention of other people. We do not usually smell so much as to affect, for better or for worse, the noses of our neighbours. Therefore, there is not usually anything to note, as far as the distance between patient and therapist is concerned. Nonetheless, certain extreme situations can sometimes be of interest.

Someone can smell, more than our accepted etiquette would allow. Obviously, if we are in a mechanics' garage, I would expect it to smell of oil and metal; if you are turning over manure, it probably will not emit spring smells; if you are washing tripe, it will not smell of lily of the valley. Such extremes in a therapy meeting are out of the ordinary. Therefore, if our interlocutor smells, we have to value the overlying message: they might have problems with their glandular system, they might have anosmia and not perceive their own odour, perhaps they do not wash themself, they might want to stay away from people, they might mistreat themself believing that they are unworthy of being presentable, there could be other explanations. A large quantity of significant information.

Then, there are specific odours. The smell of alcohol or nicotine on the breath. These are significant indices of information that should not be underestimated.

At the other extreme, there are people who have a smell that is too good. Someone wrapped in a cloud of perfume, either cheap or expensive, has chosen to say something, albeit with varying degrees of awareness. From blatant seduction, to "come close to me to smell me", to, at the same time, "I'm not really me, I'm my (expensive?) perfume, my meticulous hygiene", to the need to hide themself because of insecurity behind an accentuated stimulation of the nostrils.

There is, in any case, a vague sense of artefact, of the ingenuine, or, even, of evident trickery: you have my odour, not myself. Since a certain proximity is required to smell the odour, we can envisage certain types of messages: if you come close I fear your judgement, I am insecure and I cover myself with a nice smell, I stun you to attract you but ultimately to keep you away, I do not know how to regulate that which my body emits, and so on.

Touch

ITAP therapy is essentially verbal, and it does not capitalize directly on the body as do other models that prioritize it in a systematic way. Therefore, touch is not involved in a primary manner. There are, however, situations in which it might be present. Even the most detached and abstinent psychoanalytic models involve shaking hands at the end of the session. Hand shaking is also a good informer on the state of the patient. We can read it as a symbolic act and not one of closeness, of contact. Therefore, the movements undertaken in relation to the act of hand shaking are indicators of the intention to enter into a relationship: does it happen actively? Passively? With desire? With reluctance? Quickly? Slowly? Spontaneously or deliberately? We are talking about movements near the brief, preordained, tactile exchange. The body, the face, and voice all participate, each with their own expressive qualities.

Once one hand is holding the other, what happens? In this case touch, proprioception, and balance take part directly in signaling something, they are a gestalt with inescapable expressive qualities. It is impossible not to communicate, even during hand shaking. If the interlocutor expects, looks for, or avoids hand shaking, how will our physical contact be? If their handshake is firm, is it as a result of their work or is it a voluntary act? Or, if it is limp, it is because they are physical weak or is it a deliberate choice? Is it active or passive? Hot or cold? Fleeting or lingering? Accompanied by the body or solitary in its presence?

Once more, the therapist, a novice Monsignor Della Casa, is not expected to draw up a treatise on the good etiquette of hand shaking, rather they are made aware that there are many ways with which they can be informed concerning the state of their interlocutor.

In the moment of our farewell, a young man, who was in the depths of his suf-fering, calmly crushed my hand in a hard, relentless hold; similarly, during our hour-long session, he talked insistently and incessantly, with a tense voice, with-out giving me any space. Gradually, as this barrier melted, I started to have more presence in our verbal exchange and, at the same time, I was not rebuffed in our athletic farewell handshake.

In this case, the two indicators were so interdependent and they reinforced each other to such an extent that a scientifically-mind colleague could have con-structed a simple experimental design with a resulting significant (statistically and clinically) correlation between giving space (or not) in the verbal exchange and accepting (or not) the handshake.

Other times the messages are not so synergistic and they can lead to considera-tions such as: how come a person who is usually so fleeting . . ., or so bashful . . ., or so present . . ., or so warm . . ., or whatever . . ., then through their hand-shake sends me the message that, I'm here . . ., I'm escaping . . ., I'm cold . . ., and so on? This complex communicative structure is rich in information. It tells us that the front presented by the interlocutor is not homogenously compact, but that there are openings. These openings can be embraced by the therapist with awareness and, therefore, probably something similar to the considerations listed above will be said. Alternatively, the openings are processed at a less aware level and, therefore, our therapist will have some indications, present but not yet organized in a strong gestalt, that the front is not compact, that there is a glim-mer, that somewhere there should be a little aperture, that something can pass through, and so on.

Another form of touch is present in the session. It is a sort of touch that has synaesthetic qualities. Just as a high note is more likely to be clear and lumi-nous and a low note dark and sullen, just as the smell of wisteria has pastel colours and the smell of musk makes you think of the colour ochre, in the same way the general expressive quality of our interlocutor can say to us, "I am soft", "I am hard" and consequently they add, "touch me" or "stay away". Therefore, simultaneously, the response can be, "I embrace you", "I reject you", "I caress you", "I distance you from me", thus deploying that portion of touch that is conveyed by the voice and the eyes. The patient who tells of how their mother treated them so coldly so as to feel unworthy of the smallest tactile manifesta-tion on the part of their listener, generates in the listener a gestalt that brings tactile qualities, both as verbal content and expressive qualities. The therapist could respond adequately in terms of verbal content but unwittingly enter into alliance with the mother on the "tactile" front, reacting with an attitude that retraces, albeit from afar, the old experiences of the interlocutor, avoiding any "cuddles" and leaving them in deprivation. Obviously, it is not a case of hav-ing to dispense regressive and parental psychological pats on the head. Rather, it involves managing the complexity of communication in order to construct a corrective emotional experience on all communication levels, to which the therapist is able to access.

Proprioception and balance

The general indications also hold true for proprioception and balance: the therapist is not required to be a kinesthesiologist nor a posturologist – rather a certain sensitivity is expected regarding non-verbal messages that the patient conveys using their body.

The position that the patient assumes while sitting can convey many expressive qualities that are able to inform the attitudes that are rarely expressed directly, because they are rarely brought to the level of awareness. For example, you can sit in a manner that is relaxed, appropriately relaxed, over-relaxed, sunk in the armchair. Or, you can sit in a manner that is tonic, appropriately tonic, or overly tonic, on the edge of the seat as if you are about to leave. The balance of the body can be favourable to exchange, or it can inhibit it with, for example, an attitude of fighting, ready for a fight but also for flight. The general attitude of the body can tell us that the person has sufficient access to the force of the Ego and that they are able to deploy energy to oppose the threats of the external world. Or, alternatively, it can tell us that they have given up on their own affirmation and that they are not able to exercise their own powers (see Chapter 6 on the diagnosis of anxiety).

The young manager, rich (and spoilt) after inheriting a fortune, sat slanted on the armchair, with his legs dangling down over the upholstery of the arm. At the same time, he told of the most recent girl he "procured" for the night during a party. The defiant position was an extreme negation of his own impotence, never to be recognized, of sustaining a relationship with a real woman. The proprioception and the balance adopted by the person can be perceived not only statically, but also dynamically. The most meaningful moments are when, at the beginning of the hour, the person goes from the entrance, or from the waiting room, towards their place or, at the end, when they get up and move to leave. Once more, it is not the usual modalities that catch our attention but the modalities that are characteristic of that particular person: they are choosing their own way of placing themselves in a space in relation to us. If everything goes smoothly, there is nothing to report. If, however, there are "excesses", we can place attention on them and understand how the patient might be a submissive person or someone who is overly confident, needing to control their own movements due to insecurity, or overly keen to mark out their personal space. Not to mention people who, not infrequently, trip or who keep their balance by holding onto supports.

Holding and alliance

We have described the ways in which an alliance is entered into by following a tripartite distinction: non-verbal, emotional, cognitive. We have done so for reasons of clarity and to facilitate understanding. In reality, these levels overlap with much more nuanced borders than the explanation might suggest. Generally, the form that we attribute to our experience is pretty much observable at the non-verbal, the emotional, and the cognitive levels, with feedback between them all. We can imagine that, probably, there is first a general gestalt, which then manifests itself non-verbally, emotionally, cognitively and, also, behaviourally. Therefore, our tri-partition is a convenient educational ploy that helps to increase awareness of the forms that we give to our experience.

Sometimes the different levels do not correspond, and they generate fractures in the overall gestalt. It might be, for example, that I express myself cognitively in a very "warm" way, but that my feelings are "cold", or that I have "light" emotions whereas my expressions are "heavy", or any other disparity between two or more levels. We are facing an experiential modality that can provide interesting information, precisely because it does not follow the standard congruence between the expressive levels.

This fact is of such interest to the therapist that, in order to describe it, they have coined the term "defence". The permeability between the levels, the fracture between them, can become rationalization or intellectualization in the case where we sideline the emotional level, or it might become an emotional intensification in the case where the level of thought withdraws. It is not necessary to refer to a model (even if there are plenty to deal with the defences) capable of defining this communicative misalignment in order to understand its experiential importance. Furthermore, the modelling of this phenomenon through the concept of defences has the tendency to keep track of non-verbal modalities of communication in an indirect manner, and it can arouse in us the propensity to evade the immediacy of communication.

This chapter might give the general impression that the alliance is favoured by the level of similarity that the therapist manages to construct with the patient; a similarity that we have laid out in relation to its various levels. The more the therapist feels similar to the patient, the more they will feel a closeness. We are using the terms "close" or "similar" in such a way that straddles everyday experience (in which they take on the weight that we attribute to them in a naïve way) and a more aware use in which they acquire the value that comes from theoretical reflection. Indeed, the first two principles that Wertheimer (1923) indicate as factors of phenomenological unification are closeness and similarity. In our clinical world, the unification does not occur between simple, geometric figures used by gestaltists to highlight their forms of thought; rather it occurs between two worlds that are very complex, that of the patient and that of the therapist. The principles that "unify" are the same, the events that are unified are much more multi-faceted, almost indescribable. Even so, the operations followed by the therapist make them similar and near to the patient, generating the clinical results that can be observed. The reason for this is due to the fact that "similar" events or "near" events tend to constitute an organized gestalt. Accordingly, the ways in which the therapist is similar to the patient, the ways with which they "move closer", are indicators of experiential units to which, with varying degrees of awareness, the patient is alerted. In clinical terms, this unit of experience is conveyed by alliance. Alliance, therefore, is a clinical way to observe how two interlocutors "unify" their experience in a gestaltian way. So much so, that the loss of the alliance comes about, to use clinical language, through "ruptures", which in turn might be overcome by corresponding "repairs". "Ruptures" are easy to translate in the absence of unification, an inadequate gestalt, and "repair" is the reconstitution of a lost unit, the gestalt returns to its good state.

If the alliance is achieved, there is an open space in which the therapist can enter with an advantage over the patient. They do not have the same history and, therefore, organize the world in a different manner (in clinical terms, they do not defend themselves in the same way) and, therefore, the therapist can move with greater freedom because they are less conditioned. Given that the therapist has an Ego that is free of conflicts, they are less conditioned, their reality testing (the Adult Ego state is functioning) is not contaminated.

The therapist, at this stage, has the task of occupying, staying, guarding, being there, in this position. Furthermore, they are required not to have fears, reticence, or other doubts because they would represent an important way of importing their defensive aspects into the relationship. If they manage to honour this position (we say honour it because it is a "privilege" offered by the relationship), it will soon reap rewards. Through a sort of implicit functioning, the patient feels that the issue that characterizes them is guarded by the therapist, and, therefore, they have permission to let it go. The issue does not have the same impact as before (they abandon or let down their defence) because someone else has taken on the responsibility. It is as if the patient could, almost momentarily "go on holiday", "lighten themself" with regard to the dysfunctional balance that bought them into psychotherapy.

The signal that the patient is passed through this experiential transformation is provided on the level of creativity, whatever the level or intensity, from the most insignificant to the extraordinary. The "closeness" of the therapist, the alliance, their "presence", facilitate the restructuring of the problem and, consequently, frees energy for new tasks.

The general idea that describes the therapist's attitude in this case is holding: the capacity to hold as a result of having comprehended what the patient is presenting. And as we have said, it is not merely a cognitive holding, the therapist also understands emotionally and they understand on the non-verbal, expressive level.

The sense of this holding can be illustrated by referring comparatively to concepts of systemic therapy. At its roots, Milan systemic approach (Selvini & Palazzoli and collaborators) constructs a model of therapy based on conceptual assumptions proposed by Bateson. In Bateson, the formation of suffering, generally epitomized by the term "schizophrenia", is due to a paradox. This paradox can be explained by the contradiction between two communicative levels: the rational level (today we would say cognitive) and the analogical one (which in this book we label as non-verbal). The object of this contradictory communication is in a position of impasse because they do not know which of these two levels to refer to, in any case they would be making a mistake. It is necessary to verify another condition: the contradictory situation cannot be avoided, albeit without incurring serious suffering. Therefore, at the origin of the paradoxical situation that produces suffering, it is necessary for there to be a contradiction on the communicative level as well as the behavioural impossibility of avoiding it.

In the case of the ITAP technique, these same elements can be used in a different manner. The communicative contradiction is necessary to facilitate the emergence of the problem rather than to keep it apart or give rise to suffering. Furthermore, the intensity of the relationship sustained by the therapist creates an inescapable situation: it is a constraint with good aims. The patient cannot choose the retreat into their usually modalities of defence or abstention, they are contained so as to remain within their "communicative contradiction", their conflict. The therapist ventures into contradiction in order to take it to the surface and to offer the possibility to "get out". Therefore, the hold has the aim of avoiding the regression and favouring the creativity.

These words concerning the alliance through holding are a reminder of the importance of using intuition. The patient needs our intuition. As therapists, we find ourselves in a role that offers two opportunities, which are not so present in the role of the patient, and it is for this reason that we can exercise operations on the patient's experience with greater ease than them. The patient finds it harder to have a creative point of view on their own experiences because they are structurally immersed (they defend themselves) as well as being temporally immersed (the problem is part of their history). The therapist is outside of both of these constraints: they are exposed to the problem in the here and now and they see it from another point of view (more functional defensive asset). Therefore, this different perspective allows them to create connections (intuition) that the patient can reach with greater difficulty. Indeed, their psychic movements engage them in a different way and it becomes impossible to have a "clear" vision of the variables in play. The therapist, being "rented out" within the therapeutic contract, and having a different history and different psychic movements, has the role of providing to the patient their own sensibility, intuition, and creativity so as to provide the result that their interlocutor, for now, is not able to provide.

This concept of lending functions to the other who, momentarily, does not have them, is not a question of love, of human fraternity, of just being good. It is not an attitude that is merely motivated by values, rather it is a purely technical question: putting to use the advantages that come from the specificity of the therapist's role. As secondary results, there are all of the positive emotions that arise when two human beings meet in the deepest sense of the word. Therefore, within the therapeutic couple, love directed towards the other, whatever the extent or manifestation, when it is not supported by sufficient management of technical aspects, becomes a therapist's need, whatever its extent and manifestation, rather than something that is functional for their interlocutor. We will address once more this theme in Chapter 9, the chapter on transference and countertransference.

The more acceptable and intense positive emotions towards the other are, the more solid and aware the relational structure is in which they are formed. The litmus test is the degree of liberty that generates them in both members of the couple.

Therefore, the sensibility of the other is not merely affection, but it also lends them the competence that is momentarily overshadowed; this generates a deep empathy, which "naturally" brings with it intensive, positive consideration, which we call in different ways; in our cultural climate it is labelled, not without reluctance, as "love".

Note

1 This chapter was written by Marco Sambin.

References

Dychtwald, K. (1977). *Bodymind*. New York: Pantheon Books.
Lowen, A. (1975). *Bioenergetics*. New York: Coward.
Rogers, C. (1951). *Client-Centered Therapy: Its Current Practice, Implications and Theory*. London: Constable.
Weiss, E. (1960). *The Structure and Dynamics of the Human Mind*. New York – London: Grune & Stratton.
Wertheimer, M. (1923). Untersuchungen zur Lehre von der Gestalt. *Psychologische Forschung: Zeitschrift für Psychologie und ihre Grenzwissenschaften*, 4.

8 Pressure[1]

The concept of pressure is a general way to indicate the activity of the therapist in the relationship. The relentless therapist is "on your heels", "neck and neck", "up to date" regarding the material produced by the patient; they are active and intense. The technical reason for this attitude is based on numerous aspects: avoiding regression; decreasing the space of the "repetition compulsion", that is, of the tendency of the patient to reiterate maladaptive relational schemata; keeping the relationship in the here and now as far as possible, with the correlated consequence of activating the sane parts of the Ego, those that are free of conflicts (Adult Ego state not contaminated). Pressure is a way of exercising that which is called relational holding.

If the therapist closely "duets" with the patient, they are inducing them to engage their energies in the here and now. The therapist is so present on the scene that they have little chance of enacting old schemata. Therefore, the patient is called on, by the relational modalities of the therapist, to not use defensive aspects. If the old schemata are followed, the therapist will point it out by making the patient aware of their own movements. This activity does not involve the therapist acting as a substitute for the patient. The therapist does not "steal the scene" from the patient, they do not occupy the patient's spaces. The therapist's activity, their relentlessness, are contractually in the service of the patient. Nothing is taken from the patient, quite the opposite. Having to keep track of "another" person who is so present in the relationship means there is little room to repeat the old schemata. Indeed, the constant presence of the therapist invokes the functioning parts of the Ego. The Ego can exercise its resources creatively by freeing itself, both from the baggage of the past and from the expected constraints of the future. The relationship is characterized by an unusual intensity, it is a "new" relational experience in as much as it is able to introduce change (corrective emotional experience, Alexander & French, 1946).

The activity of the therapist is not considered by itself, but in relation to the production of the patient. It cannot be measured in number of words, frequency of interventions, length of turns, or other parameters of this sort. Rather, it consists in the pressure to introduce change. The dynamic balance of the patient can allow small as well as large changes. The therapist's relentlessness is not mirrored by the degree of change, but rather by capacity to not miss out on the chances for introducing it.

The exercise of not leaving any respite is not related to the varying degree of power and/control that the therapist has. It is about being present, achieving a relational modality in which the other feels the presence of the therapist, and where this presence is necessary for the patient to have a "reckoning" with their own non-adaptive behaviours. Being firm, therefore, does not only mean conspicuous confrontation, a colossal battle with the internal saboteur (head on collision, Davanloo, 1990), it also means inexorable exercise in the comprehension of the other (Fosha, 2000). In this unconditioned acceptance (accompanied by immovability), it is as if the therapist sends the patient a relational message: your game cannot get me, I understand its necessity though, here we must and we can adopt other behaviours.

Pressure, therefore, is that sum of the therapist's behaviour which shows them to be in a close relationship with the events that occur in the experience of the patient. This type of presence of the therapist achieves, by itself, the request of another way of entering into the relationship.

Pressure is an originator of the alliance. The patient feels that the therapist is "close", even if this closeness requires the patient to engage in unusual work, the effort of overcoming resistance, the suffering involved in becoming aware of something that has been displaced, the commitment necessary to stay out of the conflict zone. In reality, the alliance is constructed because the patient feels that all of these efforts, which the therapist also undertakes, albeit with a different role, are focused on the change, i.e., the object of the therapeutic contract.

In the following pages, we will look at the different types of pressure, using as a guide various types of empathy, and therefore of alliance, espoused in the previous chapter.

We will follow the reverse order and begin by looking at pressure on non-verbal manifestations.

Pressure at the non-verbal level

Given that non-verbal responses are not constructed from rational thought, or secondary processes, but rather from a more immediate language, or primary process, pressure will also not need articulated verbal expressions. It is enough to say that the expression has been observed, or to ask for explanations of those expressions. This is sufficient to make the patient feel that we are observing them fully, that we are interested in all of the ways in which they are present, including non-verbal messages. The pressure consists in placing great attention on this level of communication. It is as if we are looking after a young child. With a young child, we do not talk in an "adult" manner, but we are aware of the non-verbal communication that they convey to us. Crying can mean cold, hot, food, wee-wee, poo, fear, hunger. And the tones and the expressions help us to decode this unsymbolic language. An adult speaks, though not always, in symbolic language, or also conveys pre-symbolic messages (Bucci, 1997) that put us in touch directly with our internal states and our needs. This type of attention does not aim to induce regression, it does not try to lead the patient to previous stages in their evolution.

Rather it aims to highlight all communicative levels and, if anything, encourages awareness to favour evolution.

We can ask ourselves if a confrontation on the non-verbal level exists. Generally, in the case of defensive aspects, the way to treat the defences is that of confronting it: conducting cognitive operations with the aim of modifying the point of view of the patient, increasing their capacity of reflection on their own functioning. In Transactional Analysis, this set of operations is described with the term "decontamination". In the case of non-verbal communication, the cognitive aspects are a tool to become more aware with respect to one's own non-verbal modalities.

We can envisage two classes of interventions. One can be attributed to awareness. The family of interventions of this sort goes something like this: "[H]ave you noticed that when you said, you remembered, you described . . ., that your voice tremored, that you looked left, that you sunk into the armchair, . . .".

A second family of interventions is more confrontational and aims, more directly, to introduce change. We can summarize them in the following way: "[A]t the moment, you are close, behind a way, complaining, frozen, absent, contrasting (hopefully not all at the same time). In what way is this connected to what we are saying?" Or: "[W]hat does this attitude say about us?" This second family is more interpretative than the first. It is not content with bringing non-verbal aspects (which are observable but not visibly expressed) to awareness, rather they define a way of being (closed, complaining, frozen, etc.) and how they connect to the here and now experience and to the history of the patient. This type of intervention makes it necessary to refer to the definition of something that is not expressed, not even at the non-verbal level. The possibility to affect this intervention is linked to the use of intuition (transactional analysts would say A_1) and it is a complex process that involves countertransferential aspects (see chapter 9).

The families of interventions indicated here have implicit content as well as explicit content. They are expressed by highlighting non-verbal aspects of communication, while the unexpressed part, while equally significant, has the role of informing the patient that we are listening and observing carefully, that we are with them, even with regards to the less evident aspects of their expression. This type of attitude, on the part of the therapist, conveys another set of non-verbal expressed communications: as a therapist, I will not be kept out by your non-verbal modalities, I am not afraid of venturing into unexpressed aspects, in fact I find this zone of your experience interesting. Consequently, the patient draws up a model that can be summarized in this way: your problem does not frighten me, distance me, confuse me, weaken me . . . and if I show that I am not affected, you can also give yourself a chance to deal with it, perhaps with my accompaniment.

Naturally, all of this is communicated in a non-verbal manner.

Emotional pressure

Emotional pressure, a bit like non-verbal pressure, does not consist of verbal confrontations, in as much as it is a way of staying close to the patient. This side of the clinician allows the entrance in resonance with the emotional state of the patient, and, therefore, to know them better, while on the side of the patient, it has the effect of feeling the interested presence of the clinician, even on emotional aspects.

The clinician does not have any need for a treatise on emotions. Furthermore, the literature on emotions is complex. A normal knowledge of emotions is sufficient, accompanied by an "accentuated" inclination to listen to countertransferential matter originating from the patient.

Although it might be too simplistic, we could divide the emotions into two large categories, positive ones and negative ones. With a clinical distinction, we believe that positive emotions are achieved in the zone that is free from conflicts, while we believe that negative emotions arise from the part of the Ego that is occupied by other instances, which effectively aim to perpetuate repetitive behaviours. Sadness, dismay, anger, depression, etc., in a "healthy" Ego are positive emotions: a situation is being achieved where it is plausible for the person to feel sad, dismayed, angry, depressed and so on. Furthermore, given the conditions of that situation, not to feel sadness, dismay, and so on, would be an indicator of poor functioning on the emotional level.

Therefore, an emotion is not positive or negative per se, but rather it is determined by the context experienced by the person and the internal conditions they find themself in.

In the same way, an emotion that we would normally judge to be positive, such as happiness, sereneness, contentedness, fulfillment etc., could be detrimental for the psychic development of the person. Happiness, sereneness etc., can be experienced in inappropriate conditions and, therefore, confirm an inadequate level of intrapsychic functioning. We can envisage a situation that is emotionally charged – for example, if my best friend lashes out at me, I find out my partner has betrayed me, my employer has a go at me (hopefully not all at the same time). If things are in this state, and I feel serene, my motives might be two. Either I have reached full enlightenment (something I would exclude straightaway, certainly in my own case and, looking around in general, I have some doubts) or I am having a dysfunctional emotional reaction. I am repeating a learnt behaviour that has, so far, allowed me to overcome difficulties, all of which, probably, will have certain repercussions: a somatic release such as a headache, dermatitis, digestive problems, and so on, with the infinite ways with which we transfer onto the body that which we do not want to feel at an emotional level. Alternatively, without referring to the somatic sphere, we can see at the relational level that my friend might attack me physically, my partner might not talk to me again, my employer might fire me. All reactions where the other has managed an escalation with which to "shake" me, because I did not give an appropriate emotional response. Also in this case, the apparent positivity of the emotion is, really, a cover for emotional illiteracy.

Transactional analysts make a distinction between "good" emotions and "bad" emotions" within, what they call, the racket system. They see "good" emotions as genuine, and "bad" ones as parasitical or extortionate (Erskine & Zalcman, 1979).

The distinction between the two classes of emotions, in terms of Transactional Analysis, can be traced back to the difference between the state of the Free Child Ego state (FC), and the Adapted Child Ego state (AC). These two ways of organizing one's own experiential energies have a fitting parallel in the distinction between true self and false self of Winnicott (1965). The true self and the FC can be understood as a manifestation of the person free from external conditions in which the expression of their own vitality does not encounter obstacles, it develops in a natural way, it achieves the potential of that particular individual. On the other hand, the false self and the AC are characterized by the expressions of energy of a person, who is adapting both to external instances, such as parents, authority figures, education and culture, as well as internal instances, introjection of any authority; in this case, the fulfilment of the person does not occur in autonomy but in dependence.

Positive emotions are the expression of a true self (FC), negative emotions are expressions of a false self (AC). While the distinction is useful, it is also overly schematic. The true self, as is the case for the state of the Free Child Ego state, represents unrealizable myths, utopia; To stubbornly pursue them entails maladjustment. Even a manifestation that is free of vital energies must account for the conditions that allow its expression. It is necessary in order to achieve forms of regulation, of containment. On the other hand, total deference (Adapted Child Ego state) to instances of external or internal control, leads to paralysis, to the absence of one's own feeling. Paradoxically, in order to adapt, I have to understand what I am adapting to, that is, I have to possess my own feeling that takes account of the other's feeling. At the same time, in order to engage on spontaneity, I have to have the capacity to attune to the demands of dependence.

Therefore, the true self and false self, FC and AC, are two pure and unachievable extremes, but they constitute a continuum on which people are situated. The dysfunctionality consists in an excess. For the false self, there is a narrowing of individual feeling, wanting, and thinking. For the true self, there is exaltation without taking into consideration the context.

The emotions mirror this distinction. They are adequate if they achieve a good balance between fulfilment of the self and their context. They are inadequate if they undermine the relationship between the self and the context.

The clinician, therefore, has the task of confronting the inappropriate emotions and of enhancing those that are conducive to the balance of the person in that moment. The confrontation occurs through the use of the ITAP triangles. It can remain "intrapsychic" by highlighting the connection between I (impulse), A (anxiety), D (defence), or it can become interpersonal by analyzing the emotional aspects with regard to the relational history of the patient. Capitalizing on the appropriate emotions can occur through an analogous procedure, highlighting it as in the evolutive emotions situated within the triangle, both I A D and C (current life situation of the patient), P (past), T (therapeutic relationship). The general attitude involves creating holding through emotions. The patient "feels" that the therapist is present, that they have a vision of their emotions, that they will not be left alone. A sense of being understood, accepted, and protected derives from this sensation. Therefore, the patient can give themself the permission to "look" at their emotional world with a new prospective. That is, they exercise more strength of the Ego, more Adult Ego state, concerning what they are feeling, and therefore the Ego becomes freer of conflicts, it decontaminates itself.

Pressure on cognitive aspects

As far as cognitive aspects are concerned, the therapist has more room for maneuver. It is principally at this level where the most distinctive confrontations occur. The cognitive expression allows a verbalization and an immediacy that the previous levels do not. The therapist has two possibilities if the patient expresses themself through dysfunctional, non-verbal modalities. For example, they always have their head bowed or they whisper, or they stare at the therapist, or they are physically ill (or any other non-verbal aspect). The first possibility is that the therapist remains at the non-verbal level, and therefore they adopt some non-verbal behaviours that can help the patient to change: they will be able to hold their head with reference to how the patient holds theirs, bowed or conversely bent back, they could "stare back" at the patient or consciously "avoid" their gaze, they could speak in an even lower voice or raise it a little more than usual, and while the therapist cannot manifest somatic symptoms they could imagine what it means to somatize in such a way. All of these operations only touch the dysfunctional aspect indirectly, they represent ways of accentuating a sort of balance (that which is displayed by the patient), and to propose possible changes by offering at the non-verbal level elements that can be accepted (or not) by the patient but which are able to bring about new conditions within the field that is generated between the two. It is like inviting the other to take that which they are spontaneously able to achieve in that moment. It is an offer that leaves the freedom of their movements intact and therefore generates little defensive activity; the other does not feel attacked, they are taking the initiative.

The second option for the therapist consists in skipping a level and passing to the cognitive one.

As far as pressure applied through cognitive aspects is concerned, the operation of the therapist is more evident, they enter an equilibrium with the patient clearly and consciously with the aim of changing them. It is therefore a direct appeal by the Adult part of the patient to become aware of the dysfunctional aspect that they are enacting. It is not an offer of nurturing, but rather a "forced" nurturing. The patient, in order not to receive it, has to resist and employ energy for defence that is proportionate to the therapist's "intrusion". If the "tug of war" between the two overcomes the barrier put in place by the defence, the "nurturing" will arrive in such a way that the patient finds it impossible not to take it into account. The therapist, in the act of applying pressure at the cognitive level, has a range of options that derive from the characteristic of the equilibrium that they want to develop. Indeed, on the one hand, the therapist can enter into explicit alliance with the functioning part of the interlocutor's Ego, and, therefore, the couple collaborates to obtain the result. On the other hand, the therapist can expect to pass through the system of defence, that is, the implicit parts of the intrapsychic functioning that gets in the way of the change. While rapid results can be gained, it is "paid for" by the work necessary to overcome the defence. Work, or overcoming resistance, is enacted using energies present in the couple: both the interlocutors are engaged in modifying the dysfunctional equilibrium. It is interesting to note that this work required effort, and this is felt both by the patient and the therapist. In the patient, the exercise of this effort is experienced personally as effort towards change but also as satisfaction for the objective reached. All this happens with varying times and modalities (see Chapter 4 on insight as an indicator of change). The effort undertaken by the therapist to introduce change by overcoming resistance also has a personal dimension. This effort can generate in the therapist the unwarranted conviction of being the agent of change and, therefore, it can force them to take on a role as protagonist that is not theirs. If even if both take part in the change, it is the patient who changes: the power lies with the patient, it is they who "re-decides" by mutating their equilibrium (Goulding & Goulding, 1978, 1979). Therefore, the important explicit activity needed in order to apply pressure at the cognitive level should not mislead the therapist into incorrectly evaluating the effort they personally contribute, erroneously attributing to themself any personal merits. It is at this juncture that the weight of the therapist's transference can come to bear by colouring the relationship of something that, in reality, does not belong to them (see the Chapter 9 on countertransference).

The range of options that the therapist has on offer at the cognitive level depends on the diagrams of the ITAP triangles (Figure 3.2, Chapter 3). These diagrams constitute a guide to the pressure operations that the therapist can enact. Indeed, each of the sides of the various triangles indicates a possible confrontation. The theorization through the use of psychic equations is a way of organizing the pressures that the therapist can adopt at the cognitive level in order to favour change.

Note

1 This chapter was written by Marco Sambin.

References

Alexander, F., & French, T. M. (1946). *Psychoanalytic Therapy: Principles and Application*. New York: Ronald Press.

Bucci, W. (1997). *Psychoanalysis and Cognitive Science: A Multiple Code Theory*. New York: Guilford Press.

Davanloo, H. (1990). *Unlocking the Unconscious: Selected Papers of Habib Davanloo, MD*. New York: Wiley.

Erskine, R., & Zalcman, M. (1979). The racket system: A model for racket analysis. *Transactional Analysis Journal*, 9(1): 51–59.

Fosha, D. (2000). *The Transforming Power of Affect: A Model of Accelerated Change*. New York: Basic Books.

Goulding, R. L., & Goulding, M. M. (1978). *The Power Is in the Patient: A TA/Gestalt Approach to Psychotherapy*. San Francisco: TA Press.

Goulding, M. M., & Goulding, R. L. (1979). *Changing Lives Through Redecision Therapy*. New York: Brunner/Mazel.

Winnicott, D. (1965). *Ego Distortion in Terms of True and False Self: The Maturational Process and the Facilitating Environment: Studies in the Theory of Emotional Development*. New York: International University Press.

9 Transference and countertransference in the therapeutic relationship[1]

In this chapter, we provide a general vision of what happens in the therapeutic relationship. In order to do this, we first present a brief excursus on transference and countertransference and, then, introduce a general framework that helps us to graphically synthesize what happens in the relationship.

The terms "transference" and "countertransference" are controversial in psychodynamic thinking. They represent a central phenomenon of the therapeutic relationship that involves both participants, often beyond their level of awareness.

Given it is one of the major catalysts for change, if not the principal one, it is understandable that there are various points of view regarding it, that it is not entirely understood, that the conceptual instruments that we use to read it have undergone variations and evolution in the course of theoretical development.

The ITAP technique makes use, to a great degree, of the countertransferential reactions, precisely because it is particularly sensitive to what happens in the therapeutic couple.

The terms "transference" and "countertransference" are part of a wholly psychoanalytical language with which we aim to describe the complexity of what happens at the relational level, indicating, not so much explicit aspects such as conveyed contents or emotions or affect (of both the interlocutors present in the therapeutic couple), but above all the less conscious aspects, those that are not yet illuminated by the vision of the Ego (once more, of both interlocutors).

Probably a portion of this phenomenon of interaction between the two components of the dyad will remain outside the awareness of the two participants, even in the meetings that go very well on the psychodynamic level. The way in which we influence each other as human beings, and more so within a setting where the meeting of two people is facilitated, certainly includes levels that are cognitive, emotional, affective, but also inevitably interactions that are less perceptible, less accessible to reason and, nonetheless, enjoy great importance in the osmosis of the psychic functioning that occurs between the two. It is not necessary to delve into mysticism, or into shamanism, or into various types of less conventional thinking (which, recently, our cultural climate feels the need to justify by citing models of subatomic physics) to have experiences that lead us to feel the anxiety of our interlocutor on our body, or to perceive their psychological and physical wellbeing, or lack thereof, or to have premonitions that come true, regardless of their probability. Many of these levels of interaction are normally accessible to the "psychic" functioning of our dog or our cat. The examples are countless. They were probably also accessible to us in our phylogenetic history, when reasoning was less important for our survival but when "holistic" perception of our field of life was much more valuable. So, it is because of this that we became "friends" of cats and dogs, and less so of eagles and deer.

At the level of the body, there are many phenomena that bring us together in the relationship, even beyond our awareness: breathing, heartbeat, hormonal balance, defensive assets at the level of the immune system. Without getting into more complicated things, we can find interesting information at the level of skin conduction. In a couple of speakers, the meanings expressed in the verbal exchange are correlated with patterns of synchronization of the variations in skin conduction (Messina et al., 2013).

This level of reciprocal influence bears great weight on the "colour", on the "atmosphere", that is created in a relationship, all the more so in a relationship that is as intense as a therapeutic one.

With these words, we have merely aimed to provide a sense of how many possible phenomena occur in the meeting of two people. Given that we are talking about a complex phenomenon which manifests itself on numerous levels, and which should not and cannot be the object of rational investigation (indeed, sometimes it is better to consciously not do so), we can therefore return to the terms of "transfer" and "countertransfer" to briefly look at their development within psychodynamic thinking.

Tranference and countertransference[2]

It was Freud who first talked officially of transference and countertransference, referring to these recurrent phenomena while describing and defining the method and scope of analytical treatment. Indeed, while trying to prompt free verbal associations and the emotional reactions of the patient through which it was possible the highlight the link between symptoms, present feelings, and past experiences, Freud notes the occurrence of a series of changes in the attitude of the patient towards themself and the emergence of strong emotional components that obstruct and interrupt the process of free association. This is what Freud defines as translation, the process through which psychic material that had been displaced – such as impulses, fantasies, and feelings that are linked to desires and significant people from the patient's past – starts to re-emerge in the analytical situations while bonding with the analyst (Freud, 1901). Precisely because of the therapist's power to block the free associations of the patient, it could only be considered by Freud as an obstacle to his work. Some years passed by before Freud was able to re-evaluate it as a therapeutic factor and, therefore, a resource in analytical operations. Indeed, gradually he became aware of how transference included aspects that were not entirely obstructive, but even positive, useful, and free from hostility, but above all how often its characteristics were closely linked to the specificity of the patient's neurosis. What's more, these aspects shed light on previous significant relationships (Freud, 1909, 1914). Consequently, the attention concerning transference became of primary importance, and its analysis in the course of treatments became an absolutely effective technique not only for Freud but also for his successors, who perfected and extended the concept. If the reflection on transference involved a rapid and spontaneous evolution from merely representing obstacle and resistance to being a principal and indispensable resource of clinical work, the same cannot be said for countertransference, a process that worried Freud, who was aware of how the patient's past emotional experiences activated by the analytical work can, in turn, stimulate them in the analyst with consequent repercussions on the quality of treatment. The transference operated by the patient, Freud clarified, would mean stimulating and reawakening, in the clinical work, the past experiences that had been relegated a long time ago to their unconscious, and that, because of their problematic nature, might represent a hindrance if it is not kept under control. He specifically refers to complexes and resistances, this is conflicts, difficulties, problems that have not been processed or displaced, unconscious defences enacted so as not to allow them to emerge, which inevitably make it difficult, if not impossible, to grasp with clarity unconscious aspects of the patient. In his view, therefore, countertransference is something that is entirely undesirable. It is therefore necessary for the analyst to know to "keep quiet" their own unconscious, with the aim of being able to understand that of their patient, mastering the responses of their internal world through continuous self-analysis and personal analysis with colleagues (Freud, 1910). Freud's reflection, however, is not totally without issue: if, on the one hand, it is clear in its suggestion to silence the therapist's unconscious, on the other hand, it is necessary to recognize as his own the principal and indispensable instrument of comprehension that it represents – the "receiving organ" par excellence of that which comes from the internal world of the patient. Furthermore, he realized how the unconscious inevitably communicates, influences, and is, in turn, influenced by the unconscious of another. Loyal, nonetheless, to the ideals of positivism and neutrality of his time, he continues to suggest that the clinician has to be on the same level as the "scientist", a neutral and removed observer of their object of investigation; as the "surgeon" who leaves aside their own personal experiences with the sole aim of executing the operation correctly; or as the "mirror", so opaque that it can only reflect that which is placed in front of it (Freud, 1912, 1915, 1937). So, in Freud, a certain ambivalence can be recognized, a duplicity in his consideration of the unconscious, an object of knowledge but, at the same time, an instrument with which to reach it. This leaves room for the possibility of describing countertransference in a similarly duel manner. Countertransference is an instrument that can blind and, at the same time, illuminate analytical comprehension. As various reviews of psychoanalytical literature and numerous important contributions attest, the period immediately following the declarations of Freud was marked by a certain silence regarding countertransferential phenomena, except for a few interventions, which were not considered significant enough to restart the debate. Indeed, interest was not renewed until 1950, the year in which the reflections of Paula Heimann brought in a phase of breakthrough and rediscovery of the characteristics and potential of countertransference. This set the stage for a boom in the literature on this topic, including new and multiple indications, and prompting various authors such as O. Kernberg (1965), L. Epstein and A.H Feiner (1979), G.O. Gabbard (2001), and C.J. Gelso and J.A. Hayes (2007, 2011) to recognize four preponderant and recurring perspectives, which they defined as actual "approaches" to countertransference. They are categorized as classical, totalistic, complementary, and relational on the basis of various positions of significant authors:

• Authors such as A. Reich and R. Fliess, defined as "classicists" due to their loyal Freudian positions, refer to the phenomenon in terms of reactions to the transference of the patient or transference of the analyst on the patient. The effort activated in the analyst due to the influence exerted by analyzing their displaced conflicted experiences, while inevitable, is held to be absolutely undesirable in as much as it constitutes an obstacle to the analytical comprehension and a block to the clinician's work.

• Authors such as P. Heimann and R.E. Money Kyrle, characterized by an approach to countertransference known as totalistic, define the construct as the sum of all the feelings and the experiences that the therapist encounters in response to the patient, highlighting that they should not necessarily be avoided nor should they invoke feelings of guilt. Rather, countertransference, if it is not too intense and it is adequately processed, can constitute useful clues to be used to truly understand the processes and experiences of the patient.

• Authors motivated by a complementary approach, such as H. Racker and M.L. Moeller, share the open position demonstrated by the totalists and, dedicating themselves to treat certain aspects of countertransference in a specific manner, suggest it has the nature of a complement, a counterpart to transference and to the relational style of the patient. They reaffirm its role as a useful instrument not only for the comprehension of the patient's self, of how they feel, but also of their internal relational objects. In addition, countertransference aids the understanding of the patient's relationship with those objects, which they continue to experience in their own internal world.

• Finally, the authors, such as V. Lingiardi and N. Dazzi (2001), C. Helferich (2008), and G.O. Gabbard (1995, 2001), who best express the relational soul of analytical thinking that has evolved increasingly in this direction, refer to countertransference as a joint creation between patient and analyst in the interaction between them, fruit of a continuous and inseparable dialectic of transference-countertransference.

When considering these various definitions of the construct, which are not necessarily mutually exclusive but rather integrate with each other by way of increasing reflection through time, we cannot ignore the fact that they are not the product of chance, but expressions of presence, upstream, of various modalities of conceiving the same nature of the analytical situation. Indeed, the more this is considered to be an actual relationship between two people, the more we are forced to entertain a less restricted vision of the processes that characterize it.

In the conceptualization proposed by the classical authors, it can be noted that there is a purely monopersonal conception of the therapeutic contest: strongly motivated by the ideals of neutrality, objectivity, and anonymity of the analyst, they wish for the therapist to be as detached as possible, and to manage to keep their own emotions and experiences outside of the relationship with the patient. Only what originates from the psychic world of the patient is a very important fact. Without a doubt, the position of the authors with totalistic and complementary approaches is different. Indeed, their conception is recognized as being bipersonal in that it highlights how the analytical situation consists in a relationship between two authentic personalities, both with their pasts and presents, their healthy aspects and their problematic ones, their difficulties and their resources. Not only is it impossible to cancel the feelings and experiences of the clinician, but, in their view, they have to be seriously taken in consideration as potentially useful instruments for their work.

Finally, still more emphasis is placed on the reciprocity that animates the therapeutic meeting by authors with a relational approach: they conceive it as a relationship that is jointly created by the patient and the analyst, in a continual interaction between their respective subjectivities, which constantly influence each other; overcoming the classical positions focused, above all, on the role of drives and on the conflict between itself and the Superego, these theorists increasingly hold the conviction that it is precisely the richness of the analytical interaction that is the authentic motivational force of the psychic life and, therefore, a factor of change.

If we do not decide, *a priori*, to back only one of these four positions – something that does not seem to be indispensable – we will get a more complete idea concerning countertransference, preserving, as far as possible, something of the complexity of the phenomenon: the involvement of aspects of the patient and of the analyst, whether they be healthy or problematic, aware or unaware, disturbing or useful, linked to the past or to the present reality, specifics of the two's subjectivity, or fruit of their specific interaction. All of this might lead us to ask ourselves whether it is opportune to continue to use the term "countertransference", or if, on the other hand, it is now inadequate as a conveyer of a wholly classical and negative conception of the phenomenon, reducing it to a contrastive reaction by the clinician, or reducing it to transference on the patient, based on problematic and unresolved elements of their past.

Aside from the definition that we decide to give to it, whether it be narrow or wide, there seems to be a general agreement on the importance of the capacity of the therapist to monitor their own subjective responses and to manage them with the aim of supplying the patient with the most effective responses possible (Gelso, 2004). Furthermore, theoretical indications regarding the technique are proposed in order to suggest to the clinician the principal focuses to have in their work, citing, for example, personal analysis and supervision, the acceptance and the valorization of one's own internal experiences, knowing how to be involved in an empathetic way with the patient while maintaining a zone of their Ego that is sufficiently removed, the ability to be and to stay in contact with oneself, experiencing the processing understanding as a continuous and progressive formulation and the verification of hypotheses on the basis of what, moment to moment, is grasped of the patient and of the self. Indeed, the therapist is invited to observe and listen, analyzing themselves and that which emerges, outside and within the self, as a product of the interaction; to provide a possible explanation of what is intuitively perceived; to decide and to enact the most opportune interventions; to continue with listening and observation to verify to what degree their positions manifest themselves again.

The therapeutic relationship represented in a diagram

We can construct an overview of the whole process of the therapeutic relationship in its components and in its dynamic, referring to a schema that represents, in synthesis and in a fragment, what happens in the relationship. A way of going back to the phenomenon after we have developed a framework on the theories which describe it.

Let us read the schema and its various components.

The t's on the left of Figure 9.1 are indications of the time in which the communicative acts within the couple occur, the arrows on the left under t1 through t5 are indicators of subsequent movements. Here, a brief sequence of five events are represented that are represented as "frozen" on the temporal "snapshot": t1 through t5.

The circular figures on the left are a representation through a Venn diagram of the patient's experience. As we can see, each whole is divided into two sectors: on the left, the experience zones constitute the Ego, in this case the patient's Ego, on the right the experience zones constitute the external world in which the objects appear. By "object", we mean any portion of experience able to organize itself sufficiently to surface, even partially, awareness (even the deepest unconscious has a portion of consciousness, otherwise it would be impossible to put it into words). Between the two zones there is a certain amount of communication represented by the permeability of the vertical line.

The circular figures on the right represent the experience of the therapist. This is also divided into two zones. On the left, there is the zone where objects of the therapist's experience appear; on the right, the portions of their experience constitute their Ego. In this case, we bring about a further distinction between a portion of the Ego of the therapist as a professional, indicated with the letter T, by another portion related to the personal Ego of the therapist, indicated with the letter P.

The arrows at the centre that alternate between patient and therapist are a graphical representation of the communicative acts that are exchanged between them and that we can summarize with the term "Transactions"; in this way, we indicate the verbal and non-verbal exchanges that occur between the two. In t1, the patient communicates something to the therapist, in t2 the therapist communicates something to the patient, and so on.

The vertical arrows indicate direct variations of the states of the Ego. For example, the vertical arrow between t2 and t3 represents a variation of the states of the

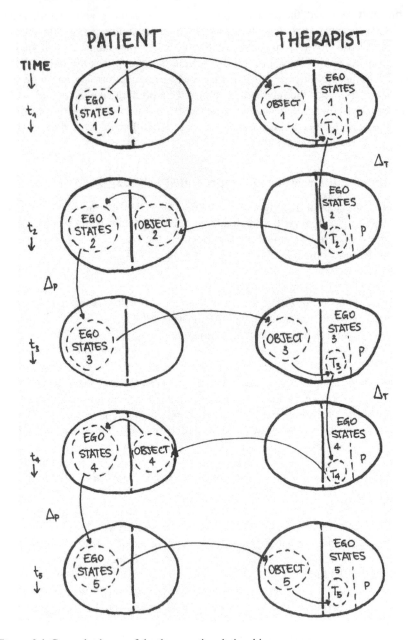

Figure 9.1 General schema of the therapeutic relationship

Ego brought about by the patient, between t3 and t4 there is a similar operation enacted by the therapist.

Now that we have espoused the "anatomy" of the schema, let us look at the "physiology", its function.

In t1, the patient emits a communicative act towards the therapist. For example, they say, "I am depressed", or any other affirmation. Here we are interested in the schema of the interactions, the clinical content is for explanatory purposes only. The transaction of P in t1 is received by the therapist as an external object that "strikes" their experience, it therefore forms the object 1 in T in the time of t1. Object 1 has an influence on the state of the therapist's Ego. We can reasonably expect it not to completely change it; nonetheless, even if it does not generate radical changes, it leads to some sort of variation, albeit small. This fact is indicated by the arrows between T1 and T2. On the basis of this variation, the therapist in t2 emits transaction 2 in the direct of the patient. For example, they might say: "How long have you felt depressed?"

This transaction is received by the patient, who in t2 constructs object 2. Object 2 is the schematic representation of the way in which the patient receives, in their experience, the communication of the therapist. Object 2, in turn modifies, to varying degrees, the state of the Ego of the patient. The arrow between t2 and t3 represents this variation. On the basis of this change, the patient in t3 emits transaction 3 towards the therapist. We can, again to provide an example, imagine that it is: "Oh dear! At least six months". This transaction "impacts" on the experience of the therapist generating object 3 which, even if in a small way, touches the Ego of the therapist in t3 by modifying it. The arrow between t3 and t4 synthesizes this variation, whether it is a micro-variation or a macro-variation. Following this variation, the therapist emits the transaction in t3, which is received by the patient and gives origin to object 4. Object 4 modifies the state of the Ego of P, as represented by the arrow between t4 and t5.

The sequence proceeds with subsequent steps as time goes on, and our example does not require us to follow any more of them.

Why should we schematize the events that occur in a therapeutic relationship in this way? What can this "physiology", this modality of functioning, offer?

We will now synthetically indicate the reasons.

The formation of the objects in the patient

The first point is supplied by the formation of the objects in the experience of the patient. We see the relationship between their self and their objects. The schema indicates schematically, if you will, that the variations of the objects lead to variations of the Ego. Even though it is represented in a way that verges on the banal, the underlying hypothesis is that the Ego is the sum of its objects. It is a point of view developed by the psychology of the Ego. The most synthetic affirmation can be derived from Federn: the Ego is its investments (1952). Denominating the investments of the Ego as objects, we can underline the interaction between the external world, the objects, and internal reality, the formation of the Ego. Both appear in a single group because both objects and the Ego form part of the patient's experience. Therefore, variations of the Ego are accompanied by variations of the objects. The modalities of this interaction among the Ego and its objects is now only represented schematically. It is clinical work that, as it introduces meanings, shows through facts how the syntactical structure that we are describing can emerge, in various ways of exchange, between the Ego and its objects. The little arrow, that in t2 or in t4 of the patient transits from the object to the Ego is a graphical indicator that displays, in a very synthetic way, these exchanges. As we will see subsequently, the object–Ego arrow can help us to place in this schema any defensive operations adopted by the patient because they constitute a transition between the external world and the internal reality.

The exchange between the objects and the Ego in the patient is a schematization of what occurs in our everyday experience: the Ego is "nurtured", either well or badly, by its objects; from the simplest object such as clothes, food, environmental conditions, to more complex ones, such as object relationships: parent, children, partners, significant other.

What happens in the therapeutic relationship? Even in the therapeutic relationship a similar "nurturing" occurs, albeit with an extra distinguishing feature.

The variations of the patient's experience, that is, their changes, occur because in the interaction with the therapist, the object of the patient is "metabolized" and restored by passing through the Ego of the therapist. We can adopt the metaphor "maternal": in "lending" their Ego, the therapist "softens up by chewing" the objects that are then restored to the patient, just as a mother during weaning sometimes chews the new food for the infant. Obviously, not every transaction has such a "grandiose" process; nonetheless, globally it is as if the therapist were to help the digestion that is required of the patient with the "gastric juices" of their own Ego. In this sense, the Ego of the therapist is "lent" to that of the patient. This nurturing exchange between the two Egos is also present in the normal object relationships, even if, on the case of the therapist, it is characterized by a precise structural condition that distinguishes, within the therapist, between the Ego P and the Ego T. In contrast to what happens in the object relations, in "lending" their Ego, the therapist makes available to their interlocutor only their Ego functioning, not their personal history. The historical aspect of the Ego of the therapist remains separated from the functioning of the professional Ego. This fact in the scheme is indicated by a dashed line that divides into two, although not completely, the therapist's Ego. Between the two Egos (T and P), there is not an impassable barrier, but we can picture an exchange, an influence, a permeability, an osmosis; it is for this reason that the border is indicated by a dashed line. As we will see in a couple of paragraphs, the distinction between P Ego and T Ego relates to the countertransferential aspects.

Returning to the variations of the patient's experience, and leaving aside the "nutritional" metaphor, we can observe the evolution of the variations. In the beginning, t1, in the patient objects and Ego achieve an equilibrium; in t2, subsequent to the reaction of the therapist, the patient is exposed to a new object that, by influencing the Ego, will change, albeit only a little, the aforementioned equilibrium on t1. This new equilibrium will be taken to t3, the patient expresses themself so as to elicit that response from the therapist who will then expose the patient to the possibility of introducing a new balance in t4. By adopting this point of view, the patient's change consists in the capacity of utilizing the inputs of the therapist to generate progressive changes in equilibrium. Therefore, in the same vein, the defence consists in a lessened capacity to highlight the possible changes. The topic of defence will be addressed again in a few paragraphs.

The co-construction of the experience

In this way of exposing the patient–therapist exchanges, the co-construction undertaken by the therapeutic couple is highlighted. The schema is little more than an indicator of the process that passes between the two. In order to get to the insight, that is to the reorganization of the experience in P, which, undoubtedly, had warning signs in T, it is necessary to have much more than the three or four little arrows depicted in the diagram. Indeed, the diagram is only a very small piece of a much larger syntax, which, in turn, is nothing more than a skeleton on which semantics are placed. However, while this syntax is not yet fleshed out with the semantics, it still highlights the role of the two interlocutors and their close interaction. In an intense therapy (ITAP), each transaction between patient and therapist brings about something new, albeit of varying degrees of importance, in line with the aim of introducing change.

Therefore, we are seeing "syntactically", that is, at the level of the relational structure, what might be the role of the therapist: they contribute to the variations of the patient's Ego, but they do not determine them. The contribution consists, as we have just seen, in placing the functions of the therapist's Ego at the service of the material produced by the patient. The function of the therapist is that of a catalyst that creates the preconditions for change, but does not determine them. It is the patient who, in effect, enacts the change. From this perspective, the passivity of the psychoanalyst (Menninger, 1958) underpins the presumption of being the author of the change: I abstain so as not to interfere in your processes. If, on the contrary, I am intimately aware that you, as my patient, are the one who enacts the change, then I will not encounter obstacles when helping you in every way possible. The agent of the change remains you, and when helping you, I will not be afraid of the regression, of the dependence, of the symbiosis, nor will I be afraid of interfering in your processes of change, which remain your own.

The structure of the therapist's ego

Let us turn our attention to the therapist. We have already addressed the reasons for their "divided" self. Of course, this has nothing to do with aspects of splitting, on the contrary. If the therapists are very clear about this type of division, they will be much freer to interact with their patient: they are merely "lending" the patient a way of functioning (T Ego), so that the patient can decide what to do with their experience. The patient, in any case, remains free. If anything, the more the therapist manages to convey good Ego, the more aware and autonomous the patient's choice will be. Accordingly, the therapist will only undertake the role of catalyst. If we do not like this chemical metaphor, we can adopt a more "human" one: the therapist is like a midwife. They are there at the birth, they help, they participate emotionally; but the protagonist remains the mother – despite sharing them, the joy and pain remain hers. It is not possible to give birth by proxy. If the therapist has an attitude which is anything but respectful sharing, it constitutes a misappropriation, even theft.

We can say something about the relationship between P Ego and T Ego. The personal story of the therapist intervenes in the clinical relationship only remotely, in the background, and it has allowed the construction of the T Ego, but it does not appear directly on the clinical stage. Self-disclosure (the presentation of personal aspects from the therapist in the therapy), even in its most pleasant and friendly forms, takes the form of an intrusion from a third party who is not involved in the clinical relationship (a third party, albeit embodied by the therapist themselves). The therapeutic dyad forms in order to examine the history of the patient. Patient and therapist cooperate to observe and "do something" for the patient, not for the dyad, and certainly not for the therapist. The material introduced by a self-disclosure is extraneous to the contact that they have in common. Therefore, it risks distracting the patient from their responsibilities but also from their power, or, in any case, their passivity can be incentivized. If self-disclosure is absorbed in the therapeutic relationship in a positive way, it probably does not originate from the P Ego but from the T Ego: that is, it only has the semblance of self-disclosure. It is not activated to expose personal aspects, rather to refine functioning, in this case that of the patient.

The personal story of the therapist is not only a means of helping them to improve their professional competence. Human affairs and learning pathways are a way of enriching their work instrument: a sufficiently well-functioning self. The functioning of the therapist's Ego is, therefore, the main instrument for measuring what happens in the relationships and the change that occurs. There are no other ways to "record", "process", or "compute" such data as complex as that generated in a therapeutic relationship (Messina & Sambin, 2017; Sambin et al., 2015). Any contribution that the personal events of the therapist can have in the clinical relationship is welcome, but not in the sense of a history to add to the relationship, rather a refinement of the therapist's professional skills. A therapist who has dealt with depression (or with any other critical aspect of their history) is probably more competent in dealing with a depressed patient, but the therapist certainly would not recount their actual experiences!

From countertransference to co-transference

At this point, we can utilize the distinction between the T Ego and the P Ego to construct a perspective on countertransference.

The therapist, as we have seen, reacts to the object brought by the patient. It is part of their professional task to "lend" their functioning to the patient. The chapters on the alliance and on pressure (Chapter 7 and Chapter 8) have given us an idea of the various ways in which the therapist "reacts" to the object presented by the patient. From the schema, we know that the communicative act that originates from the patient is brought into the experience of the therapist as an object. As we know, the Ego is modified by the presence of the objects. Therefore, in our case, we ask ourselves what the changes induced in the T Ego are and how they should be used in the relationship.

The initial precondition is due to the availability of T to receive all levels of communications emitted by P. In T, an object can appear that P had not intended to generate. This availability of T opens up to P the possibility of coming into contact with communicative aspects that P does not know and does not want to externalize. Sometimes P communicates implicitly, they are not fully aware of what they are putting in the relationship. This disparity between the explicit and implicit communication constitutes the defence. It is due to the defence that P is not aware of their own levels of communication. In implementing this modality of communication, P "plies their trade", "plays their game"; they entered into the therapeutic relationship precisely for this reason. They have a problem, something that is not clear, in the infinite ways a patient says it to themselves.

In the face of P's communicative modality, the therapist is required to understand it. Let us see what happens, with the help of the schema. The states of the T Ego are modified by the objects of P. T is "sensitive" to the communications of P. Sensitivity is a way of indicating that T has greatly modified their own Ego through training. The "sensitivity" derives from their personal experiences and from the formation, in synergy. Metaphorically, we can say that the states of the T Ego are a seismograph that records all of the states of P.

Given this attitude, T will be grateful to P, whatever their communicative modality is, explicit or implicit, very or not very defensive, because this puts the therapist into contact with P's way of experiencing things, of constructing objects and of being influenced by them.

This first attitude, which we can define as being an opening, corresponds with the next one, which we can synthetically say is a sort of response. In what way does the therapist respond to the patient? The distinguishing factor that makes T's response professional is their awareness that, as far as possible, P's communication is at least two-fold: it says something, and it implies something. The therapist cannot, therefore, "respond" on one level. If they did so, they would give up the functioning of T Ego, thus remaining bound by P Ego. They would react, quite rightly, as any of us would in everyday life. The "everyday" reactions are needed to enter into attunement with the patient, but they are not needed to guide the responses. The function of the T Ego consists, therefore, in managing to utilize the reactions (P Ego) within the therapeutic relationship. Schematically, we could say that the P Ego is necessary to "feel" (and it is not only the state of the Ego as it would seem at first glance, but it is all of the Ego state that we can indicate as the integrated Adult Ego state), while the T Ego is necessary to "respond". Starting from the first, then going on to the second, we pass by the processing enacted by the therapist which, a few pages ago, we defined as a "pre-mastication" or "softening" enacted by their "gastric juices". If you, as my patient, make me feel boredom, anger, love, curiosity, turbulence, confusion (and an infinity of other messages that you might send me), my first operation is that of valorizing what I am feeling, even if it is vague and imprecise. Subsequently, I will undertake some movements to consolidate the impression received, and later still I will ask myself what you are showing me, what boredom, anger, etc., says about you. All of this constitutes the first phase and occurs in the totality of the therapist's Ego, both on the part of the therapist and on the part of the personal. Subsequently, the therapist should evaluate how they can give back to you, the patient, in relation to the resources that you are displaying in this moment, and I will enact only my T Ego.

The process of involving the various functions of the therapist Ego can occur in brief moments within the functioning of T, or it can be made explicit step after step in the interaction with P. This depends on the context and the resources present in the therapeutic couple. It is the specific task of the T Ego to evaluate the modalities of response.

Using psychoanalytic terms, the transferential movements enacted by the patient constitute the material of the relationship. The therapist is not asking to undertake movements "against". If the therapist executes movements "against" it is because it is not clear to them the distinction between their functions of receiving and of responding. In this case, just as P does not have full awareness of its own levels of communication, T also does not have full awareness of its own functioning; it hooks itself onto the operations of P, and, therefore, is driven to respond "against" so as to defend itself.

In a good relationship, the response of T is not "against", but it is "with", therefore we should really define it as co-transference. This opening of the therapist to transferential information, and not only, produced by the patient is the richest instrument to understand the other. We do not possess more precise or more reliable "measuring sticks"; furthermore, it is the principal guide in the therapeutic process because it provides information on how to proceed. For these reasons, we can define it as co-transference: far from being a defensive movement of the therapist (against), rather it is a precious instrument for their work.

The capacity to separate P Ego from T Ego protects the therapist from their own transferential movements and, therefore, frees them from their personal history. Consequently, on the one hand, the P Ego has a full possibility to explore in greater depth and valorize the empathetic reaction because it is freed from the task of "everyday" responses. On the other hand, the T Ego is free from responding because it has a more functional management of its own empathetic responses (co-transference), and, therefore, it does not need to defend itself by continuing to abstain.

These structural observations on co-transference allow us to draw certain conclusions that have repercussions for the technique. We have seen that co-transference is a response of the therapist to a communication, which contains an implicit component, enacted by the patient. The exchange that occurs between the two is complex and involves aware aspects, and aspects that are less aware. In a short time, many processes occur that cannot all be brought to awareness, otherwise the process slows down and becomes rigid. Therefore, the therapist is required to undertake a continuous evaluation concerning what can and must be returned to the patient of the transferential aspects and co-transferential repercussions that they generate and what can be left aside because it would require too much energy to be brought to the surface. Too much energy for the patient to surface their transferential aspect, but also too much energy for the therapist to become aware of themselves and to organize a good use of their own co-transference. A therapist that knows how to appropriately use their own co-transference has continuous material to use to avoid blocks and stagnation in the therapeutic process; furthermore, it adds quality and efficacy to a therapy that is already going well.

A suggestion for therapists who utilize co-transferential data is to make use of it immediately. The co-transferential process is so transient and delicate, while being of great importance in understanding the patient, that it fades and soon afterwards it is submerged by other information. For this reason, in intense therapy, such as ITAP, a "quick sharing" technique is adopted.

The timely use of co-transferential data leads to great advantages for the evolution of the therapy, above all if the therapist is aware of what is linked to the present therapeutic relationship and what originates from their own personal past: the distinction between the T Ego and the P Ego. We will return to the topic of "quick sharing" in the final paragraph of this chapter.

Transference of the therapist

What must not happen is a transferential reaction of the therapist; that is, the irruption of personal needs in the setting. This is certainly an operation "against" because it pollutes the setting with aspects from the therapist's history. Therefore, the therapist must not allow their P Ego to intervene in the relationship. If the rule applies, as already suggested, even for an innocuous self-disclosure, it certainly should be avoided if this engagement in the session is determined by the insufficiently under-control needs of the functions of the Ego of the therapist.

The schema can help us to see this type of response by T. In Figure 9.2 this situation is represented.

The object of the patient not only "strikes" the T Ego of the therapist, but by going beyond the internal barrier it activates the P Ego not only in its sensitivity, but it also elicits a direct response from the P Ego. Consequently, the reformulation of the object that the therapist returns to the patient is determined not only by its therapeutic function but also by their personal needs. This is represented by the two arrows that "return" to P.

This modality is destructive in the relationship because T is responding on two levels; therefore, the two levels of communication are unconsciously mixed up, thus acting as a mirror to the patient who, given their "role", has permission to have communication on several levels. The patient has no "weapons" to defend themself from the therapist's "infraction" because the therapist, in this way, has introduced something into the relationship that was not agreed in the contract. P and T agreed to meet to take care of P. The breach of P Ego's needs breaks the contract because the roles are inverted: the patient is asked to take account of the personal aspects of the therapist.

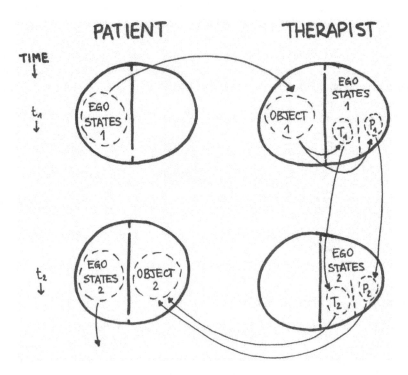

Figure 9.2 Representation of the relationships in the case of transference of the therapist

The representation of the defence

Let us now turn our attention to the defensive aspects of P. What happens if the Adult is contaminated? If the Ego's strength is weakened by the presence of other instances? If it defends itself?

We can imagine how to represent the defensive operations adopted by P in our diagram. Given that defence is an operation that straddles the external world and the internal reality, we can imagine a graphical way that shows that "anomaly" in the passage between formation of the object and the way in which it impacts on the Ego. In Figure 9.3 there are two ways of representing the interaction between experience (the objects) and the person (the Ego). Graphically it can be conveyed through a dotted arrow or by zig-zags. Two conventional ways of indicating a different way of connecting object and Ego. They differ one from the other because they represent ways of defending themselves, that is, of connecting the external world and the internal reality.

The connection between defence and transference

The schema in Figure 9.3 allows us to highlight what happens in a situation where P adopts defensive aspects. That which is graphically represented in the little

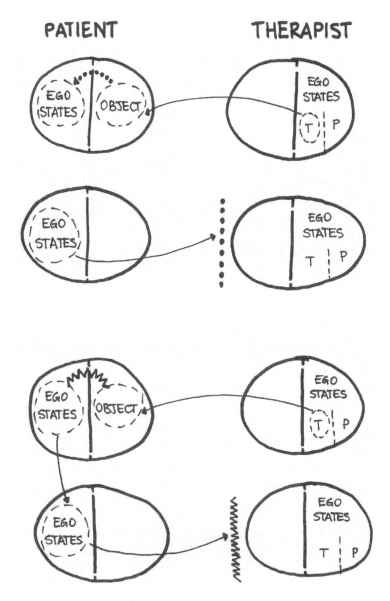

Figure 9.3 Graphical representation of the defensive operations (two examples)

arrows of the defence (dotted lines and zig-zagged lines) reflects, or is brought into (projected), the relationship with the therapist. The malfunctioning at the entry point becomes malfunctioning at the exit, and, therefore, the relationship is coloured with the modalities of defence. If I have a fear (unjustified, past, contaminated Adult) that derives from the real or imagined idea of being attacked, now in relation to you (current or therapist), I will make sure that this fear carries weight: I will unjustifiably fear being attacked or I will unjustifiably attack. This type of relational modality is described by J. Weiss (1993) as "testing the therapist".

Alternatively, in another case, if I need to be recognized because back then (past) I was not sufficiently accepted, now (current and/or therapy) I put myself in relation with the other, believing it to be an omnipotent dispenser of psychic wellbeing, or keeping score of what will be recognized and what will not. And so, I will relate to T, or impersonating the Parent not giving recognition or the malnourished Child, hypersensitive to the reactions of others (yet another test of the therapist in the theorization of Weiss).

And so on, with other ways in which the defensive asset determines the transferential relational object.

I transfer the structure of the defence (world entering in) to the structure of the relationship (contact with the world). This transference, as we have seen from the brief examples reported earlier, does not occur in a linear manner, with a "scientist's" logic, but it is a retelling (more or less "faithful" and engaged with) of the original scenario. And of the original scenario, as a patient, I can choose varying elements, roles, certain angles; those that are particularly meaningful for me in this moment and that I want to, unconsciously, show to my therapist the most. The therapist is a "screen" on which to "project" one's own film. Graphically, in Figure 9.3, this is represented by the zig-zags and the dotted line that interpose between P and T. P is not in relation with T, but with its projection: a consequence on the relational level of its internal defensive movements. This projection is the transference of the patient and, as we have already said, it is fully present in psychotherapy practice: it is a way of constructing the world that characterizes the patient and their problems.

The concept of therapy intensity

The schema of Figure 9.1 allows us to provide a description of what intensity in a relationship means. There are two factors that contribute. The first is due to the frequency of the verbal exchanges. A relationship with brief verbal exchanges, equally distributed between the two, will increase the probability that it is intense, even if frequency and intensity are not linearly correlated. The second factor is due to the quantity of "novelties" brought about by the transactions, both of the patient and of the therapist. A sequence of transactions will therefore be at maximum intensity where each remark is accompanied by something more, something that contributes to proceeding towards change. On this level, the patient will tend to be more "conservative", precisely because he/she is affected by personal schemata that tend to repeat themselves, while the therapist ought to be "innovative", that is, bring about through the therapist's interventions aspects that were not contemplated in the vision of the patient's world. The "innovation" brought about by the therapist is not absolute, it cannot be untied from the context, but instead founded on the type of response that the patient provides, that is, on their ability to deal with the evolution of the communicative exchange. A communicative exchange in which the therapist introduces a lot of innovation that, however, the patient does not follow, cannot be considered intense and perhaps not even an exchange. Therefore, the intensity is determined by the maximum change possible that can be introduced, transaction by transaction, and sustained by the therapeutic couple. Paradoxically, it might be that the most driven innovator is the patient, and that the therapist does not manage to pick up these movements, rare but not impossible. Therefore, as we said in the first pages of this book, intensity and brevity are correlated, but not in a linear fashion. It is probably that a brief therapy is also intense, but it could also be intense as well as being longer, and this happens because there is a lot of change brought about by the transactions of the couple. Intensity, therefore, does not have an absolute value, but it is relative to the conditions under which it occurs.

This will allow us to highlight, through Figure 9.1, what constitutes change. We can describe change as progressive micro-variations that are introduced, step by step, from the interaction between the two interlocutors. In Figure 9.1 there are the symbols delta P and delta T in the vertical arrows that characterize patient and therapist, a way of indicating the change that occurs between one transaction and another (the horizontal arrows). Given that the object of change is the patient and only secondarily the therapist, those that are of interest to the therapy are the delta P. The sum of the P delta is the change enacted by the patient, that is, the result of progressive changes introduced by the interaction with the therapist. In order for the patient to be able to introduce their experiential delta, the therapist must also progressively enact corresponding delta that are derived from the transactions manifested by the patient. If, unfortunately, the therapist is not able to create T delta, the therapy will fail or stagnate. The therapist is asked to take the perspective that each intervention opens the possibility that the patient changes, perhaps in very small ways, but that there is change. This is the indicator of intensity: the quantity of delta enacted by the therapist that can be absorbed by the patient: continuous nutrition.

This point of view on the aggregate of the delta of the patient goes hand in hand with what we said about insight (Chapter 4). The insight is a reorganization of the field – that is, a creative way of reorganizing their own experience. As we have seen, there are insights for the various levels of functioning: intellectual, emotional, corporeal, even if it is easier to describe the cognitive insights. Similarly, the delta is a schematic indicator that something has happened between the two temporal moments and that it has introduced a change, whether it be small or large. The sequence of the delta is an indicator of subsequent changes to experience that might bring about insight. Not every step, not every delta, brings about a visible insight, but every delta can represent moving closer.

It is interesting to think of the sequence of the P delta in connection with the T delta. The more the two sequences proceed in parallel, the more productive and smooth the process of the therapy will be. If we take for granted the fact that the therapist has good functioning, then the slowing development, in line with the P and T deltas, originates from the defensive aspects of the patient, which are not able to achieve those innovative suggestions that the therapist proposes. In this case, the patient slows down the development of the transactions, they create resistance; but as soon as this braking is taken off or mitigating, things proceed towards change and the course continues. Therefore, the functioning of the delta is correlated and involves the side of the therapist as a proactive source of delta, and the side of the patient as more or less able to keep up with the proposals that arrive. If the course of the T deltas undergoes any stops or limitations, the whole process suffers the consequences. This leads us to understand that psycho-therapy has to be active, and the therapist has to produce T deltas by reprocessing the information presented by the patient and extending it in a way that helps the patient to take them on, delta P. If this activity does not occur in this way, then the therapy will experience the negative consequences because the therapist shied away from their task, perhaps pinning it on the patient.

If we use a nutritional metaphor, the therapist has the role of offering the necessary food. If the patient, because of their predisposition, lacks appetite or is "allergic" to certain foods, this does not give the therapist the right to not prepare other food, nor to ask the other to cook their food on their own.

From the observation of the schema, another suggestion arises. The events that occur are many on numerous levels placed in a temporal flow that advances and that requires effort to be stopped or pursued. That which the two exchange is a continuous construction, one of communicative facts presented by the other, which takes place with such richness of levels that it intensely involves the cognitive and emotional resources of the therapist. In the therapist's work as a "recorder" of communication originating from the patient, there remains little energy to conserve impressions to return subsequently. The patient produces so much information that the therapist is also asked to be immerged in the communicative flow, otherwise the co-construction of the experience is lost. This is true, above all, for the co-transferential aspects. They are a highly ephemeral (delicacy does not mean not existing!) and transitory phenomenon; therefore, putting them momentarily aside and proposing them again after a few moments risks damaging or losing the phenomenon irrevocably. It was there, it was beautiful and iridescent like a soap bubble, but it is no longer. That is why it is necessary to get back to the patient immediately (in terms of time and manner), otherwise that information will get lost. In reality, it might allow certain pieces of information to settle in the therapist, which might then emerge consciously later on, following numerous exposures to the transient phenomenon. Without waiting for this more structured moment, we can immediately utilize information, albeit not well formed, suggested by co-transferential aspects in intense therapy, while taking account of the patient's resources. This attitude of the therapist, which is ready to return to the patient certain well-formed, transient, ephemeral aspects, is indicated with the term "quick sharing". I share with you what you are generating in me, even in its most delicate aspects, otherwise it will be lost. The underlying messages are numerous: I place at your disposition all of my modalities of reacting, to get an idea or an impression of what you are presenting me; second, you also have the resources to do it, you can read what your communication generates; third, you are not alone in your experience; fourth, if I do not return something consolidated to you, undoubtedly you will have more space for your creativity.

The technique of "quick sharing"[3]

Much has been written about countertransference and its use in psychotherapy. I will merely add some further considerations to better describe how we use it with our patients within the ITAP methodology.

The complex field of relationship that is created in the meeting between two human beings involves the significant exertion of physical, psychological, and emotional energy. The meeting between two complex worlds shifts balances in both the actors of the relationship, who influence each other reciprocally. It is the task of the therapist to listen to their patient attentively, observe their movements, and understand the mechanisms of mental functioning so as to achieve meaningful change. Each patient is unique, each therapist is unique, and each meeting you will have together will be unique. As in life, there are no rehearsals, you "arrive on the scene" knowing that, in some way, you will have to improvise. Theatrical actors who dedicate themselves to improvisation think of this form of artistic expression as a field of play with some basic rules. I will not describe them in detail, but I am interested in one in particular: the rule of "never saying no". When someone arrives on the scene in the theatre, these (brave) professionals or amateurs do not have any scripts to follow, rather they tackle the scene "armed" only with their imaginations, their intuition, and their faith in their improvisational partners. The very first movement of the actor in front of the public is known as the "proposal", which can be addressed to themselves (monologue), to the public, or to another actor. In this precise instant, the rule of "never say no" comes into play. Whatever the invitation, the story, or the setting that characterizes the "proposal", the second actor will accept it without hesitation, letting themself be guided without casting any doubt on what they perceive, hear, feel, and intuit. To give a brief example, we can imagine an actor entering the scene exclaiming: "Good day sir, do you by any chance know what time the number 13 for the centre gets here?" It is easy to guess that the "proposal" is addressed in a clear way, and the response will be something like: "I'm sorry to say that the number 13 has just passed by . . ." or "I have been here waiting for it for 10 minutes already and I've already lost hope, in what direction are you going? Maybe we can share a taxi . . .". When this rule is respected, therefore, from that point onwards, once the reality, that has been co-constructed and shared, is accepted, the play, and the adventure, can commence. Not respecting this rule, on the other hand, could represent a break in the dialogue, confusing the reality of both and, following this, there would necessarily be a repair with an obligatory reformulation of one or more participants or the intervention of a third. It is usually difficult to move from one world to another instantly: on the street or in the cinema, in medieval times or in the future, lover or politician, old person or child. It is, therefore, difficult to have to identify yourself with what, in that moment, the other person wants to convey to us about them.

Just like the improvisers, we believe that it is fundamental for the therapist to accept what emerges from the relationship without ever "saying no" to what you feel, perceive, remember, or imagine during the interaction. The position of acceptance may seem similar to: "I accept what you're proposing to me and I will let it flow through me; I realize that it originates from your world and from our meeting and it is a form of communication addressed to me. I will listen to it carefully and without any judgement".

Returning to our friends from the world of the theatre, one further fundamental aspect in order to guarantee a successful theatrical performance is the speed of the response of the shared improvisations. Imagine an actor who enters the scene "proposing" to the other a cue such as: "Hands in the air, this is a robbery!" (perhaps miming someone holding a gun). A good response for this type of communication might be an abrupt raising of the arms and an immediate plea to spare their life, we can suppose. However, such a good response has to occur instantly so as not to lose the "proposal" and the message of the first actor. Can you imagine the second actor waiting 20 seconds or so and thinking about it before delivering their line? The whole scene loses its sense, the "proposal" is lost, the first actor would probably have veered away to other meanings and the emotional "contact" between them would be lost (not to mention the disappointment in the audience). In psychotherapy, there is no audience (apart from possibly a one-way mirror or through the recording of the meetings), but there are all of the elements that we have just mentioned that render the two "stages" so similar. The relational proposal of the patient, which is created in the relational field, has an immediate impact on therapists who are sufficiently in tune with their own reactions. Waiting too long to make sense of what has been perceived is fatal, as it also is in the theatre. "Delayed" responses to unconscious communication arising in the dyad, rather than "live responses", can be alienating and it can be perceived, as in the theatre, as a break that will necessitate a repair (Safran & Muran, 2000). In this regard, we should mention the work of Marco Mazzetti on the use of countertransference in therapy and his three fundamental questions for self-supervision: What am I feeling during the session? Why do I feel what I am feeling? Why does the other person want (unconsciously) to make me feel what I am feeling? (Mazzetti, 2012). We can add a fourth one to these three fundamental questions: is it useful for this specific patient, in this precise moment of the therapy, for me to share with them my sensation or thought or reflection that has emerged between us? Responding in the short time available between one remark and another is a difficult skill to acquire but it is not impossible (as it is difficult but not impossible for the improviser to learn to trust their own sensations and respond in a few moments). Once more: training, sensitivity, intuition, awareness of the functioning of the patient, and trust in the relationship seem to be the principal elements for good outcomes from the intervention.

From the theatre analogy, however, another fundamental difference arises between the improvised lines on the stage and the therapeutic "lines": the possibility to take time to think. After many years of training, the expert actor is capable of reacting in different situations in ways that are guided by instinct; the actor's skill is due to the impossibility of doing otherwise (in this context, there is no time to think and reflect) and to the damage that any error might cause. In the process of therapy, however, there is, and there must be, the possibility of doing otherwise. The "quick sharing" is not an obligation, it is a precise relational choice. If on one hand, the excessive period of waiting before verbalizing a "transferential object" can easily reduce intensity and efficacy, on the other hand, the impulsivity of "throwing it into the mix" can create rupture or detachment, or in the long-term even the failure of attunement and loss of alliance. In this regard, it is worth underlying how the criteria of immediacy of sharing must be subordinate to that of the protection – in this case, of the whole relationship with the patient (Berne, 1972).

Notes

1 This chapter was written by Marco Sambin; a section was written by Davide Facchin, and another by Francesco Scottà.
2 This section was written by Davide Facchin.
3 This section was written by Francesco Scottà.

References

Berne, E. (1972). *What Do You Say After You Say Hello? The Psychology of Human Destiny*. New York: Grove Press.
Epstein, L., & Feiner, A. H. (1979). Countertransference: The therapist's contribution to treatment – An overview. *Contemporary Psychoanalysis*, 15: 489–513.
Federn, P. (1952). *Ego Psychology and the Psychoses*. New York: Basic Books.
Freud, S. (1905[1901]). Fragment of an analysis of a case of hysteria. In J. Strachey (Ed. & Trans.) (1953). *The Standard Edition of the Complete Psychological Works of Sigmund Freud*, Vol. VII (pp. 3–112). London: The Hogarth Press and the Institute of Psychoanalysis.
Freud, S. (1910[1909]). Five lectures on psycho-analysis. In J. Strachey (Ed. & Trans.) (1957). *The Standard Edition of the Complete Psychological Works of Sigmund Freud*, Vol. XI (pp. 3–49). London: The Hogarth Press and the Institute of Psychoanalysis.
Freud, S. (1912). Recommendations to physicians practising psycho-analysis. In J. Strachey (Ed. & Trans.). (1958). *The Standard Edition of the Complete Psychological Works of Sigmund Freud*, Vol. XII (pp. 109–120). London: The Hogarth Press and the Institute of Psychoanalysis.
Freud, S. (1914). Remembering, repeating, and working-through. In J. Strachey (Ed. & Trans.) (1958). *The Standard Edition of the Complete Psychological Works of Sigmund Freud*, Vol. XII (pp. 145–156). London: The Hogarth Press and the Institute of Psychoanalysis.
Freud, S. (1915). The unconscious. In J. Strachey (Ed. & Trans.) (1957). *The Standard Edition of the Complete Psychological Works of Sigmund Freud*, Vol. XIV (pp. 159–204). London: The Hogarth Press and the Institute of Psychoanalysis.
Freud, S. (1937). Analysis terminable and interminable. In J. Strachey (Ed. & Trans.) (1964). *The Standard Edition of the Complete Psychological Works of Sigmund Freud*, Vol. XXIII (pp. 209–254). London: The Hogarth Press and the Institute of Psychoanalysis.
Gabbard, G. O. (1995). Countertransference: The emerging common ground. *International Journal of Psycho-Analysis*, 76: 475–485.

Gabbard, G. O. (2001). A contemporary psychoanalytic model of countertransference. *Journal of Clinical Psychology*, 57: 983–991.

Gelso, C. J. (2004). Countertransference and its management in brief dynamic therapy. In D. P. Charman (Ed.), *Core Processes in Brief Psychodynamic Psychotherapy*. New Jersey: Lawrence Erlbaum Associates.

Gelso, C. J., & Hayes, J. A. (2007). *Countertransference and the Therapist's Inner Experience: Perils and Possibilities*. New Jersey: Lawrence Erlbaum Associates.

Hayes, J. A., Gelso, C. J., & Hummel, A. M. (2011). Managing countertransference. In J. C. Norcross (Ed.), *Psychotherapy Relationships that Work: Evidence-based Responsiveness* (2nd edn., pp. 239–258). New York: Oxford University Press.

Helferich, C. (2008). *Due animali in una stanza: Diario di controtransfert [Two Animals in a Room: A Countertransference Diary]*. Milano: Franco Angeli.

Kernberg, O (1965). *Notes on countertransference*. London: Sage.

Lingiardi, V., & Dazzi, N. (2011). Il movimento relazionale: ascendenze teoriche e fecondazioni culturali [The relational movement: theorical ascendancies and cultural fecundations]. In V. Lingiardi, G. Amadei, G. Caviglia, & F. De Bei (Eds.), *La svolta relazionale: Itinerari italiani [The relational change: Italian itineraries]*(pp. 3–31). Milano: Raffaello Cortina.

Mazzetti M. (2012). On receiving the Eric Berne memorial award. *The Script*, 42(9): 9–11.

Messina, I., Palmieri, A., Sambin, M., Kleinbub, J. R., Voci, A., & Calvo, V. (2013). Somatic underpinnings of perceived empathy: The importance of psychotherapy training. *Psychotherapy Research*, 23(2): 169–177.

Messina, I., & Sambin, I. (2017). *Valutazione delle psicoterapie. Dalla metodologia della ricerca alla pratica clinica [Psychotherapy Evaluation: From Research Methodology to Clinical Practice]*. Milano: Franco Angeli.

Safran, J. D., & Muran, J. C. (2000). Resolving therapeutic alliance ruptures: Diversity and integration. *Journal of Clinical Psychology*, 56(2): 233–243.

Sambin, M., Palmieri, A., & Messina, I. (2015). *Psiconeurodinamica [Psychoneurodynamics]*. Milano: Cortina Editore.

Weiss, J. (1993). *How Psychotherapy Works*. New York: Guilford Press.

10 Our idea of relational holding[1]

We understand the term "holding" as being close to the concepts of empathy and alliance (see the following pages in this chapter), and so we believe that it can extend through the entire duration of a therapy course. In the ITAP (Intensive Transactional Analysis Psychotherapy) approach, we consider holding not as phase or as an intervention strategy in moments of vulnerability or regression, but as a basic relational attitude, not simply for support but also as a role that we can define as the construction of a facilitating and holding environment (Winnicott, 1953, 1967). Consequently, we believe that the patient can learn to remain for as long as possible outside of the spaces of scripted "noise" (script maintenance systems and racket reactions of anxiety).

In line with this, we can cite the words of Cornell & Bonds-White (2001, p. 74) which are similar to our conception regarding this basic relational attitude:

> Berne offered a model of challenge, alignment with the Adult, and thoughtfully timed interventions to free the client to think and feel autonomously. He did not close the "as if" space of the therapeutic process by becoming a parental figure, but he did draw on the force of the parental attitudes of permission, protection, and potency to create a psychological space within which the client has the opportunity to develop autonomous functioning.

Other authors talk about holding in a more detailed way by referring to a specific phase of treatment or to an intervention. For example, according to Hargaden and Sills (2012) there is a specific phase of therapy defined as "supporting" (holding). The authors state that: "it is important to be aware that sometimes the client simply needs an intervention aimed at doing no more than offer the steady containing presence of a non-judgmental therapist who is perceived as having the potency to offer the protection and permission needed. This is known as 'holding'" (p. 195).

In our view, however, the relational attitudes can be summarized in a perspective in which holding applied by the therapist through the course of the therapy is described by a conceptual instrument present in the sphere of Transactional Analysis called "the triangle of the three Ps": permission, protection, power. This instrument, which contains elements already outlined by Berne (1972), can be effectively placed in a relationship with the triangle of conflict within the ITAP therapy process. Indeed, each vertex of the triangle of conflict corresponds to one of the vertices of the triangle of the three Ps (Figure 10.1).

We will now briefly describe the attitudes of the therapist within the ITAP model.

Power: The attitude of potency in relation to the script maintenance systems (D – defence) is intended as a communication to the patient that the therapist has the strength and the instruments necessary to remain outside the dysfunctional dynamics of the patient and that, at the same time, the therapist has the energy necessary to deal with them together. The result of this attitude is the function of modelling, as if to say "you can stay out of your defensive system and equally you can maintain a relationship".

Protection: The attitude of protection in relation to the racket reactions of anxiety (A) is fundamental in order to allow the patient to perceive that the change also brings with it useful instruments of self-preservation inside and outside the therapy room. The challenging of the scripted mechanisms leaves the patient "exposed", in an imbalance, functional in terms of change, but at the same time still not solid enough to be perceived as safe. Therefore, it is fundamental to know how to protect the patient from the possible anxious reactions that, along the way, can present themselves during therapy and in everyday life.

Permission: The attitude of creating an environment in which permissions for the Child's emotions can emerge (I – impulse) is conceived here as a therapeutic terrain in which authentic emotions can flourish – for example, through a look that communicates closeness, support, acceptance, openness (and much more besides if we are fully present in the relationship). We can provide the relational space necessary, so that the other can feel sufficiently safe and experience what was previously not allowed in their history.

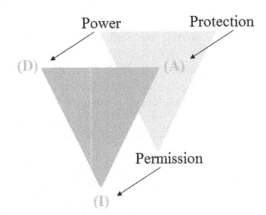

Figure 10.1 The triangle of the three Ps

It is the task of the therapist to deploy the three Ps and, furthermore, do it in such a way that, over the course of the therapy, the patient can make it their own, over and over again. In this sense, we can consider them to be lost "functions", forgotten or never actually acquired from the patient's parent.

In contrast, the risk of keeping these attitudes for oneself, without the aim of subsequently passing them to the patient so that they can take them with them in life, might lead the therapist to instigate a less egalitarian relationship (I am OK/ You are not OK), with the consequent lack of construction of necessary autonomy.

The chapter on pressure (Chapter 8) showed us the many levels at which the therapist can be present in the relationship. At this point, we can explore in greater depth that which has only previously been mentioned regarding our idea of relational holding.

The terms "holding" and "hold" mean different things, each of them helps us to clarify our concept of relational holding. For each meaning, we have provided some technical reflections that we describe here:

- To hold: to remain, in a physical sense, solid and listening to oneself and "anchored" to the ground. To remain firm in the position of being OK.
- To hold: the grasp the defence (D)/the scripted mechanisms as soon as they manifest and as soon as possible in the relationship, based on the strategic moment of the therapy and the resources of the patient.
- To hold: to contain. The room, the body, and the words of the therapist are tools for the movement of the patient in a safe physical and relational space.
- To hold: to embrace. In the moment of the expression of the authentic emotion, it is important to make the patient feel that we are with them with our whole self and just as with a child, we give them the permission to express themself, inviting them to stay in the difficult intimacy of one's own self and with the other, metaphorically holding them to us.
- To hold: to wait. Patience is fundamental so as not to incur reckless accelerations, but it can represent a hindrance if it becomes passivity or a block.
- To hold: to sustain. Deep and unexplored emotions sometimes explode in the therapy room without warning. It is fundamental to show the patient that we are solid by showing that such emotions touch us deeply but do not set us off balance too much. We do not want to give the impression of an "icy", emotionless, unknowable therapist, quite the contrary. We do, however, want to underline to what degree the patient sometimes asks us, whether consciously or not, to sustain or deal with that which they find difficult to confront. The implicit message could be this: "This thing that you are communicating to me/that you are experiencing is really difficult to confront. At the same time, I will show that it can be looked at and overcome".
- To hold: to grip. It is important to recall Osimo's concept of solidly "gripping" (2001) the defence. It is important not to let the defences leave the field of our attention thereby getting the better of the relationship. A solid grip also means, in some cases, confronting them severely if we believe that it can help our interlocutor and that they are ready to overcome them.

- To hold: to stow away. The historical memory of the therapy course is mainly in the hands of the therapist. The therapist, hopefully, should follow from above the evolutions of the pilot (patient) who is handing their airplane (unconscious contents), which often misbehaves. In following the route and trying to guide it towards faraway places, they are sometimes asked to act as the deposit for contents that emerge and are then "mysteriously" neglected, of images and moments of breakthrough that happened months or even years ago. The capacity to "stow away" such memories, emotions, and thoughts for brief or long periods is necessary to provide the patient with a historical memory of their own journey and of their own "evolutions" and progresses, and to be able to subsequently pass them on, at an appropriate time, to the patient.
- To hold: to resist. The quantity of relational pressures that a therapist is exposed to every day (every hour, every minute) is surprising. Occasionally feeling overwhelmed by such forces is a common experience. Being able to recognize them as not necessarily being one's own is a skill to be refined in moments of self-reflection and supervision, and it characterizes the work of a good clinician. Increasing one's own resistance to the relational pressure is one of the objectives which makes it fundamentally important for ITAP practitioners (but also other techniques that involve structural changes, especially deep ones) to have undergone or to undergo a solid and in-depth course of personal therapy.
- To hold: to endure. Sometimes it seems that change does not occur despite our best efforts, our studies, our passion, our commitment, and that of our patient. The patient, exhausted and disheartened (at least as much as us!), can invite us to give up, to quit, mostly doing so unconsciously. However, it is important to maintain faith in our work, in our acting "in science and conscience", in our belief in that quality of the world defined as "physis". In this regard, we remember the words of Berne (1957, p. 89), who defines it as "the growth force of nature, which makes organisms evolve into higher forms, embryos develop into adults, sick people get better, and healthy people strive to attain their ideals and grow more mature". He also admits that "perhaps Physis does not exist at all, but in spite of our inability to be definite about this subject, there are so many things which happen *as if* there were such a force, that it is easier to understand human beings if we suppose that it does exist". Berne's faith in this mysterious force is fascinating and wonderful and it echoes affirmations by English (2008) on the *vital impulse* that "compels people unconsciously toward more life" (Cornell, 2010).
- To hold: to defend. Defending our patient's progress, even when they will feel the impulse to attack them, to underestimate them (directly or through an attack on us). Defending our neutrality when we are subtly invited to abandon it. Defending the setting in the moments when it is called into question. "Defending" the defences (convalidation) as the only solution possible in the "there and then" of the script decision in the moments when the patient tends to blame themself for this, or they might want to eliminate them as an act

of magic capable of cancelling that which "isn't working" in them and that causes them pain.

- To hold: to occupy. As permission for the patient to occupy the space (physical and relational) necessary to take care of oneself in the therapy environment. The permission to occupy the mind of the therapist without it being damaged, wounded, or overpowered, to occupy the time necessary to take what is needed while keeping track of the limits of the setting.

By indicating all of these meanings in the term "hold", we want to convey that the therapist is present in the relationship in many ways. The terms present many nuances, they establish themselves, and they also change through time; in any case, these considerable variations indicate the capacity of the therapist to "be present" fully in the relationship. Rogers (1980) describes this attitude as congruence of the therapist, nowadays something of this attitude is present in the term "mindfulness".

Note

1 This chapter was written by Francesco Scottà.

References

Berne, E. (1957). *The Layman's Guide to Psychiatry and Psychoanalysis*. New York: Grove Press.

Berne, E. (1972). *What Do You Say After You Say Hello? The Psychology of Human Destiny*. New York: Grove Press.

Cornell, W. F. (2010). Aspiration or adaptation? An unresolved tension in Eric Berne basic beliefs. *Transactional Analysis Journal, TAJ*, 40(3–4): 243–253.

Cornell, W. F., & Bonds-White, F. (2001). Therapeutic relatedness in transactional analysis: The truth of love or the love of truth. *Transactional Analysis Journal, TAJ*, 31(1): 71–83.

English, F. (2008). What motivates resilience after trauma? *Transactional Analysis Journal, TAJ*, 38.

Hargaden, H. & Sills, C. (2002). *Transactional Analysis – A relational perspective*. London: Psychology Press, Taylor & Francis Group.

Rogers, C. R. (1980). *A Way of Being*. Boston: Houghton Mifflin.

Winnicott, D.W. (1953). Transitional objects and transitional phenomena; a study of the first not-me possession. *International Journal of Psychoanalysis*, 34 (2): 89–97.

Winnicott, D.W. (1967). Mirror-role of the mother and family in child development. In: P. Lomas (Ed.), *The Predicament of the Family: A Psycho-Analytical Symposium*. London: Hogarth Press.

11 The triangles of the sky[1]

In this chapter the structure of an "ideal" ITAP therapy course is delineated. There is also a brief description of the phases identified and the specific objectives and methodologies for each phase.

Introduction

The technical framework using Malan's triangles has enjoyed, through the years, numerous confirmations concerning the validity of its affirmations and the practicality of its use in psychotherapy. He observes:

> I call it the *Universal Technique*, because I find that, no matter what part of the world a reasonably well-trained therapist comes from, this is most frequently the technique that he instinctively uses. Moreover, the language that he uses is that of everyday human interaction, entirely free from jargon. But above all, what he is doing is actively pursuing two triangles, using rapport as a guide, instinctively knowing which corner or corners he is seeking, all the time using much of his own personality, which includes eye contact, questions, humour, and his own comments and associations – as always, entirely in the service of the patient . . . I have formalized the principles, but in fact I will have described no more than what every such therapist already does.
>
> (Malan, 1979, p. 94)

Many hundreds of therapists have made use of these initial intuitions in modalities and styles that are very different one from the other, yet they never lose or neglect the basic sustaining principles. Indeed, we have always considered the triangles as a structural base on which to proceed in the construction of the ITAP (Intensive Transactional Analysis Psychotherapy) model. At the same time, we have developed the idea that while such instruments were complete as such, they also provide a partial vision of the patient.

The triangles of the sky

In our view, the idea of framing the human being sitting in front of us in the therapy room, utilizing only the three vertices of the triangle of conflict has, over time, left us less than satisfied. Defence, anxiety, and impulse represent the vertices of conflict, but not the entire person and their possible evolution according to the areas identified by those same vertices. It is as if a doctor, when examining their patient, were to consider only the broken leg to "fix" without taking care, over time, of how that leg can start to work again, perhaps thanks to a process of physiotherapeutic rehabilitation. Once the bone is "firm", it is not necessarily the case that the person is able to start to walk again. The "classic" triangles provide the photograph, moment by moment, of how the patient moves in their dysfunctional patterns, while remaining within a problematic vision. Once the patient has let their defences down, they have observed the limitations in the here and now, they have felt the weight and evaluated the abandonment, how do they restart their developmental journey along each of the vertices identified? In the intrapsychic process, how can an evolutionary and positive vision of the defence materialize? Once the anxiety has been understood and integrated, how does it evolve into a good activation? During the moment of full experience of the impulse, what objective do we have concerning its expression in the relationship? We have imagined that the answer to these questions lies in a triangle that is no longer "of the earth", bound to the dysfunctional conflict, but rather connected to a triangle "of the sky", bound to the resources and the constructive use of lived experiences, understood moment by moment in the course of the therapy.

We say that a triangle is "of the earth" when it has its vertex pointed down and is used to describe suffering or things that are not working. In contrast, a triangle "of the sky" is one with the vertex pointing up, which aims to describe the constructive, evolving, resilient aspects of the person.

From this perspective, if we examine the triangle of the conflict, we can construct another one that has been turned on its head, which we will call the triangle of autonomy. So, the impulse (I) can become autonomy (Au), intended as the intimately authentic, expressive relationship of emotions and experiences with oneself and with the other. Autonomy (Au), therefore, is in the superior vertex of the triangle of the sky, a new possible connection with that which the person is now ready to live, to instigate, to experience, thanks to the contact with their authentic emotions. Their three fundamental components, self-awareness, spontaneity, and intimacy, constitute the ultimate objectives of ITAP psychotherapy, in accordance with the work of Berne (1966).

The defences (D) can become changes (Ch) in the acceptance of getting back power over one's own life direction, modifying the limiting decisions of survival taken in childhood. Changing in such a way can mean, for example, replacing a first self-limiting decision (defence D), with a new decision (change C), which takes account of all of the person's Adult resources (Goulding, & Goulding 1979).

Anxiety (A), considered in the triangle of the earth to be an automatic parasitic reaction, can be revisited and reconsidered in a process of transformation towards Arousal (Ar) (activation), as a natural, healthy warning bell that tells us about a danger and invites us to implement the new decision.

In the triangle of autonomy (see Figure 11.1) there is a shift towards a positive vision of the human being that moves away from a schematization based on pathological conflict and, instead, places itself in a dynamic equilibrium of

Figure 11.1 The triangle of autonomy

functioning that is sufficiently satisfying, stable, and coherent. The equilibrium is no longer centred on an Ego (we can also refer to the concept of Adult in Transactional Analysis) merely crushed by conflict, but it gradually moves towards a central position among useful activations, good changes, and experiences of intimacy. The task of the therapist is not only that of guiding the patient within the vertices of the triangle "of the earth", but also to guide them to get out of it, as far as possible, to enter the triangle "of the sky" in a gradual but constant process of self-experimentation and re-education.

Following a good intervention within the intrapsychic triangle, in relation to one of the vertices of the interpersonal triangle, the patient is able to energize their Ego to a greater extent. This movement, shifting the internal boundaries, leads to the calling into question of a modality that, albeit dysfunctional, has, for a long time, been the only one we have known of.

Trying out different modalities becomes, therefore, the main aim of the therapeutic process, while considering that each step taken in the direction of acquiring new awareness of dysfunctional modalities leads, naturally and inevitably, to a moment of "fertile vacuum" to be filled with the new energy available.

It is not only the triangle of conflict that can be "turned on its head", but also the triangle of persons.

According to the classic formulation, the patient moves on the basis of past relationships and reaches the present by restarting old, dysfunctional schemas, in the here and now or in the recent past, with others and with the therapist. A possible reflection is also similar for this triangle. Is everything we can observe truly here? Is this truly the only vision that we want to have of the person sitting in front of us? What if, in the relationship with the therapist (T), it was not only scripted or transferential repetitions that occurred, but there was also a role for positive introjection of the therapist (something that we know takes place)?

We can, therefore, formulate the triangle of development in which we construct, on the basis of the vertex of the therapist/transference (T), a new vertex of positive introjection (Pi) of a caring figure. This leads us to consider the process of growth towards health as an important element to be thought of without seeing it all merely as a pure repetition of the script. Through the concept of enlivening transference (Gerson, 2003), we remember how transference is not a mere repetition of the past, quite the contrary. Transference, when conceived as a means to creatively synthesize experience, can be thought as a form of language that not only includes practical instances of communication but also performative instances, that is, practices with the aim of making real what was previously only imagined.

In this type of transference the focus is on the rediscovery of what Berne called autonomous aspiration (which we can place on the vertex F – Future) (Berne, 1972), rather than on the past (vertex P): "aspiration may be the strongest determinant in personal, social, and global change" (Clarskon, 1992, p. 206). The top vertex of the triangle of development F is, without doubt, the least tangible, but certainly the most fascinating, at least in our opinion. It represents an orientation, a tension, a journey, more than it does a true objective. The general reorientation of the person occurs on the basis of the restructuration (of perception) of the past and on the change of the present, it aims to modify the vision and new construction of the future. The future is, however, moment by moment, a development discovery based on the predisposition to open up to experience. If such an opening occurs and there is the possibility to create an internal space of acceptance (breaking free of past baggage and freeing up energy), we could say, in accordance with Berne, that "all men and women have their secret gardens whose gates they guard against the profane invasion of the vulgar crowd. These are visual pictures of what they would do if they could do as they pleased" (Berne, 1972, p. 157).

In support of the passage between the triangles of the earth and the triangles of the sky in the ITAP process of change, we can refer to the concept of "retrospective attribution" of meaning, in the sense of being able to look back afterwards as a moment of reorganization of personal meanings, as, for example, it was interpreted by Thomä & Kächele (1988) in the wide debate of psychoanalysis.

Within the framework introduced by these new triangles, in accordance with Gregoire, we can see how the work in the direction of consolidating the triangles of the sky is not only a matter of content alone but also of process. It is the process of creativity and of construction, together with the spring of change. The individual becomes aware of their own resources and of the power they have over their own life and the way in which they give it sense (Gregoire, 2007).

Moving forward in the direction of the construction of the triangle of development (see Figure 11.2), we can consider the relationships in C (Current) and think of them from the perspective of change concerning the vertex Sp (Significant people). Shifting attention onto this vertex, we invite the patient to rediscover, in

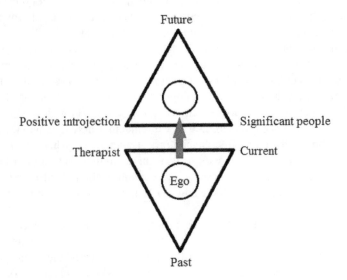

Figure 11.2 The triangle of development

present relationships, an expression of the self that is, as far as is possible, outside of the repetitive and dysfunctional schemas, and, as far as possible, in contact with the authentic sharing of one's own feeling, thinking, and behaviour in relation to other significant people.

It is worth considering, at this point, which opposing forces are encountered in this process of coming out of the triangles of earth. On the one hand, these forces are pushing in the uphill direction towards the triangles of the sky: the motivation for change, the therapeutic alliance, the therapy process in general, and the physis of the patient. On the other hand, a push in the opposite direction comes from the scripted processes (compulsive repetition) and from stress (understood as a sum of factors of emotional, cognitive, somatic, and relational pressure of varying degrees), which we deal with in everyday life. In this dynamic of forces, the progress towards a positive treatment outcome is achieved when the progressive proceeding of the patient is aimed at and consolidated within the triangles of the sky, despite possible momentary and physiological oscillations.

The process of ITAP therapy

In approaching a clinical case, or more generally in order to construct one's own professional practice, it is sometimes useful to have a sort of "plan of action". The strength of the plan of action lies in the (necessarily) simplified schematizations of something that is much more complex. These schematizations allow us to perceive something intuitively that normally would require more time to be processed. Creating a plan of action or an ideal work process allows us to keep at hand a useful compass for orientating ourselves in the phases of work that, hope-fully, take place with our patients. However, the plans of action also have evident limitations in as much as they reduce, to sterile points, the magnificence, the infi-nite complexity, and the elegance of the meeting between two human beings.

Aware of both these peculiarities, we present our idea of the ideal ITAP thera-peutic process in Figure 11.3.

As we can immediately note, the phases following each other consequentially and consecutively involve an advancement by degree, taking as the starting point the acceptance of the patient and moving towards the conclusion of the pathway. At the same time, however, the whole process "spirals" towards the bottom (in the first part of the therapy when we descend towards the triangles of the earth) and towards the top (in the second part when we ascend again to construct or consoli-date the triangles of the sky); this is because, in each moment, if necessary, it is possible to return to previous phases to complete and then re-follow the pathway.

We have inserted at the side of the schema a line that goes through the whole pathway. It acts as an invitation to think of the therapeutic alliance as a vital element to be nourished for the whole duration of the journey, regardless of the specific phase that the couple is going through.

Synthetically, we specify the objective and the process for each phase of the treatment.

Phase A: Objective: Welcoming the patient with the problems they bring and having the most precise idea possible of their psychological structure.

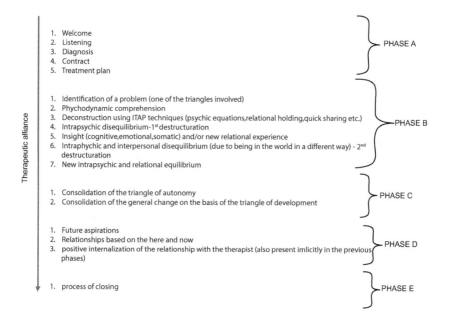

Figure 11.3 ITAP therapy process

Process: Listening and data collection, formulation of a diagnostic hypothesis, formulation of an administrative and therapeutic contract, drafting of a treatment plan in line with previous reflections.

Phase B. Objective: Energizing the Adult sufficiently to have awareness of one's own emotions/impulses (I), expressing them intimately (In), to manage one's own anxiety (A) considering it to be a useful activation signal (Arousal), changing (C) one's own scripted decisions (Defences) by increasing one's own capacity for management unforeseen events in an adaptive manner.

Process: Analysis of the triangles of conflict for each area of the triangle of persons using the ITAP technique (psychic equations, quick sharing, relational holding, confrontation of the limiting defensive systems, regulation of anxious experiences, permissions for intimacy etc.).

Phase C: Objective: Reinforcing a sense of global equilibrium in such a way as to help the patient to experience intimacy (In), to increasingly consider anxiety as a signal of activation (Ar) while at the same time increasing the capacity to manage unforeseen events in an adaptive manner (Ch).

Process: Providing the patient with an expanded and coherent self-image that underlines the changes. Delivering changes, in its widest sense, through all the triangles in which the process occurred. If the technique of the psychic equations is valid for the deconstruction, it is, in the same way, valid for the reconstruction of a solid and coherent self-image, pointing out to the patient the congruencies and the strengths in the various areas that are, little by little, being built. The promotion of resources, supporting changes with a view to consolidating the growth process.

Phase D: Objective: Favouring the exit of the patient from the triangle of persons towards the triangle of development. Consolidating the process of change through the construction of a vision that is no longer only problematic in relation to situations but also proposing a type of functioning within a vision focused on wellbeing.

Process: Gradually decreasing attention on the dysfunctional past and taking it towards the future aspirations of the patient (I wish . . ., I would like to . . ., I have always wanted to . . ., I have always dreamed of . . ., I want to . . ., Why don't I try to. . .) so that the change achieved is increasingly structured and consolidated in all the areas of the person's life.

Phase E: Closure of the therapy course, processing of the detachment, celebration of the results achieved, acceptance for the imperfection of the journey and for the areas of work that will possibly emerge in the future, which will have to be dealt with.

Process: Retracing the pathway taken in its main phases, underlining the fundamental passages. Helping the patient to recognize in their active role within the change process and helping them to take back control responsibility for their own future wellbeing (keeping open the door for future possible therapeutic pathways).

Note

1 This chapter was written by Francesco Scottà.

References

Berne, E. (1966). *Principles of Group Treatment*. Menlo Park, CA: Shea Books.
Berne, E. (1972). *What Do You Say After You Say Hello? The Psychology of Human Destiny*. New York: Grove Press.
Clarskon, P. (1992). Phisis in transactional analysis. *Transactional Analysis Journal, TAJ*, 22(4): 202–209.
Gerson, S. (2003). The enlivening transference and the shadow of the deadliness. Paper delivered to the Boston Psychoanalytic Society and Institute, Boston, MA.
Gregoire, J. (2007). *Les orientations récentes de l'analyse transactionelle [The Recent Orientations of Transactional Analysis]*. Lyon: Les Éditions d'Analyse Transactionelle.
Malan, D. H. (1979). *Individual Psychotherapy and the Science of Psychodynamic*. London: Butterworth & Co. Publishers.
Thomä, H., & Kächele, H. (1988). *Lehrbuch der psychoanalytischen Therapie. 2: Praxis*. Berlin-Heidelberg: Springer Verlag (Trad. It.: *Trattato di terapia psicoanalitica. 2: Pratica Clinica*. Torino: Bollati Boringhieri, 1993).

12 ITAP and Transactional Analysis[1]

This chapter aims to create an integration between models – on the one hand, the conceptual technical instruments of Transactional Analysis (TA) and on the other, Malan's triangles (1979).

All of the TA terms that we use here are present in the Glossary in Appendix 1.

As we know, the first triangle, which is defined as intrapsychic, summarizes the concept of the dynamically understood conflict. There are some impulses/desires/needs (I) that cannot be freely expressed. Such impulses generate reactions of anxiety (A), which is understood as a form of inhibition and as a set of various physical reactions. The physical and psychic cost derived from having to support such a load of anxiety is sometimes too high to sustain, making it necessary to resort to unconscious mechanisms such as defences (D) with the function of reducing or blocking such reactions.

The second triangle derives from the work of Menninger (1958) and is defined by Malan as the triangle of the persons; it depicts the main significant figures within the life of a person. The first vertex, P (Past or Parents), refers to all significant figures, such as parents. The second vertex C (Currents) represents all of the significant figures presently in the subject's life. The third vertex T (Transference or Therapist) represents the relationship with the therapist and the consequent transference that is subsequently established.

The idea to place the two triangles side by side with the aim of using them for therapeutic means can be credited to David Malan (1979), one of the theoretical and methodological founders of brief dynamic therapies. In Figure 12.1, you can find the graphical presentation of the triangles as reported by Malan.

A particular characteristic of ITAP (Intensive Transactional Analysis Psychotherapy) is that of implanting an intrapsychic triangle in each of the vertices of the triangles of the persons, making the two ways of describing suffering all the more integrated, and consequently offering options for the therapy.

Let us now see how such instruments can be utilized and integrated with TA.

First, let us start with an important consideration. The continuous movement between the two triangles, presented in Chapter 4, the chapter dedicated to the psychic equations connected to the "triangle diagram", supports the possibility for the ITAP model to move on various levels. Venturing further in the world of TA, in accordance with Gregoire (2007), we can see how there is a continuum

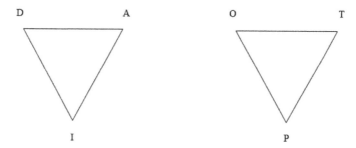

Figure 12.1 Malan's triangles
Reprinted with permission

that sees, on one end, TA authors who place greater attention on observation and interventions at the conscious and preconscious levels, while on the other end, recent movements that have increasingly proposed the idea of concentrating on transference and on the relationship. The model of the "triangle diagram", which as we shall see can be "read" from a TA perspective, can be placed in a position that we can define as integrated, because it tends to comprehend both poles of the continuum. Indeed, Cornell states (2006, p. 4):

> It is my clinical experience that most psychotherapies are a constant back-and-forth weaving among the client's concerns [*psychic equations within the triangle diagram*] about daily life and relationships outside of the therapy session [*vertex C of the triangle of persons*], the client's intrapsychic conflicts as they emerge over the course of treatment [*triangle of conflicts*], and the matrix of transference/countertransference dynamics within the therapeutic relationship itself [*vertex T of the triangle of persons*]. [. . .] The relational perspectives have brought important advances in transactional analysis treatment approaches. Many clients need a therapeutic model – and a therapist – open to multiple levels of intervention.
>
> (our notes in italics)

We believe that the ITAP model, through the use of the "triangle diagram" tool, is near to such a conception.

Vertex I: authentic needs present in the child

As we have previously explained, vertex I refers to primary needs, impulses, and emotions. It represents the unnoticed element, the unconscious, which the patient and the therapist have to reach. This element activates anxiety (A) from which the defences (D) emerge. The principle objective is that of bringing to the surface the emotions and the contents present in I in the largest quantity that the patient is able to tolerate in each session. Through this process it is possible to bring into the territory of emotional experience and consciousness those unconscious impulses that activate anxiety and maintain the defences.

Vertex I represents in TA what is called the innate needs of the C_0. It is also called the Somatic Child and the authentic needs of C_1 (Child in the Child or Natural Child) at the structural level, defined as the sources of needs and feelings unconditioned by the parental figures (Moiso & Novellino, 1982). Furthermore, this part derives from desires and authentic natural emotions of the body, and it contains the memory of our past experiences (Woollams & Brown, 1978).

In TA functional analysis, we can define this same vertex by comparing it with the concept of the positive Free Child, which expresses itself authentically, spontaneously, and free from parental dictates.

Vertex D and the four defensive categories of ITAP

Vertex D represents, as we have said, the vertex of the defences. While there are many ways that defensive mechanisms can be described, we will not be summarizing them here. In our integration, we have decided to adopt a particular model that can be placed within the intervention method of Intensive Short-Term Dynamic Psychotherapy (ISTDP) technique, founded and developed by H. Davanloo (see Chapter 1). This specific categorization can be articulated through the subdivision into four different types of mechanisms, which Davanloo (1990) himself distinguishes as:

- Tactical: There are obsessive types, such as rationalization, rumination, vagueness, retraction and so on, and there are character-based types, such as, passivity, detachment, obstinacy, provocation, and challenge.
- Major: such as resistance against emotional closeness, isolation, and instant repression.
- Regressive: such as complaining, weepiness, irritability, and the tendency for temper tantrums.
- Primitive: such as projection, internalization, projective identification.

Other authors who gravitate towards the ISTDP technique, such as Baruh (2010) and Abbass (2015), only make a subdivision between tactical defences and major defences, positioning them on a continuum, like the one in Figure 12.2 (Abbass, 2015, p. 24).

From the perspective of the integration proposed in this chapter, we present, for each defensive category identified by Davanloo, a possible range of concepts from TA. Given the diversity of ways with which defences are described, what follows represents a possible, basic integration, which can be modified, specified, amplified.

The *tactical defences* can be compared to TA concepts, such as:

- Redefinition transactions: bypass or blocking transactions
- Carom or gallows transaction
- Thought disorders: overdetailing and overgeneralization

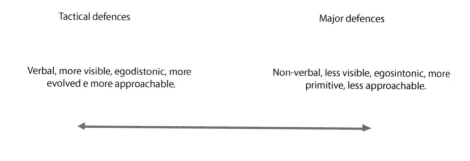

Tactical defences

Major defences

Verbal, more visible, egodistonic, more evolved e more approachable.

Non-verbal, less visible, egosintonic, more primitive, less approachable.

CONTINUUM

Figure 12.2 Continuum of tactical and major defences

As we can see, they are all modalities with which people can "distance" themselves from others. They diminish or reformulate the problem they present or that emerges, they confuse and shift the central point of the discussion. The function of these dysfunctional systems is, therefore, that of not allowing the other to move closer to oneself or to the problem; using movements with the aim of shifting, interrupting, diminishing, confusing.

The *major defences* can be compared to TA concepts, such as:

- Limiting script decisions
- Injunctions
- Drives
- Contaminations
- Impasses
- First-degree or second-degree games

As we can note, these represent all of the modalities with which the individual structures their own vital field and their own internal and external processes, according to dysfunctional modalities. These systems represent the foundation of the personality structure, they are acquired in childhood, structured through the course of life, and constitute the central defensive nucleus in the face of those prohibited, authentic emotions in the here and now. Access to these psychic and relational contents is protected by the tactical defences that represent the "front line" to be overcome to be able to then get to the TA mechanisms which we have linked to the major defences.

The *regressive defences* can also be compared to TA concepts, such as:

- Discounting
- Passivity: doing nothing, overadaptation, agitation
- Symbiosis
- Racket emotions

It is possible to maintain positions based on the there-and-then, that is, of the regressive kind, through passive modalities or discounting the self or others, which aim to keep oneself in a symbiotic relationship (Schiff et al., 1975). Through processes of discounting, for example, the person does not fully consider their own resources in recognizing or modifying the difficult situations of their own life and they tend to diminish their own responsibility by satisfying their own needs through the external world, often thereby increasing their own passivity.

The topic of racket emotions is slightly different. They are learned and maintained on the basis of the impossibility of being able to express authentic emotions. They therefore represent "socially acceptable" substitutes for inexpressible emotional experiences, because they are deemed dangerous and frightening by the significant figures. Crying in a continuous and imploring way (Davanloo would call it "weepiness") while retelling a scene in which we were rudely overtaken in a supermarket queue can represent a moment of regression to the extent that the authentic expression of anger, of a well-integrated Adult anchored in the here and now, is hidden.

The *primitive defences* can be compared to TA concepts such as:

- Somatic impasses
- Early script decisions (protocol)
- Passivity: incapacitation or violence
- Third-degree games

Basic conflicts, with implications for the somatic level and script decisions taken in the earliest months of childhood, can be read as primitive ways of dealing with anxiety. We have also included violence here as a primitive modality of extreme dysfunctional protection, which can be seen as comparable to third-degree games, in which resorting to violence often leads to serious safety issues for the individual and for others: detention, suicide, and murder.

Vertex A, racket manifestations (reported internal experiences), unbound energy, behavioural diagnosis

Knowing the anxiety discharge pathways of the patients allows the therapist to evaluate autoregulatory capacity of the same anxiety, to evaluate the capacity of the adaptation of the Ego, and consider the degree of severity of the pathology. Furthermore, correct evaluation of anxiety allows the formulation of a valid diagnosis and an efficacious treatment plan (see Chapter 6 for an in-depth exploration of this topic). Here we will limit ourselves to considering how vertex A can be compared in TA with the concept of the racket manifestation of reported internal experiences and of observable behaviours inherent in the script present within the model of the script system (Erskine & Zalcman, 1979; Erskine, 2010). By reported internal experiences, we mean those pains, discomforts, or physical tensions that can be linked to unbound energy expressed through the body; they represent a more general description of that which is the internal classification of vertex A, as specified and explored in this volume.

The TA instrument that is able to recognize the manifestations connected with the vertex of anxiety A of the triangle of conflict, is the *behavioural diagnosis* utilized within the therapeutic relationship T of the triangle of persons. Through this diagnosis, we can identify what Ego state our interlocutor is in, in any given moment, by observing behavioural manifestations, such as: words, attitudes, gestures, posture, tone of voice, expressions, and anxious manifestations. In order to conduct an accurate behavioural diagnosis, it is necessary to possess an uncontaminated Adult, an aware Little Professor, and knowledge of the peculiar signs that characterize each Ego state. Naturally, the behavioural manifestations are different from person to person. By definition, the acquired experiences are unique and unrepeatable. We can add that no one behavioural signal is sufficient for a diagnosis, but rather, the sum of several clues can justify a diagnosis. Through this type of diagnosis, it is possible, among other things, to pick up on the signals of anxiety described. The accurate observation of physical manifestations of discharge gives us a more accurate diagnostic approach and also allows the TA therapist to have a more refined instrument of examination and control, moment by moment, of the activation state of the patient. Alongside the classical TA behavioural diagnosis, there is also the careful observation of anxiety channeling (as described in Chapter 6), allowing the therapist to calibrate better the interventions, making them more efficacious and targeted.

The triangle of persons and other diagnoses in TA

As well as behavioural diagnosis, Berne (1961) identified three other modalities of diagnosis, in order to recognize the Ego states, which we can place alongside some vertices of the triangles:

- *Social diagnosis*, the use of transference in TA and vertices T and C
- *Historical diagnosis* and vertex P
- *Phenomenological diagnosis* and vertex T

The second type of diagnosis is defined as *social diagnosis* and refers to the Ego state that people provoke in their interlocutors. The basic assumption lies in the fact that often people tend to relate to others according to the complementary Ego state as it relates to that which the other person is energizing. Therefore, by noting the Ego state with which I react to, I can deduce the energized one from my interlocutor and vice versa. This type of diagnosis can be placed alongside vertex T of the triangle of persons, considering that both can take the relationship as a point of reference, in the here and now of the relationship, between patient and therapist. It might also be placed alongside vertex C, demonstrating how the same mechanism can also be observed in relationships with significant figures of the present.

Within social diagnosis we can examine in greater details vertex T, because it offers points for further discussion. Some of the most important work in the sphere of TA concerning transference and countertransference is, in our view, that produced by Carlo Moiso and Michele Novellino.

Moiso (1985) developed the idea that, in the transferential process, the patient externalizes their own internal Parent–Child dialogue, thereby impeding the relationship from being based on data originating in the here and now. Referring to Novellino's analysis, we can summarize the idea of transference in TA in the following way:

- At the theoretical level: transference is a repackaging of the original impasse, in which the patient projects the parental pole of that same impasse (Moiso, 1985; Novellino, 1990);
- At the operative level: the analysis of countertransference takes on fundamental importance as an instrument of comprehension of phenomena of the therapist's unconscious identification towards the patient's unconscious (Novellino, 2004).

The mechanism of projection in vertex T involves, according to the theorization of Moiso:

- The transference of P2: which can be negative if the client plays psychological games with the therapist that tend to provoke in the client the same type of frustration received once by their parents and, in this way, to reinforce the limiting aspect of their script *(vertex of defence D in relation to T)* (Gregoire, 2007). It can be positive if, on the other hand, the patient proceeds towards a search for permissions and recognitions that have not arrived in the past *(enlivening/positive transference vertex of change of the triangle of the sky)*. For Carlo Moiso, the transferential transactions are further transactions.
- Transference of P_1: in which the protection is unconscious and is applied to an archaic Parent (known as P_1) split into two sub-structures (known as P_1+ e P_1-). In the split, the object (the parental figure) is separated into two opposite and isolated elements, which the individual is incapable of taking into consideration simultaneously at the conscious level. One is experienced as exclusively good: it is Melanie Klein's (Klein, 1932) good object, which Berne calls the fairy godmother, or the good giant when these dynamics are applied to the father. The other aspect, in contrast, is experienced as being exclusively bad: the bad object, or according to Berne, the witch or the ogre. Similarly, the self is split: the person considers themselves as a good object (called C_1+) when in contact with the image of the good mother, and as a bad object (C_1-) in the face of the bad mother (Gregoire, 2007).

Within the world of TA there are various authors who, from the 1990s onwards, have begun to consider the analysis of transference as a central element. These include Moiso and Novellino, but also, among others, Clarkson (1992), Erskine (1991), Allen and Allen (1991), who have brought a significant contribution to the classification of transferential phenomena. We refer you to their works, which provide further exploration.

We now come to the third type of diagnosis. Through the *historical diagnosis* we can confirm and reinforce the previously examined diagnoses. It results from the awareness that the present behaviour and reference schema have a precedent, both in the sense of a memory of a similar behaviour from a significant past figure (P), and regarding memories of similar previous experiences and behaviours from one's own childhood (C) (Moiso & Novellino, 1982). Through gathering data on the past life of the person, we are able to structure a precise impression of the origin of such behaviour and, taking account both of the process and the content of the phenomenon, to verify our diagnostic hypotheses. The historical diagnosis can be compared to vertex P of the triangle of persons, which considers the meaningful relationships of the past and how these have contributed strongly to the structuring of the pathology of the patient in the present.

The last to be examined is the *phenomenological diagnosis*, which consists in reliving, in the here and now, the moment in which a certain experience of an Ego state is experienced for the first time in the then and there. While it is the most subjective, it is also most precise and has the highest emotional impact of all of the TA diagnoses. We place this TA concept alongside vertex T of the triangle of persons, in as much as this diagnosis can be achieved only in the therapist–patient relationship.

Triangle of persons and relational TA

Continuing from the perspective of integration between models, we believe it is important to continue our journey by tracing a bridge that links the triangle of persons with relational TA, as defined by Charlotte Sills and Helena Hargaden (2002). The authors identify intersubjectivity as a cardinal principal in their model of psychotherapy. It can be defined as a meeting and reciprocal interaction of two subjectivities that create a relational field. Such a meeting involves, therefore, the possibility of change for both the subjects of the relationship who modify each other, creating new possibilities for creative development. The basic idea is that both therapist and patient are, to some extent, reciprocally "changed" by proceeding in such a relationship. Concerning the topic of the relationship in therapy, it is possible to distinguish between primary and secondary intersubjectivity. We refer you to the original book of the authors (Hargaden & Sills, 2002) for an in-depth examination, while we will limit ourselves to looking at the concept of primary subjectivity in a specific and synthetic way.

Primary intersubjectivity and vertex T in the ITAP technique

In this first typology, the two subjects are conscious of their reciprocal subjective past, but only as far as is concerned the qualitative aspects of the relationship in the here and now, and their present lived experience within the same relationship. The access to primary intersubjectivity means it is necessary to have a reflexive relational capacity that develops from birth through to the first six months of life and is configured as the capacity to comprehend that the other people have a mental experience that is separate from their own (Hargaden & Sills, 2002). It is preverbal, emotional, non-symbolic, and unconscious. It continues to exist throughout life and, in any case, underlies each relationship or human communication. It is still present even when its content, after the appearance of secondary intersubjectivity, it is partially verbalized, symbolized, rendered conscious, and expressed in cognitive terms by the subjects (Gregoire, 2007).

The contents presented so far regarding primary intersubjectivity indicate a model of reciprocal influence, in the here and now, that might lead to a deep modification of the primitive relational schemas of the there and then. In accordance with this, and in reference to the triangle of persons, we can say that each modification in primary intersubjectivity that occurs in the T vertex also modifies, both in the therapist and in the patient (we hope much more in the latter), the processual schemas in P and in C.

In adult life, there is the tendency to look for fusional or prereflexive experiences in objects or in life experiences. From these experiences, there is an expectation for a psychophysical transformation of the self or of the surrounding world. Such searching not only lacks awareness, but it is also founded on an understanding of the self and of others that is mediated by affective and sensorial exchanges; by a true psychophysical "idiom"; made up of bodily and emotional sensations, as well as of gestures, movements, and actions (Favasuli, 2010).

In vertex T it is possible, therefore, to work with all those components of primary intersubjectivity and co-construct what Bollas (1987) calls the "healing idiom", meaning the capacity of the therapist to give shape and content to the needs and the requests of the patient. Such a "healing idiom" takes shape and solidifies in the ITAP technique through introducing the added value of the intensity to the quality of the patient/therapist relationship. It has already been discussed elsewhere in this manual, the value and meaning of such relational attention of continual "presence", the aim of which is to stimulate the patient to put aside their own defence mechanisms and to monitor constantly their own anxiety so that it becomes gradually more aware, in a process of progressive energization of its Adult Ego state.

As far as primary relationships are concerned, we believe that the process of relational intensity, taken with the modalities presented in this volume and the clarifications already described in this chapter, is similar to the idea of a good enough maternal presence (Winnicott, 1953, 1967). This maternal presence is capable of providing the necessary zone of proximal development (Vygotskij, 1978) without forcing the patient but also without leaving the patient alone in the relationship. Finding this type of distance is certainly the arduous task of the therapist and it cannot always be achieved naturally. At the same time, we are convinced that it is possible to refine such attitudes with clinical practice and supervision, above all, through the careful observation of videos of therapy (better still with ourselves in the role of the therapist).

Note

1 This chapter was written by Francesco Scottà.

References

Abbass, A. (2015). *Reaching Through Resistance – Advanced Psychotherapy Techniques*. Kansas City, MO: Seven Leaves Press.

Allen, J. R., & Allen, B. A. (1991). Concepts of transference: A critique, a tipology, an alternative hypothesis and some proposals. *Transactional Analysis Journal, TAJ*, 21(2): 77–92.

Baruh, L. (2010). Prolegolemi alla diagnosi in Psicoterapia Intensiva Breve Dinamico-Esperienziale (PIBD-E) [Prolegomena to diagnosis in brief dynamic-experiential brief intensive psychotherapy]. *Psyche Nuova*, 2010: 117–121.

Berne, E. (1961). *Transactional Analysis in Psychotherapy*. New York: Grove Press.

Berne, E. (1964). *Games People Play*. New York: Grow Press.

Berne, E. (1966). *Principles of Group Treatment*. Menlo Park, CA: Shea Books.

Berne, E. (1972). *What Do You Say After You Say Hello?* London: Corgi.

Bollas, C. (1987). *The Shadow of the Object*. London: Free Association Books.

Clarkson, P. (1992). *Transactional Analysis Psychotherapy*. London: Routledge.

Cornell, W. F. (2006). Another perspective on the therapist's stance. *The Script*, 36(3): 4.

Davanloo, H. (1990). *Unlocking the Unconscious: Selected Papers of Habib Davanloo, MD*. New York: Wiley.

English, F. (1976). *Analyse transactionnelle et émotions [Transactional Analysis and Emotions]*. Paris: Desclée de Brouwer.

Erskine, R. G. (1991). Transference and transactions: Critique from an intrapsychic and integrative perspective. *Transactional Analysis Journal*, 21(2): 63–76.

Erskine, R. G. (2010). *Life Scripts: A Transactional Analysis of Unconscious Relational Patterns*. London: Karnac.

Erskine, R. G., & Zalcman, M. (1979). The racket system: A model for racket analysis. *Transactional Analysis Journal*, 9(1): 51–59.

Favasuli, M. A. (2010). La rappresentazione – forme e contenuti della mente [Representation – Forms and Contents of the Mind]. *Corpo Narrante*, 2: 1–17.

Goulding, M. M., & Goulding, R. L. (1979). *Changing Lives Through Redecision Therapy*. New York: Grove Press.

Gregoire, J. (2007). *Les orientations récentes de l'analyse transactionelle [The Recent Orientations of Transactional Analysis]*. Lyon: Les Éditions d'Analyse Transactionelle.

Hargaden, H., & Sills, C. (2002). *Transactional Analysis – A Relational Perspective*. London: Psychology Press, Taylor & Francis Group.

Klein, M. (1932). *The Psychoanalysis of Children*. London: Vintage Publishers.

Malan, D. H. (1979). *Individual Psychotherapy and the Science of Psychodynamic*. London: Butterworth & Co. Publishers.

Menninger, K. (1958). *Theory of Psychoanalytic Technique*. New York: Basic Books.

Moiso, C. M. (1985). Ego states and transference. *Transactional Analysis Journal*, 15(3): 194–201.

Moiso, C. M., & Novellino, M. (1982). *Stati dell'Io [Ego States]*. Roma: Astrolabio.

Novellino, M. (1990). Unconscious communication and interpretation. *Transactional Analysis Journal*, 33, 3: 223–230.

Novellino, M. (2004). *Psicoanalisi Transazionale [Transactional Psychoanalysis]*. Milano. Franco Angeli.

Novellino, M. (2014). *Dizionario Didattico di Analisi Transazionale [Dydactic Dictionary of Transactional Analysis]*. Roma: Astrolabio.

Schiff, J. L., Schiff, A. W., Mellor, K., Schiff, E., Schiff, S., Richman, D., Fishman, J., Wolz, L., Fishman, C., & Momb, D. (1975). *The Cathexis Reader: Transactional Analysis Treatment of Psychosis*. New York: Harper and Row.

Stuart, I., & Joines, V. (1987). *TA Today: A New Introduction to Transactional Analysis* (2nd edn.). Nottingham: Lifespace.

Vygotskij, L. S. (1978). *Mind in Society: Development of Higher Psychological Processes*. Cambridge, MA: Harvard University Press.

Winnicott, D. W. (1953). Transitional objects and transitional phenomena: A study of the first not-me possession. *The International Journal of Psychoanalysis*, 34(2): 89–97.

Winnicott, D. W. (1967). Mirror-role of the mother and family in child development. In P. Lomas (Ed.), *The Predicament of the Family: A Psycho-analytical Symposium*. London: Hogarth Press.

Woollams, S., & Brown, M. (1978). *Transactional Analysis*. Dexter: Huron Valley Institute.

13 Neurobiological evidence for the ITAP model[1]

In the present chapter, we describe empirical evidence gathered in the field of affective neuroscience that converge with the ITAP (Intensive Transactional Analysis Psychotherapy) model, thereby reinforcing the empirical basis that characterize it as an evidence-based model. In particular, we will consider: (1) the neural systems responsible for the semantic representations associated with the concept of the interpersonal triangle, conceptualized as projections of generalized representations constructed there and then in the interpretation of life events in the here and now; (2) the neural mechanisms underlying the learning of conditioned responses and of the non-voluntary regulation of such responses in association with the concept of the intrapsychic triangle; (3) physiological attunement as a resource for the maintenance of the alliance and holding on the therapeutic relationship.

Interpersonal triangle and semantic representations of relationships

Let us summarize the relevant material from the previous chapters. The ITAP technique based on the interpersonal triangle envisages the exploration of the patient's modalities of relating to the relational figures of the present (C), including the therapist (T), and the relational modalities experienced in the past (P). The idea of the intervention based on the interpersonal triangle is that the individual possesses internal self-representations in relation to others, constructed in the course of their experience, which guides them in current relationships. The perception of current relationships, therefore, depends both on the perception that the individual enacts in the here and now (Adult), and on internal representations constructed in the there and then (Child and/or Parent). In emotionally difficult situations, the perception of the present relationships is influenced in an exaggerated or dysfunctional way by internal representations (Child and/or Parents). In these situations where there is a predominance of the Child or the Parent on the Adult – which in Transactional Analysis terms are called "contaminations" – the therapist can act by stimulating the perceptual aspects of the patient, guiding the patient in the observation of their relational modalities in the here and now in C (for example, "does this also occur with their partner?") or in T (for example, "is this happening here with me as well?"). These operations have the functions of leading the patient to gradually increase their awareness of the relational schemas that they repeatedly enact and to expand the chances of giving meaning to their own experience. Therefore, if before the therapy a person tends to interpret their own relational experiences in a rigid and repetitive manner, after the therapy we would expect a greater richness of meanings when the patient makes sense of their own every day, relational experiences.

In the field of neuroscience, the semantic functions underlying the attribution of meanings to experiences – which include all those semantic memory processes of recovery and manipulation that the individual constructs by capturing aspects that appear with some regularity in the external world – we can trace back to a set of areas known as the "semantic system" (Binder et al., 2011; Binder et al., 2009). Studies in this area have explored the exact cortical location of various categories of actions and concrete objects (Martin & Chao, 2001), while only recently researchers have started to study the neural correlates of complex semantic representations, which might also be of clinical relevance, such as those that govern representations of the self and social interactions. For example, Zahn and his colleagues (2007) have studied the activations of the semantic system in a group of subjects during a task that involved the expression of judgements associated with social concepts (for example, the concept of honour) as compared with concepts that describe general functions in animals or objects (for example, the concept of "usefulness"). They observed that the presence of emotional aspects in social judgements modulated the activation of medial semantic areas, while the richness of detail with which the social constructs were described (but not the emotional concept) modulated the activations in the temporal lobes. Therefore, both these areas and their associated functions seem to play a key role in guaranteeing the flexibility of social behaviours through the integration of abstract conceptual knowledge of social behaviours (dependent on temporal semantic areas) and the emotional and motivational aspects (dependent on the more medial semantic areas).

The interest in these topics has grown alongside the further description of the default system (Raichle et al., 2001; Raichle & Snyder, 2007), a group of cerebral areas that coincide with the areas of the semantic system. These areas demonstrate a functioning that is internally consistent, they are normally active when the brain is resting (when no specific task is being asked of the subjects). The name "default system" (which we can consider to be a synonym of "semantic system") refers precisely to this peculiar functioning through which the activation of these areas is anti-correlated with the activation of areas responsible for executive and perceptual processes normally involved in completing tasks (Fox et al., 2005). This description corresponds to the dynamic between the activation of the Adult (perceptual and executive functions in the here and now) and the activation of the Child and/or Parent (semantic representations) (Messina & Sambin, 2015a). Furthermore, returning to the idea of contamination as a prevalence of semantic aspects originating in the there and then (Adult), an excessive activation of the default system has been demonstrated in patients affected by depression (Messina et al., 2016, Sheline et al., 2009) or by disorders of anxiety (Zhao et al., 2007, Gentili et al., 2009).

Leaving aside researching studying the brain in a resting state, the activation of the default system has been associated with cognitive tasks that have notable clinical relevance. These tasks include those involving representations of self, such as tasks that require the subject to judge whether adjectives are descriptive of themselves as people (Northoff et al., 2006). Furthermore, the default system has been associated with self-projection, described as the capacity to mentally project oneself into the past or into the future but also onto other people's perspectives (Buckner & Carroll, 2007; Spreng et al., 2009). Self-projection is associated with numerous clinically relevant processes, including access to autobiographical memories (projections of the self into the past), future plans (projection of the self into the future), and also the capacity for empathy and theory of mind (projection of the self onto other points of view).

The neural dynamics that underlie the semantic processes described up until this point suggest other fundamental clinical implications that are central in the work on the interpersonal triangle in the ITAP model. The first level of work on the interpersonal triangle concerns the stimulation of the Adult perception of current relationships, through interventions that aim to direct the patient's attention onto aspects of the here and now, to contrast the influence of semantic representations formed in the there and then. In this way, the therapist intervenes by favouring a greater release of energy in the neural areas responsible for perceptions in the here and now, which function in a way that is not correlated with semantic networks and therefore also limit them.

A second level concerns the reprocessing of semantic representations that the individual uses to give sense to their own relational experiences, favouring the development of increasingly complex and varied semantic networks that allow the individual to flexibly orient themself within their own relationships. An example of this level of change concerns contrasting the rigid modalities and schemas of experiential representation that characterize personality disorders in which others, and/or the self, are seen as being completely good or completely bad, with a reduction of the complexity of the relational objects. The work on semantic representations does not only concern work in the past but it also influences scripted aspects of the projection into the future. In this regard, the work on the triangles of the sky can also be seen as being about semantic representations.

Finally, a third level concerns the emotional reactions associated with semantic representations. This level cannot be based merely on work at a cognitive level but requires relational experiences (initially with the therapist) that modify the anxious reactions, associated with the emergence of impulses, which could not find expression in the relationships of the past. These processes, which depend on the medial areas of the semantic system, will now be explored in greater detail.

Intrapsychic triangle: emotions and regulation

The ITAP model inherits from previous psychodynamic models the idea that anxiety functions like an internal signal that warns the individual of the necessity to defend oneself from a growing emergency of unpleasant emotions. The emotions that are generated by interaction with the environment, therefore, do not always produce a coherent behavioural response but are first processed or modified in line with the needs of the homeostatic balance of the individual's mind through the enacting of defence mechanisms (Messina & Sambin, 2015b).

The intrapsychic triangle offers a clear vision of this intrapsychic vision, consisting of a certain type of emotional activation (impulse), which causes the activation of anxiety in the individual in such a way that, rather than the emotion being used as a guide for their own behaviour, the individual avoids it by using individual defences. From the neuroscientific point of view, there is evidence that supports the existence of this type of dynamic and which, in turn, constitute indications that are central to the ITAP intervention model.

Impulse and anxiety

In order to examine the theme of signal anxiety (or anticipatory anxiety) from a neuroscientific perspective, it is useful to refer to the behaviourist theories of learned anxiety, which formed the basis on which the main neurobiological models of anxiety were constructed. The behaviourist models concerning anxiety go back to the associative learning theories of Pavlov (1927), according to whom animals and human beings acquire a fear of potentially dangerous objects through association between previously neutral stimuli and dangerous stimuli through a processed known as "conditioning". According to this model, the extinction of the anxiety responses seems to depend to a large degree on exposure to the original traumatic situations, a technique which forms the basis of behaviourist therapies (Mowrer, 1960). The efficacy of this technique, however, is generally limited to certain symptoms (such as specific phobias). The underlying neural structures of these processes have been described adequately from various points of view. A representative contribution by Kandel (2008) studied a very simple nervous system (that of the aplysia) and managed to describe in detail the variations in the synthesis of proteins within its neurons, and therefore the expression of its genes, which have the effect of producing a response of anticipatory anxiety on the basis of the interaction between brain and environment.

Moving on to the more complex human neural system, LeDoux (1998) described certain fundamental characteristics of the responses of anticipatory anxiety, which are generated following traumatic events. From his studies, certain fundamental elements emerged. Firstly, the author described the amygdala as the cerebral area responsible for the registration of emotional reactions that the individual has during a traumatic event, while the conscious memory of such events depends on other, more evolved cerebral structures, such as the hippocampus and the cortex. This means that the emotional reactions linked to the trauma depend on primitive neural processes, similar to those present in reptilian brains, which have the characteristic of activating very quickly (manifestations of anxiety can be activated suddenly) and automatically, without the intervention of complex cognitive processes. Another characteristic of responses to anxiety is that they are not very discriminatory; in other words, the conditioned response can also be activated by stimuli that are only distantly associated with the trauma. As far as this point is concerned, we can hypothesize that in the presence of semantic networks that are not highly differentiated the fear response can be easily extended to stimuli that, in an approximate way, can be traced back to similar categories. All of these characteristics of learned anxiety correspond to the forms of anxiety described in the ITAP model. In terms of Transactional Analysis, this modality of anxiety activation corresponds to the functioning of the Child, and, therefore, remains within the person, even in the presence of an Adult thought that considers it to be irrational and dysfunctional.

With the advent of neuroimaging it has also been possible to describe the processes of conditioning in terms of neural systems and areas involved. One of the areas that seems most involved with the processes of associative learning and distinction of conditioned responses is the prefrontal cortex (Milad & Quirk, 2012; Sehlmeyer et al., 2009), which, once more, represents a central element of the semantic system described in the preceding paragraphs (or default system). All things considered, these models effectively predict certain changes involving simple, associative processes, while at the moment they are not especially useful in explaining complex forms of change, such as those required in emotional and personality disorders.

In order to develop neurobiological models in this direction, it would be necessary to keep under consideration the psychodynamic approaches that, in the course of time, have produced theoretical models and gathered empirical evidence regarding the importance of relationships for the psychological development of the person (especially primary relationships). From a psychodynamic point of view, the learning of conditioned responses that intervene in most emotional disorders are not considered in an abstract way but rather are placed within the traumatic experiences that concern the relationships. This is an aspect that is fundamental if we consider that in the first years of the life of a human being, the event that, above any other, might threaten life concerns the possibility of being abandoned by the caregiver. Consequently, the conditioning processes that intervene most determinedly in the psychic development of the child are, without a doubt, those that regard the relationships with others. It is therefore the case that the child is extremely sensitive to the reactions of others to the child's behaviours and to the spontaneous expression of their impulses. From this point of view, in line with the ITAP model, we can say that the extinction of conditioned responses regarding most emotional disorders would require exposure to a similar situation in which the impulse was originally prohibited (archaic scene) in a relational condition characterized by acceptance and the absence of judgement (in terms of dynamic psychology, corrective relational experience). Therefore, the objective of the therapist is that of facilitating and promoting the free expression of impulses which, spontaneously, are generated in the individual in the course of relational experiences. However, as the behaviourist said, one of the principal obstacles to change is the tendency of the individual to avoid the surfacing of the impulse through defence mechanisms. Therefore, a large part of the therapist's work is that of confronting the defences, thereby maintaining the level of anxious activation within acceptable limits (see paragraph 3).

Defences: neural correlates of spontaneous avoidance

The enactment of defence mechanisms, therefore, has an important function for the intrapsychic balance of the individual, regulating the activation of anxiety. In order to utilize language that is closer to neuroscience, the passages from one vertex to another of the intrapsychic triangle can be seen as operations aimed at emotional regulation, defined as "the processes by which individuals influence which emotions they have, when they have them, and how they experience and express these emotions" (Gross, 1998; p. 275). Although neuroscientific research has mainly focused on forms of voluntary regulation, it is the research on non-voluntary emotional regulation, or defence mechanisms, that lend most support to the ITAP model.

The study of non-voluntary forms of emotional regulation has been neglected by neuroscience due to the methodological difficulties inherent in spontaneous processes. Nonetheless, some pioneering studies have taken this direction. In a study conducted by Benelli and colleagues (2012), an experimental design was used whereby participants, during an fMRI scan, were passively exposed to stimuli that consisted in different versions of stories (either neutral or emotional). After the fMRI, the participants were asked to describe the stories that had been read as stimuli during the fMRI experiment. Subsequently, the number of emotive words utilized by participants in their descriptions of the stories was used to calculate an index of tendency to avoid emotional content. From the analysis of individual differences in this index, there was found to be an association with lower deactivations in the areas of the default system. Similar results were identified in a study by Viviani and colleagues using perfusion weighted imaging (PWI) (Viviani et al., 2010). In this study, mechanisms of spontaneous emotional regulation were investigated using a phrase construction task in which the participants had to spontaneously avoid the construction of phrases with negative content. Also in this case, in the spontaneous avoidance of negative words, a modulation of the areas of the default system was observed. The results of these first studies provide new elements to understand what happens in the brain when an individual enacts defence mechanisms and their function in the psychic dynamics of the individual. This highlights the fact that mechanisms of emotional regulation can occur in an involuntary manner through forms of control that are closely dependent on the internal states of the individual, their innate motivations, and their needs (Small et al., 2001).

Once more, the neuroscientific evidence suggest different levels of therapeutic action (corresponding to the concepts in paragraph 1): (1) stimulation of the Adult perception to move the person to greater awareness of the defensive processes in play; (2) reprocessing of semantic representations to increase the specificity of the defensive responses, limiting them to truly dangerous environmental stimuli (diminishing, therefore, the pervasiveness of the defences); (3) favouring the extinction of anxiety responses through experiences of exposure of the impulse within an empathetic relational context of containment which favours a corrective relational experience in which the patient experiences the possibility of expressing impulses without negative relational consequences.

Physiological attunement as a resource
for the alliance and holding

As we have seen in the previous paragraphs, a fundamental point concerning the ITAP intervention regards the delicate equilibrium between the confrontation of the defences (necessary to surface the impulse) and the need for the individual to maintain a tolerable level of activation. From a technical point of view, the ITAP model suggests specific relational modalities that are based on attunement of the therapist concerning the state of their patient. Attunement seems to be necessary both to calibrate the interventions (alliance versus confrontation) and to immediately utilize countertransference, which itself is based on intuitions that are fruit of deep attunement with the other.

Interpersonal events, especially the subtle and ephemeral ones, have not been sufficiently investigated through neuroscientific methods. An fMRI study conducted by Coan and colleagues (2006) investigated relational aspects, showing how the neural response to painful stimuli (electric shocks), considered in terms of activation of areas responsible for emotional reactivity, was strongly modulated by the fact that the participants of the experiment could hold the hand of a loved one during the scan. The effect was present even if they held the hand of a stranger, although it was less strong (Coan et al., 2006). This evidence supports the importance of an environment characterized by holding an ideal condition for lowering the anxiety to a level that allows the intervention by confronting the defences.

Another area of research studies that provide evidence to support the ITAP model is that of interpersonal physiology applied to psychotherapy, which involves studying the tendency of human beings to enter into physiological attunement (Di Mascio, 1957). These studies do not only explore psychophysiological responses in single subjects, but rather they look at the interaction between multiple subjects in which psychophysiological parameters are measured simultaneously. Therefore, we are not only addressing what happens in the patient but also what happens in the therapist – how the therapist manages anxiety so as to enter into contact with the other and provide them with the relational holding that forms a basis of the ITAP method. The first studies in this sector were limited to documenting the existence of phenomena of physiological attunement between patient and therapist between their heartbeats (Malmo et al., 1957; Stanek et al., 1973) or through the combination of various measures (heartbeat, skin conductance, blood pression, EMG) (Busk et al., 1976). More recent studies have found a significant association between physiological attunement and empathy. Robinson and colleagues (1982) examined the interactions between student volunteers and counsellors during clinical interviews, revealing positive correlations between the empathy perceived by the volunteer, evaluated with a self-report questionnaire, and the concordance of skin conductance between the dyad. A similar result was found by Marci and colleagues (2007) between therapists and their patients during psychotherapy sessions. Such data were also explored in greater depth by Messina and colleagues (2013), who utilized measures of physiological concordance in order to evaluate the relational skills of psychotherapists, compared to psychologists and non-therapists. There was also a correlation in this study between physiological concordance and empathy perceived by the participants, with differences between therapist who had received training and those who had not.

These results demonstrate how the tendency for human beings to enter into physiological synchronization can be a resource to be tapped by the therapist in order to be emotionally attuned with the other. This resource, which, as we have seen, can be enhanced through specific training, is of fundamental importance both in the evaluation of emotional resources of the patient as well as essential instrument of immediate countertransference, which is mostly based on the intuitions that the therapist has in relating with the other. These intuitions are also probably influenced by the psychophysiological asset that originates from the other and towards which the therapist can be open to varying degrees.

Note

1 This chapter was written by Irene Messina.

References

Benelli, E., Mergenthaler, E., Walter, S., Messina, I., Sambin, M., Buchheim, A., Sim, E., & Viviani, R. (2012). Emotional and cognitive processing of narratives and individual appraisal styles: Recruitment of cognitive control networks vs. modulation of deactivation. *Frontiers in Human Neuroscience*, 6(329): 1–26.

Binder, J. R., & Desai, R. H. (2011). The neurobiology of semantic memory. *Trends in Cognitive Sciences*, 15(11): 527–536.

Binder, J. R., Desai, R. H., Graves, W. W., & Conant, L. L. (2009). Where is the semantic system? A critical review and meta-analysis of 120 functional neuroimaging studies. *Cerebral Cortex*, 19(12): 2767–2796.

Buckner, R. L., & Carroll, D. C. (2007). Self-projection and the brain. *Trends in Cognitive Sciences*, 11(2): 49–57.

Busk, J., Naftulin, D. H., Donnely, F. A., & Wolkon, G. H. (1976). Therapists' physiological activation and patient difficulty. *The Journal of Nervous and Mental Disease*, 163(2): 73–78.

Coan, J. A., Schaefer, H. S., & Davidson, R. J. (2006). Lending a hand social regulation of the neural response to threat. *Psychological Science*, 17(12): 1032–1039.

Fox, M. D., Snyder, A. Z., Vincent, J. L., Corbetta, M., Van Essen, D. C., & Raichle, M. E. (2005). The human brain is intrinsically organized into dynamic, anticorrelated functional networks. *Proceedings of the National Academy of Sciences of the United States of America*, 102(27): 9673–9678.

Gentili, C., Ricciardi, E., Gobbini, M. I., Santarelli, M. F., Haxby, J. V., Pietrini, P., & Guazzelli, M. (2009). Beyond amygdala: Default mode network activity differs between patients with social phobia and healthy controls. *Brain Research Bulletin*, 79(6): 409–413.

Gross, J. J. (1998). The emerging field of emotion regulation: an integrative review. *Review of General Psychology*, 2(3): 271.

Kandel, E. R. (2008). *Psychiatry, Psychoanalysis, and the New Biology of Mind*. Washington, DC: American Psychiatric Publications.

LeDoux, J. (1998). *The Emotional Brain: The Mysterious Underpinnings of Emotional Life*. New York: Simon and Schuster.

Malmo, R. B., Boag, T. J., & Smith, A. A. (1957). Physiological study of personal interaction. *Psychosomatic Medicine*, 19(2): 105–119.

Marci, C. D., Ham, J., Moran, E., & Orr, S. P. (2007). Physiologic correlates of perceived therapist empathy and social-emotional process during psychotherapy. *Journal of Nervous and Mental Diseases*, 195(2), 103–111.

Martin, A., & Chao, L. L. (2001). Semantic memory and the brain: Structure and processes. *Current Opinion in Neurobiology*, 11(2): 194–201.

Messina, I., Bianco, F., Cusinato, M., Calvo, V., & Sambin, M. (2016). Abnormal default system functioning in depression: Implications for emotion regulation. *Frontiers in Psychology*, 7.

Messina, I., Palmieri, A., Sambin, M., Kleinbub, J. R., Voci, A., & Calvo, V. (2013). Somatic underpinnings of perceived empathy: The importance of psychotherapy training. *Psychotherapy Research*, 23(2): 169–177.

Messina, I., & Sambin, M. (2015a). Berne's theory of Cathexis and its links to modern neuroscience. *Transactional Analysis Journal*, 45(1): 48–58.

Messina, I., & Sambin, M. (2015b). Verso un modello psiconeurodinamico dei meccanismi di difesa. In M. Sambin, A. Palmieri, & I. Messina (Eds.), *Psiconeurodinamica [Psychoneurodynamics]*. Milano: Libreria Cortina Editore.

Milad, M. R., & Quirk, G. J. (2012). Fear extinction as a model for translational neuroscience: Ten years of progress. *Annual Review of Psychology*, 63: 129–151.

Mowrer, O. (1960). *Learning Theory and Behavior*. New York: Wiley.

Northoff, G., Heinzel, A., De Greck, M., Bermpohl, F., Dobrowolny, H., & Panksepp, J. (2006). Self-referential processing in our brain – A meta-analysis of imaging studies on the self. *Neuroimage*, 31(1): 440–457.

Pavlov, I. P. (1927). *Conditioned Reflexes*. Oxford: Oxford University Press.

Raichle, M. E., MacLeod, A. M., Snyder, A. Z., Powers, W. J., Gusnard, D. A., & Shulman, G. L. (2001). A default mode of brain function. *Proceedings of the National Academy of Sciences*, 98(2): 676–682.

Raichle, M. E., & Snyder, A. Z. (2007). A default mode of brain function: A brief history of an evolving idea. *Neuroimage*, 37(4): 1083–1090.

Robinson, J. W., Herman, A., & Kaplan, B. J. (1982). Autonomic responses correlate with counselor–Client empathy. *Journal of Counseling Psychology*, 29(2): 195.

Sehlmeyer, C., Schöning, S., Zwitserlood, P., Pfleiderer, B., Kircher, T., Arolt, V., & Konrad, C. (2009). Human fear conditioning and extinction in neuroimaging: A systematic review. *PloS One*, 4(6): e5865.

Sheline, Y. I., Barch, D. M., Price, J. L., Rundle, M. M., Vaishnavi, S. N., Snyder, A. Z., . . . & Raichle, M. E. (2009). The default mode network and self-referential processes in depression. *Proceedings of the National Academy of Sciences*, 106(6): 1942–1947.

Small, D. M., Zatorre, R. J., Dagher, A., Evans, A. C., & Jones-Gotman, M. (2001). Changes in brain activity related to eating chocolate: From pleasure to aversion. *Brain*, 124(9): 1720–1733.

Spreng, R. N., Mar, R. A., & Kim, A. S. (2009). The common neural basis of autobiographical memory, prospection, navigation, theory of mind, and the default mode: A quantitative meta-analysis. *Journal of Cognitive Neuroscience*, 21(3): 489–510.

Stanek, B., Hahn, P., & Mayer, H. (1973). Biometric findings on cardiac neurosis III: Changes in ECG and heart rate in cardiophobic patients and their doctor during psychoanalytical initial interviews. *Psychotherapy and Psychosomatics*, 22(2–6): 289–299.

Viviani, R., Lo, H., Sim, E. J., Beschoner, P., Stingl, J. C., & Horn, A. B. (2010). The neural substrate of positive bias in spontaneous emotional processing. *PLoS ONE*, 5: e15454.

Zahn, R., Moll, J., Krueger, F., Huey, E. D., Garrido, G., & Grafman, J. (2007). Social concepts are represented in the superior anterior temporal cortex. *Proceedings of the National Academy of Sciences*, 104(15): 6430–6435.

Zhao, X. H., Wang, P. J., Li, C. B., Hu, Z. H., Xi, Q., Wu, W. Y., & Tang, X. W. (2007). Altered default mode network activity in patient with anxiety disorders: An fMRI study. *European Journal of Radiology*, 63(3): 373–378.

14 ITAP in the treatment of common mental disorders[1]

The use of ITAP (Intensive Transactional Analysis Psychotherapy) is suitable for common mental disorders (CMD), such as depression, anxiety, and mild/moderate personality disorders. CMDs are defined by the World Health Organization (WHO) and include a vast range of disorders.[2] For each of these mental disorders there are numerous manualized treatments, whose efficacy is continuously subjected to rigorous studies.[3] The underlying assumption of most of these manualized treatments is that each disorder, for example depression, represents a unique, categorical, nosographic entity, with a specific aetiology, which is diagnosable and treatable with a dedicated treatment, often focused on behavioural and cognitive aspects of the disorder.

In contrast, according to the psychodynamic perspective assumed by ITAP, mental disorders such as depression constitute the symptomological manifestation of suffering, the roots of which can be found in the intersection between the natural temperament of the individual at birth and the environment in which they subsequently developed. Consequently, the symptoms of mental disorders considered by WHO to be CMD are, according to ITAP, conceptualized as patterns of thoughts, emotions, behaviours, and somatizations that act as defences by protecting the individual from the anxiety of coming back into contact with their own impulses and the anxiety associated with unattuned responses received from the relational environment during development.

In the same way, in accordance with the specificity of the psychodynamic tradition, ITAP considers personality disorders to be a manifestation of a constellation of defences (McWilliams, 2012) that protect the individual from entering into contact with the impulses and relative anxiety.

ITAP can be placed in the tradition of Transactional Analysis, which conceptualizes the origin of psychopathology as a stratification of successive adaptations that the Natural Child (Berne, 1961) has to enact from birth onwards so as to adapt to the relational environment and survive in the world, leading to the development of the Adapted Child (Berne, 1961) and of the script (Berne, 1961). The adaptations that lead to the formation of the script, according to a psychodynamic perspective, can be conceptualized as a collection of conflicts, or subsequent impasses (Goulding & Goulding, 1976; Mellor, 1980), which have become stratified during development.

The more archaic conflicts are instilled between the genetic predispositions of the child at birth and the first unattuned responses received from the environment: the interaction between genetics and environment in the first years of development determines the temperament of the child, which constitutes the basis on which the personality will subsequently develop.

ITAP, with its focus on constellations of impulses, anxieties, and defences (intrapsychic triangle) within transference, in current relationships, and in archaic relationships (interpersonal triangle), provides an efficacious conceptual model with which to understand and plan the treatment of symptoms and the personality disorders of patients.

For example, a child who is born with a genetic predisposition to perceive intense needs for closeness and dependence, who is then systematically undervalued and humiliated because of these needs, might experience intense anxiety and develop a defensive behaviour of emotional isolation and an attitude of avoidance of relationships so as to protect themselves from suffering. In this case, the emotional detachment and avoidance are not to be considered as the manifestation of natural temperament of a "quiet" child, rather as a defensive reaction to intolerable suffering. During development, this defensive pattern can become more structured and consolidated, transforming into an automatic association between impulse, anxiety, and defence. The unfulfilled need/impulse, however, continues to be unconsciously active throughout life, and it can stimulate the associated anxiety, which instantly activates the now well-consolidated defensive patterns, able to deactivate or deviate the impulse. This continuous process of activation and deactivation of impulses/needs/desires can manifest itself through symptoms, defences, and personality. In the previous case, the child, as an adult, can show symptoms of fatigue and loss of pleasure – typically associated with major depressive disorder – defences of emotional isolation, avoidance, internalization, devaluation of self, which can constitute an avoidant personality disorder.

It is clear from this perspective that the mental symptoms or disorder, the defences, and the personality are inextricably linked, one to another. For this reason, a person who shows depressive symptoms or who has any other CMD will be understood and treated with the ITAP approach by referring to their developmental history; to their needs; to how these aspects have been expressed and perceived by the environment; to defensive patterns that have formed during development including their transformation into a style (normal), a trait (subclinical), or a personality disorder (pathological).

The ITAP provides a model of intervention that can be effectively applied to various CMDs, including depressive disorders, anxiety disorders, obsessive-compulsive disorders, disorder deriving from traumatic events, dissociative disorders, somatic disorders, as well as mild and moderate personality disorders.

Which diagnostic systems does ITAP refer to?

ITAP can be utilized to treat mental and personality disorders diagnosed using the main psychodynamic and psychiatric diagnostic systems.

The main diagnostic systems modelled on the psychiatric tradition are the *International Classification of Diseases* (ICD), published by the World Health Organization (WHO) and now in its 10th edition (ICD-10; WHO, 2010), and the *Diagnostic and Statistical Manual of Mental Disorders* (DSM) published by the American Psychiatric Association (APA) and now in its fifth edition (DSM-5; APA, 2013).

In addition to these, there are diagnostic systems modelled on the psychodynamic tradition: the *Psychodynamic Diagnostic Manual* (PDM), compiled by the Alliance of Psychoanalytic Organizations (APO), now in its second edition (PDM-2, Lingiardi & McWilliams, 2017), the *Schedler-Westen Assessment Procedure* (SWAP; Shedler & Westen, 2010), and the *Operationalized Psychodynamic Diagnosis* (OPD) edited by the OPD task force and now in its second edition (OPD-2; OPD Task Force, 2008).

Even though the psychiatric and psychodynamic diagnostic systems belong to different traditions, in the DSM-5 there is a convergence between the concepts and diagnostic systems of the psychiatric and psychodynamic orientations. Indeed, in section III of DSM-5 there is an alternative model of personality disorders that adopts a psychodynamic structure; it contemplates, in the first place, the evaluation of the level of personality functioning, and subsequently the type of personality, as described by pathological personality traits (American Psychiatric Association, 2013, pp. 761–762).

This perspective is adopted by the diagnostic process of ITAP. The same symptomological pattern, for example, a major depressive disorder according to DSM-5, should be treated in a different way based on whether it manifests itself in a patient with a neurotic level of personality organization, as opposed to a patient organized at the borderline level. Furthermore, a patient with major depressive disorder and a neurotic organization of personality will receive a different treatment based on whether they have a dependent personality or a narcissistic personality because it requires a focus on different impulses, needs, anxiety, and defensive patterns.

Finally, because two people with depressive symptoms, neurotic organization, and dependent personality type can have different developmental histories (differing in terms of attunement between parental figures and the child's temperamental needs), it might be important to also consider the precursor to personality, that is, the temperament and the genetic predispositions that influence it. ITAP originates from within Transactional Analysis, which considers of primary importance the comprehension of the Natural Child of the patient and their transformation through the development of the life script in the Adapted Child, under the pressure of adaptations developed in the course of interactions with the unattuned family environment. Therefore, in this chapter we present a model that allows the diagnosis of temperament and the conceptualization of personality as the outcomes of conflicts between temperament and environment. In this way, temperamental conflicts, on which personality disorders are based, can be conceptualized and treated utilizing the ITAP intrapsychic triangle, integrating Transactional Analysis with Cloninger's model of temperament and character (Cloninger et al., 1993).

Overall, the ITAP model has been developed taking in consideration diagnoses obtained from the diagnostic systems cited earlier, in particular:

- Diagnosis of symptoms and signs associated with a mental disorder (for example, DSM section II, ICD-10 chapter V, PDM-2 S axis, OPD-2 axis V – Mental and Psychosomatic Disorders)
- Diagnosis of basic mental functioning, (PDM-2 M axis) and/or level of integration (OPD-2 axis IV – Structure) and/or level of personality functioning (DSM-5 section III) and/or personality strengths (SWAP Psychological Health Index)
- Diagnosis of personality disorders (ICD-10 chapter V, DSM-5 section II) and/or personality syndromes (PDM-2 P axis; SWAP Personality Syndromes – Q factors) and/or pathological personality traits (DSM-5 section III)
- Diagnosis of dysfunctional relational patterns (OPD-2 axis II – Interpersonal Relations)
- Diagnosis of neurotic patterns of conflict (OPD-2 axis III – Conflicts)
- Diagnosis of genetic dispositions and temperament (Cloninger's model)

ITAP: diagnosis and indications for treatment

ITAP's diagnostic approach, which starts with symptomological manifestations and continues through mental functioning until the temperamental roots of personality, is based on previous diagnostic systems and involves an articulated diagnostic process in the following areas:

- Evaluation of mental disorders (symptoms)
- Evaluation of the profile of mental functioning and/or level of personality functioning
- Evaluation of personality type
- Evaluation of aetiopathogenesis (trauma, conflict, deficit)
- Evaluation of genetic and temperamental conflicts

The diagnostic process starts with the evaluation of the symptoms (for example, depression), then there is the evaluation of mental functions (for example, capacity for affective range, communication, and understanding), the level of personality functioning in the area of the self and interpersonal relationships (for example, moderate impairment of personality functioning), the personality type (for example, dependent personality), the aetiopathogenesis (for example, psychopathology due to trauma, neglect, or conflict).

If aetiopathogenesis has a conflictual origin, we end with the evaluation of genetic, temperamental, and developmental conflicts. The diagnosis with ITAP identifies the focuses of the treatment in each area, detecting the correspondent impulses, anxieties, and defences in past and current interpersonal relationships, both external and with the therapist.

Evaluation of symptomological pattern and mental disorder

The evaluation of the mental disorder is based on the DSM-5 classification, which can be rapidly converted to corresponding ICD-10 diagnoses, thanks to the tables in the appendix. The symptoms reported by patients and the signs observed by the clinician can apply to one or more mental disorders.

For example, let us consider a patient who reports sadness, a sense of emptiness, desperation; they say that they have lost interest and pleasure in their everyday activities; that they do not sleep anymore; that they attend the clinician's objective examination in a tearful manner, with slowed down psychomotricity, with self-denigration and excessive feelings of guilt. The clinician can evaluate the symptoms and signs that fulfill criteria 1, 2, 4, 5, 6, and 7 of major depressive disorder. Once the duration and intensity of the suffering and its pervasiveness have been verified, and the effects of substances or other mental disorders have been excluded, a diagnosis might be established of "major depressive disorder, without further specifications". In the ITAP approach, however, the attention of the clinician is not focused on the treatment of symptoms, which are, in any case, carefully considered and included in the treatment plan, but rather they proceed by gathering information on the level of organization and on the type of personality.

Evaluation of level of mental functioning and of personality functioning

Intensive and brief psychotherapies tend to rapidly show patients their own interpersonal, intrapsychic, unconscious, and dysfunctional patterns. Furthermore, they favour a change in representations of the self, of others, of the world, of life, of the past, and of the future. The change might be accompanied by insights, catharsis, expansion of awareness, which can be associated with intense, emotional activations and modify interpersonal relationships. If the contact with impulses, needs, and desires that have been unconscious for a long time has not been sufficiently processed and contained at an intrapsychic level, it can involve somatic aspects (e.g., conversion) and behavioural aspects (e.g., acting out). For these reasons, it is necessary to evaluate the level of personality functioning and the development of each of the basic mental functions, which constitute the structure of the mind. The more developed the level of personality functioning and the more developed basic mental functions are, the more rapid the change can be in the psychotherapy.

The intensity of the therapy, on the other hand, should be modulated when there are moderate or more severe compromises of the level of personality functioning or, in the case of moderate or more severe limitations and alterations, in mental functioning.

Various diagnostic systems exist in the literature that provide instruments and procedures for evaluating the level of personality functioning and the level of mental functioning. Among them we consider:

- The alternative model for personality disorders included in section III of DSM-5
- The profile of mental functioning of PDM-2
- The Axis IV – structure of OPD-2

In section III of DSM-5 an alternative model of personality disorders is proposed that includes two phases: the evaluation of the level of personality functioning and the evaluation of the presence of pathological personality traits.

> The level of personality functioning evaluates the area of functioning of the self and the area of interpersonal functioning.
> The area of the self is subdivided into identity and self-directedness, while the interpersonal area subdivides into empathy and intimacy.
> Identity considers the following dimensions: unitarity experience of the self, borders between the self and the others; self-esteem, capacity for self-evaluation, range of emotions, regulation of emotions.
> Self-directedness considers the following dimensions: pursue existential objectives in the short and long term, internal behavioural standards, capacity for self-reflection.
> Empathy considers the following dimensions: comprehension of experiences and motivation of others, tolerance of difference, comprehension of effects on others.
> Intimacy considers: depth and duration of relationships, desire and capacity for closeness, reciprocal respect.
> Each dimension is evaluated on five levels, from healthy (0) to mild (1), moderate (2), serious (3), extreme (4), impairment of personality functioning (5).
> ITAP is suitable for people with mild or moderate levels of personality functioning compromise.

The PDM (first edition, 2006) considers the personality by evaluating the level of organization and the type of personality disorder. On the P axis (personality), the level of personality organization defines the seriousness of the personality disorder (healthy, neurotic, borderline) and is evaluated considering seven capacities: (1) identity; (2) object relations; (3) emotional tolerance; (4) emotional regulation; (5) integration between Superego, ideal Ego, and Ego ideal; (6) reality testing; (7) Ego strength and resilience. At the healthy level all characteristics are present, at the neurotic level most are present and one or two areas can be problematic, at the borderline level the first four capacities are strongly compromised and sometimes the fifth is as well (in narcissistic, psychopathic, and antisocial personalities), while the sixth is compromised in a transitory way only in situations which are emotionally intense and only in more severe borderline disorders.

Utilizing this diagnostic system, ITAP is suitable for people with a personality organization from the healthy level, to the neurotic level, up until the less compromised borderline level.

The second edition of the PDM manual, the PDM-2 (2017), has a revision of the levels of personality organization, adding the psychotic level of organization and distinguishing between high- (bordering on neurosis) and low- (bordering on psychosis) borderline level. Furthermore, in the second edition the criteria for the evaluation of personality organization level presented in axis P of the first edition, were integrated and unified with the criteria proposed in axis M. Therefore, compared to the PDM, in the M axis of PDM-2 the categories for the evaluation of mental functioning increased from 9 to 12. Table 14.1 proposes a comparison

Table 14.1 Comparison among DSM-5, PDM, and PDM-2

DSM-5		PDM	PDM-2	
Self Identity	Experience of oneself as unique, with clear boundaries between self and others	Capacity for regulation, attention, and learning	Cognitive and Affective Processes	Capacity for regulation, attention, and learning
	Stability of self-esteem and accuracy of self-appraisal	Capacity for relationships (including depth, range, and consistency)		Capacity for affective range, communication, and understanding
	Capacity for, and ability to regulate, a range of emotional experience	Quality of internal experience (level of confidence and self-regard)		Capacity for mentalization and reflective functioning
Self-Direction	Pursuit of coherent and meaningful short-term and life goals	Affective experience, expression, and communication	Identity and Relationships	Capacity for differentiation and integration (identity)
	Utilization of constructive and prosocial internal standards of behaviour	Defensive patterns and capacities		Capacity for relationships and intimacy
	Ability to self-reflect productively	Capacity to form internal representations		Capacity for self-esteem regulation and quality of internal experience
Interpersonal Empathy	Comprehension and appreciation of others' experiences and motivations	Capacity for differentiation and integration	Coping	Capacity for impulse control and regulation
	Tolerance of differing perspectives	Self-observing capacities (psychological-mindedness)		Capacity for defensive functioning
	Understanding the effects of ones's own behaviour on others	Capacity for internal standards and ideals: a sense of morality		Capacity for adaptation, resiliency, and strength
Interpersonal Intimacy	Depth and duration of connection with others		Self-Awareness and Self-Direction	Self-observing capacities (psychological mindedness)
	Desire and capacity for closeness			Capacity to construct and use internal standards and ideals
	Mutuality of regard reflected in interpersonal behaviour			Capacity for meaning and purpose

Note: DSM-5 = *Diagnostic and Statistical Manual of Mental Disorders* (American Psychiatric Association, 2013). PDM = *Psychodynamic Diagnostic Manual* (Alliance of Psychoanalytic Organizations, 2006). PDM-2 = *Psychodynamic Diagnostic Manual*, second edition (Lingiardi & McWilliams, 2017).

between the elements of personality functioning considered by DSM-5 and the mental functions considered by PDM and PDM-2.

In the first edition of the PDM there is a summary of basic mental functioning, which considers different levels: from optimal or appropriate mental capacity (M 201–203) to mild limitations (M 204), moderate (M 205), or severe (M 206), to deficiencies in integration (M 207) or severe deficiencies in basic mental functions (M 208). ITAP is appropriate for people with up to moderate limitations of mental functioning (M 201–205).

In the second edition of the PDM, there is a summary of basic mental functioning that includes healthy level (M01), neurotic (M02–03), borderline (M04–06), and psychotic (M07). Each of the 12 functions can be evaluated on a scale from 1 (compromised functioning) to 5 (optimal functioning), providing an overall score between 16 and 60, associated to each level of mental functioning. ITAP can be adopted with healthy people (score 60, M01) up to the high-functioning borderline level (score 33, M04).

Finally, the axis IV–Structure of the OPD-2 proposes 24 mental functions for the evaluation of level of structural integration of personality, subdivided into cognitive capacities, regulation capacities, emotional capacities, and capacity to create attachment. Each of these capacities is evaluated from two perspectives: capacities concerning self-regulation and capacities concerning objects. The OPD-II evaluates four levels of structural integration, from high to moderate, to low, to structural disintegration. ITAP is appropriate for people with a moderate to high level of structural integration.

Suitability for treatment according to level of personality functioning

Making a diagnosis of development of mental functions and of the consequent level of personality functioning, which allows the construction of a personalized treatment plan for the patient and favours the definition of a contract with realistic objectives that are consistent with the time available, avoids in both the therapist and the patient frustration caused by unrealistic objectives. It improves attunement with the patient and enhances the therapeutic alliance.

Furthermore, identifying the level of mental and personality functioning allows the selection of the focus of priority interventions.

Healthy and neurotic level of functioning

ITAP can be applied with great efficacy; relational pressure, the therapist's activity, and confronting defences are generally well tolerated and a source of curiosity for the patient.

High-functioning borderline level

ITAP needs to be integrated with interventions that aim to enhance certain deficient structural mental functions (for example, work on capacity for impulse control and regulation might be necessary before working on interpersonal and intrapsychic triangles).

Low-functioning borderline level

ITAP can be understood as a theoretical framework that can help in the comprehension of the patient. The focus is on the development and integration of deficient structural mental functions. The use of the triangles to interpret the conflicts between impulses and anxieties that determine the defences can be introduced after having consolidated the psychic structure, verifying that, at the end of the session, the patient's reactions are of relief and not of an increase in anxiety.

Psychotic level

ITAP can be used as a referral framework to understand the formation of the patient's thought processes. Interventions are focused on the consolidation of the intrapsychic structure and on the functions of the Ego. Impulses are explored and linked to the mental representations of sensation, emotion, thought, and behaviour, which often surface and form for the first time in the course of the treatment. Defences are not interpreted with the triangle of impulses. The single vertices can be explored and connected only within specific episodes and only when the patient has reached a preconscious understanding of the defences and anxieties associated with defences. Relational pressure cannot be exercised. The triangle of persons can be used to show the connections between any two vertices, but the interpretations should not include the third vertex; for example, it can be noted how an event occurred in the past or reoccurs in the present, or alternatively that it occurs outside and inside the therapy room. In any case, the three vertices of the interpersonal triangle cannot be integrated simultaneously.

Evaluation of personality type

In the ITAP model, the evaluation of the patient's personality style, trait, or disorder allows the consideration of the main conflicts between impulses and defences that might surface during the treatment. For example, a paranoid patient can be characterized by a conflict between the need to show aggression (impulse) and the fear of being humiliated when they are aggressive (Anxieties), which leads the patient to project aggression on others and to feel threatened (Defence).

In the ITAP model, the personality of a patient is considered the sum of a constellation of conflicts between impulses and anxieties, with the relative Defences, which is formed in the archaic relationships and manifests itself in current relationships. This is similar to how the OPD-II considers the character as an active or passive expressive of seven basic conflicts, and it is also similar to how McWilliams (1994) considers personality types as the expression of a constellation of pervasive and prevalent defences.

Although brief and intensive psychotherapies such as ITAP are not presently considered to be a first choice in the treatment of personality disorders, each intensive or brief treatment that considers the constellation of typical conflicts of each type of personality can also have effects on the personality, the consolidation of which requires appropriate lengths of treatment.

Various taxonomies exist that classify personality disorders (see Table 14.2). The evaluation of the personality type is described in various diagnostic tools, for example:

* Personality Disorders in section II of the DSM-5
* Personality Syndromes in the PDM-2 axis P
* Personality Syndromes described by the SWAP (Q-factors)
* McWilliams's types of character organizations
* Prototypical descriptions of passive and active mode to express neurotic conflicts, described in the OPD-II's axis III – Conflicts

In general, working with ITAP implies exploring the association among the vertices of the intrapsychic triangle (impulse, anxiety, and defence), identifying

Table 14.2 Comparison of personalities among different diagnostic systems

DSM-5 Personality Disorders	SWAP Personality Syndromes (Q-Factor T-Scores)	PDM-2 P Axis Personality Syndromes	OPD-2 Axis III – Conflict Passive and Active Mode
Paranoid	Dysphoric	Depressive (with	Individuation vs
Schizoid	(Depressive)	comment on	dependency
Schizotypal	Antisocial-	hypomanic and	Submission vs
Antisocial	psychopathic	masochism)	control
Borderline	Schizoid-schizotypal	Dependent	Need for care vs
Histrionic	Paranoid	Anxious-avoidant	self-sufficiency
Narcissistic	Obsessional	and phobic	Self-worth
Avoidant	Histrionic	Obsessive-	Guilt
Dependent	Narcissistic	compulsive	Oedipical
Obsessive-	Avoidant	Schizoid	Identity
compulsive	High functioning	Somatizing	
	Depressive	Hysteric-histrionic	
	Borderline	Narcissistic	
	(emotionally	Paranoid	
	dysregulated)	Psychopathic	
	Dependent-	Sadistic	
	victimized	Borderline	
	Hostile-externalizing		

Note: DSM-5 = *Diagnostic and Statistical Manual of Mental Disorders* (American Psychiatric Association, 2013). PDM = *Psychodynamic Diagnostic Manual* (Alliance of Psychoanalytic Organizations, 2006). PDM-2 = *Psychodynamic Diagnostic Manual*, 2nd edition (Lingiardi & McWilliams, 2017). OPD-2 = *Operationalized Psychodynamic Diagnosis* (OPD Task Force, 2008) the schemas that repeat themselves in three types of episodes: scenic episodes (in the present, in transference, in the relationships with the therapist), relational episodes (in the present, with people outside therapy), and archaic episodes (in the past, with parental figures, in the moment of the formation of associations between impulses, anxieties, and defences).

To recap, the term "impulse" includes urges, needs, desires, intentions, aspirations, primary emotions appropriate for the environmental stimuli; the term "anxiety" includes fears, painful and/or traumatic experiences; the term "defence" includes the classical psychodynamic defences, secondary emotions substituting the primary ones, dysfunctional patterns of behaviour, and, in more general terms, the personality as a whole, intended as a constellation of pervasive, maladaptive defences.

Taking into consideration the patient's personality and the typical conflicts that occur, including impulses, anxieties, and their relative defences, would allow the planning of individualized interventions, thereby improving the therapeutic alliance, adherence to the treatment, the outcome, and stability of the results. Even in cases where the patient and the therapist have an agreement to resolve a specific problem (for example, interaction with the manager at work) or they have chosen a limited focus and a brief treatment, consideration of the personality type makes it more likely objectives will be reached. For example, if the patient and the therapist have agreed to resolve a work problem with a manager, linked to not knowing how to express the patient's own needs, the treatment plan will be different based on whether the patient has a paranoid or a dependent personality. In the first case, it will probably be necessary to consider the impulses of healthy interdependence and the anxieties of submission, which might have caused defences of the rejection of authority. In the second case, it will probably be necessary to consider the impulses of autonomy, the anxieties associated with autonomy, and the relative defences of submission.

To provide an example, we will now present a typical constellation of impulses, anxieties, and defences of the personalities syndromes considered in Chapter 2 (axis P) of PDM-2, which can be referred to for further detail.

Depressive personality (including manic and masochist manifestations)

People with depressive personality experience little pleasure in life activities, in as much as the pleasure in experienced in a conflictual way. Positive feelings like joy, excitement, and pride are, consequently, inhibited and substituted with painful emotions like depression, guilt, shame, inadequacy, loss, and behaviours such as self-criticism, self-bias. The clinician must explore the inhibited positive feelings within the relational episodes and the scenic episodes and identify the causes of the inhibition by exploring archaic episodes. Often, depressive symptoms are the result of the tendency to substitute with aggression directed at oneself through self-criticism the aggression and criticism that should be directed at the parental figures due to their abuses, mistreatment, or negligence. In the scenic episodes in which the patient displays new intrapsychic patterns (that is, they express aggression, hostility, criticism directed at the therapist) that substitute the previous one, particular attention should be paid to recognize and sustain the change.

Some depressive forms manifest themselves through a hypomanic defensive style that prioritizes secondary emotions of euphoria, energy, absence of guilt, hypertrophic self-esteem. In these cases, after having excluded the presence of bipolar or cyclothymic disorder, it is a good idea to focus on the primary denied emotions, such as sadness, loss, loneliness, and to explore their antecedents in archaic episodes.

Particular attention should be paid to the differential diagnosis between depression and masochism (with the relative subtypes: masochist-dependent, masochist-narcissistic, and masochist-paranoid), since they often require different treatment plans.

Dependent personalities

Dependent personalities are characterized by excessive dependent needs, up until the point of being subjected to various types of abuse without being able to separate. Impulse are related to autonomy, self-realization. Anxiety can be associated with themes of performance, defeat, failure, refusal from others of normal needs of dependence following the achievement of autonomy, criticisms, abandonment. The defences include regression, somatization, and acting out, often in the desperate attempt to receive nurturing.

In dependent personalities, it is essential not to favour dependence with the therapist, making sure that, in the scenic episodes, the role of an expert person or an adviser is not adopted.

Among the dependent personalities, there is a noteworthy subtype characterized by hostility, defined as passive aggressive. These patients tend to not be aware of their aggression, both emotional and behavioural, expressed in an indirect way, and of the effect that it has on others. The focus therefore includes the structural aspects of mentalization and the provision of the effect on others and of the consequences of their own behaviours on current relationships, starting with the analysis of the transferential relationship.

Furthermore, there is also a counterdependent subtype, where strong needs of dependence are inflexibly denied and give rise to reactive formations.

Anxious-avoidant and phobic personalities

Anxious personalities are characterized by awareness of pervasive anxiety, often diagnosed as generalized anxiety, which includes separation anxiety, castration anxiety, anxiety concerning violation of moral norms, or disintegration/annihilation anxiety. Anxiety in this case is not generally activated by a specific conflictual impulse, rather each impulse can potentially activate anxiety. The defences typically associated are those of avoidance, withdrawal, and inadequacy. Treatment has to include exposure to feared situations, including verbally naming the emotional states, the fears, the fantasies regarding the consequences. In general, the treatment of anxious personality requires a long-term relationship, emotionally reliable and not acting as a saviour, which favours the development of a sense of internal security. There is a subtype of phobic personality, defined as counterphobic, characterized by avoidance of primary emotions of fear, their treatment requires the development of awareness of their own normal fear reactions.

Obsessive-compulsive personality

The main characteristic is the inhibition of primary emotions, which are replaced by defences of intellectualization, rigidity, order. The central conflict is linked to having to submit to others' requests, associated with emotions of anger and shame, or to having to rebel and challenge others, associated with emotions of fear of retaliation. The archaic scenes retrace episodes in which the lack of control of the impulses was blamed, both at a somatic level (control of the sphincter) and at an emotional level (spontaneous primary emotions). In treatment, it is important to deal with anxiety associated with the expression of impulses because these people fear that their impulses, and particularly aggression and pleasure, might get out of control.

Schizoid personality

In the psychodynamic tradition, the term "schizoid personality" refers to a population characterized by conflicts, different from the description in DSM-5, which is characterized by deficit and impoverishment of the cognitive, emotional, and relational spheres. In general, schizoid personalities are characterized by a conflict that can be placed at a level of functioning of the superior personality (neurotic, high-level borderline) as compared to schizoid personalities characterized by deficits and impoverishment (low-level borderline, psychosis).

The nuclear conflict of the schizoid personality is linked to the impulses of intimacy and being involved in relationships, which are associated with the anxiety of being engulfed, swallowed up, intruded on, controlled, overstimulated, and traumatized. The impulses are also associated with the defences of detachment from relationships (up until the point of being a hermit) and withdrawal into fantasies and their own internal world. Other conflicts to be explored are those between the needs for individuation and the needs for dependency (OPD-II, axis III – Conflicts), the experiences of having to (rather than being able to) be with others or alone, with the possibility of modulating the interpersonal distance manifesting their own needs for closeness and distance.

Somatizing personalities

Somatizing personalities are a heterogeneous category that includes people inclined to inhibit the verbal expression of their emotions (alexithymia) and to express their dysphoria through complaints concerning the body, hypochondriacal worries, physical illnesses linked to stress, physical symptoms that symbolically express emotions and unspeakable words (conversion reaction). Particular attention should be paid to the evaluation of the pervasiveness of hypochondriacal aspects because their presence in intensive therapies, and in particular the exploration of transferential reactions, can favour the appearance of paranoid reactions.

Somatizing personalities can probably best be understood by referring to the concept of deficit, in particular, in the development of the capacity to represent and express experiences, sensations, and emotions. The intervention focusses on creating connections among: perception, sensations, emotions, thoughts, and words, reconstructing the deficient associative chains. Often, these patients have the experience of not being listening to, and the alliance is based on providing a climate of careful listening and verbalization of messages that are often cryptic and hermetic, communicated through somatic manifestations.

Histrionic-hysterical personality

Hysterical personalities tend to experience anxiety when they come into contact with their own impulses, emotions, and internal desires, which they are afraid of being overstimulated and engulfed by. The defences that are typically used to control these impulses might include sexualization, theatricalization (laughing about expressed emotions reduces their importance), the use of an impressionistic cognitive style to reduce stimuli, conversion with a wide range of physical symptoms, attention seeking, exhibitionism, and competitiveness regarding themes of sexuality and gender. Another central conflict is the desire to be recognized in an adequate way by primary attachment figures, in particular for their gender characteristics: often hysterical personalities have experienced a feeling of disappointment and inadequacy from the parent of the same sex and overstimulation or seductiveness from the parent of the opposite sex.

Narcissistic personality

Narcissistic personalities feel anxiety from a sense of emptiness and lack of values or meaning. This sense is associated with defences that aim to externally affirm their obtained importance and value through the idealization of the self; the denigration of others; the search for admiration, success, wealth. When they are not able to satisfy their own need for external recognition, the observable defences change, tending to put down themselves and idealize the other, with intense experiences of depression, humiliation, shame, and jealousy in the face of the success of others. The impulses, associated with emptiness anxieties and the lack of value or meaning, can be traced back to the attachment period, in which nurturing figures might have been confusing, unpredictable, often revealing ulterior or secret motives, provoking a withdrawal from intimacy with and from emotional investment in others, replaced by preoccupation with the self and one's own physical integrity. Due to this excessive investment in physical integrity, there are often associated hypochondriacal themes and somatic complaints. The treatment imposed on the conflict should focus on the defences against jealousy, the shame and the healthy dependence and intimacy, according to the model proposed by Kernberg. According to the model of Kohut, the interpretation of the conflict can be effectively assisted by a systematic exploration of the original impulses that were not validated and which have not been able to be expressed with the adaptation figures. Such impulses can manifest themselves in therapy through forms of self–object transference, or internalizing transference, often associated with the idealization of the therapist. Generally, these forms of transferences should not be interpreted but rather accepted and explored, with the aim of identifying unexpressed, atrophied, or repressed impulses, which have not been able to express themselves in relationships with primary caregivers.

Paranoid personalities

The main observable defence in paranoid personalities is the attribution to others of one's own impulses, emotions, and thoughts that are perceived as intolerable and, therefore, disowned. The impulses that activate the projection are, generally: anger; dependence/intimacy; sexual attraction; as well as painful primary emotions such as hate, jealousy, shame, disdain, disgust, and fear. The anxieties associated with impulses concern the terror of trusting others, of being attacked suddenly, of experiencing humiliation and shame, which echo situations actually experienced or perceived in the past. Treatment focuses on the exploration of convictions that feeling and expressing their own impulses and painful emotions is as dangerous as acting on them in an uncontrolled way, according to the equation thought = action.

Psychopathic and sadistic personality

The PDM-2 also considers psychopathic and sadistic personalities. These syndromes are characterized by a substantial absence of anxiety, remorse, guilt, shame, therefore that subjective suffering that generally motivates the person to seek psychotherapeutic treatment is missing. For these syndromes, treatment focused on the comprehension of the association between impulses, anxieties and defences is not recommended.

Borderline personality

The PDM-2, in contrast to the previous PDM, considers both the borderline level of organization and the borderline personality syndrome. The latter is characterized by a disorganized/disoriented attachment style; emotional dysregulation; primary defences, including splitting and projective identification; mentalization deficit; deficit in the perception of continuity of self and of objects. The aetiopathogenesis is generally due to a collection of factors of a traumatic nature, precocious attachment disorders, and arrests in development. For this syndrome, the general indications concerning the treatment of borderline levels of personality organization are pertinent, therefore intensive treatments are generally not appropriate.

Evaluation of aetiopathogenesis

The aetiopathogenesis of the patient's suffering can be divided into three areas: traumatic origin, conflictual origin, and deficit origin.

Traumatic origin

Traumatic events can be determined from: (1) external factors, in general single events that are unpredictable and sudden (for example, earthquakes, accidents, bereavement) or (2) relational factors, generally repeated, continuous and with unpredictable patterns. External traumas can generally be resolved quickly with elective treatments for post-traumatic stress disorder, such as eye movement desensitization and reprocessing therapy (EMDR). Repeated relational traumas can be conceptualized as conflicts between developmental needs and varying degrees of unattuned and traumatic environmental responses, which favours the development of a dysfunctional defensive pattern.

Conflictual origin

Conflicts originate when a desire, a need, an urge, or a vital drive is obstructed by an external reality or internal object, norm, fantasy. The conflicts become pathological when they impede the expression of the vital impulses of a person, thereby inhibiting their development. Generally, the conflict is unconscious and it can be modelled through the intrapsychic triangle: when impulse is activated, an associated anxiety is also activated, which deviates the normal and rewarding expression of the impulse by deviating it towards an adapted and defensive expression. Generally, the conflicts manifest themselves through a projective type of transference.

Deficit origin

Deficits refer to those experiences that the patient should have gone through so as to complete their own development in a harmonious way (for example, the experience of the parents' pride in their autonomy), whereas they did not occur. Some deficits can be conceptualized as conflicts between developmental needs and the absence of validation.

Generally, experiential deficits manifest themselves through introjective transferences. There is a noteworthy difference between the relational traumas and deficits: in the aetiology of relational traumas there is the presence of a need that receives a traumatic response from the environment, while in the aetiology of deficits there is a need that does not receive validation from the environment:

metaphorically, it is not fullness, but emptiness; it is not an internal object to differentiate and externalize, rather the lack of a relational experience that is sought in relationships so as to be internalized.

Treatment indications based on hypothesized aetiopathogenesis

The hypothesis regarding the aetiopathogenesis impacts on the choice of treatment type.

People with relational traumas generally feel it necessary to recognize their own need and become aware of the traumatic response received from the environment and of the dysfunctional pattern that has developed as a consequence. ITAP is extremely useful in these contexts, and in patients with elevated mental functioning it leads to a rapid resolution of the suffering.

People with relational experiences characterized by neglect and abandonment, generally, need to experience their own need, to receive validation in the relationship with the therapist, and to experiment new ways of obtaining satisfaction for that need outside of the therapy. In people with an elevated level of functioning, ITAP is effective in rapidly surfacing needs that have not been validated. Generally, validation and experimentation require a certain amount of time, longer than is normal with brief or intense psychotherapies.

In most cases, people have multi-layered and complex suffering, which is rooted in all three of these aetiopathogenetical areas. Depending on the duration of the intervention, treatments can be planned that include one or more aetiopathogenetical areas.

Diagnosis and treatment of the conflictual origins of personality disorders in ITAP

In order to enhance understanding of the intrapsychic conflicts that have built up over the course of a person's development, it is useful to consider the genetic predispositions that most influence the natural temperament of the child at birth together with the outcome of successive interactions with the relational environment, which can promote the harmonious development of temperament and subsequent personality, or alternatively favour the development of traumas, conflicts, or deficits, becoming one of the aetiological factors of later mental and personality disorders.

We will briefly present Cloninger's theory of temperament and the concepts of temperamental and genetic conflict (impasse). We will conclude this section with some reflections on the use of temperamental and genetic impasses in the ITAP model.

Cloninger explores personality from a bio-psycho-social perspective, and considers it to be fruit of a complex interaction among genetic, biological, neurophysiological, psychological, relational, and environmental components (Cloninger et al., 1993). According to this model, personality can be defined as a dynamic and multidimensional system, which includes various components (traits) organized in an interdependent manner. Personality is subdivided into two distinct dimensions: temperament and character.

Temperament corresponds to the sum of innate neurological dispositions, derived from a genetic substrate, the characteristics of which define the individual differences in the basic emotional responses (according to Cloninger: anger, fear, attachment, ambition) and in the automatic behavioural responses (according to Cloninger: inhibition, activation, and behavioural maintenance) correlated to specific environment stimuli (according to Cloninger: danger, novelty, various types of reward). Cloninger and his colleagues identified four temperamental traits, which are genetically determined and inherited independently: novelty seeking (NS), which modulates the perception of novelty, the experience and expression of anger, and behaviour activation (stimulus, emotion and behaviour written in bold in Figure 14.1); harm avoidance (HA), which modulates the perception of danger, the experience and expression of fear, and inhibition in reaction to the behaviour (stimulus, emotion and behaviour written in italics in Figure 14.1); reward dependence (RD) and persistence (PS), which all modulate the perception of environmental reward, perception, and expression of attachment and ambition and the maintenance of behaviour (stimulus, emotions and behavior written in normal font in Figure 14.1). These temperamental traits, which we will explore further in the next paragraph, are inherited independently and they tend to consolidate between the second and third year of life. It can be important for the therapists to consider that right from birth each person has a unique way of perceiving stimuli and responding to them with emotions and behaviours that, in part, are genetically determined. Temperament is inherited from one's parents and can, in any case, be different from that of one's parents. Phrases such as "I don't know who you get it from", spoken by two parents with timid and tireless temperaments to a child with an audacious and energetic temperament (or vice versa), reflect the difficulty of parents in understanding and tolerating the fact that temperamental traits are inherited independently and, therefore, a genetically recessive temperament with a silent phenotype in the parents can express itself in the child due to the effect of genetic recombination at conceptions – just as children with blue eyes can be born of parents with brown eyes.

Character, according to Cloninger, matures successively in adult age; it is not influenced genetically but is based on temperament and on its interactions between temperament and environment occurring in the first years of life. These interactions contribute to the development of the conception of the self, of others, and of the universe, and of the relationship among them. Therefore, according to Cloninger, the character is modulated by three dimensions: self-directedness, that is, to what degree the person perceives themself to be an autonomous individual (included in the sense of autonomy conceptualized by Berne); cooperativeness, that is, to what degree the person perceives themself to be an integral part of humanity; self-transcendence, that is, to what degree the person feels an integral part of a universal system. It is interesting to note that Cloninger's first two character dimensions are analogous to the two dimensions which are used in the new alternative system of personality disorders introduced by DSM-5 to evaluate the level of personality functioning, self-functioning, and interpersonal functioning.

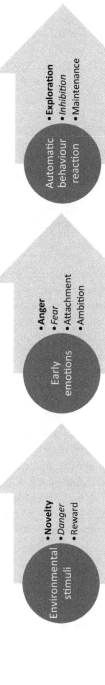

Figure 14.1 Relationship among environmental stimuli, early emotions, and automatic behaviour reactions

Note: Temperament involves heritable neurobiological dispositions to display early emotions and automatic behaviour reaction in response to environmental stimuli. Temperamental trait novelty seeking (NS) modulates the connection among stimuli of novelty, early emotion of anger, and automatic behaviour of exploration (stimulus, emotion and behaviour written in bold in Figure 14.1). Harm avoidance (HA) modulates the connection among stimuli of danger, early emotion of fear, and automatic behaviour of inhibition (stimulus, emotion and behaviour written in italics in Figure 14.1). Reward dependence (RD) and persistence (PS) modulates the connection among stimuli of reward, early emotion of attachment and ambition, automatic behaviour of maintenance (stimulus, emotion and behaviour written in normal font in Figure 14.1).

The natural temperament of the child

According to Cloninger, each person is born with an innate predisposition to select and react to environmental stimuli with specific emotional and behavioural responses, mediated by four neuromodulatory systems (Table 14.3).

Novelty seeking (NS) is a temperamental dimension that refers to the behavioural activation in reply to novelty and pleasurable stimuli. It reflects heritable variables in the activation of the approach response to novelty to reward signals or active avoidance of signs of unconditional punishment. It manifests itself in seeking new sensations, excitation in response to new stimuli, impulsivity and extravagance, the necessity of anticipating gratification, and active avoidance of frustrations (not passive withdrawal). A low NS characterizes a child who is reserved, thoughtful, sparing, stoic (who does not show their own experiences). An elevated NS characterizes a child who is explorative, impulsive, extravagant, and irritable (who shows their own experiences). A pathological presence of the NS trait is associated with hyperactivity, binge-eating, drinking, and with other behaviours of substance abuse and other new additions. Cloninger believes that the elevated presence of this trait can be found, typically, in "strange" subjects – those that can be placed in the cluster A of personality disorders in the DSM (paranoid, schizoid, schizotypal).

Harm avoidance (HA) refers to behavioural inhibition in response to unpleasant stimuli or signs of danger. It is a temperamental trait characterized by the propension to learn to inhibit behaviours that can induce danger. It includes heritable variables concerning the behavioural inhibition in response to signs of punishment or frustration, unpleasant stimuli, and signs of danger. HA appears as a pessimistic anticipatory preoccupation, quick fatigue, shyness, and fear of uncertainty. Clinically it has been found that greater behavioural inhibition predisposes for anxiety, depression, and low self-esteem. An elevated presence of HA can be found in fearful and anxious subjects. According to Cloninger, this dimension is present on cluster C of personality disorders on the DSM (avoidant, dependent, obsessive-compulsive, and passive-aggressive). Elevated HA characterizes a child who is pessimistic, timid, submissive, and weary, while low HA characterizes a child who is optimistic, audacious, energetic, and expansive.

Reward dependence (RD) refers to the maintenance of affective behaviours, contact, and intimacy. It is a dimension that is linked to the maintenance of behaviours associated with the preoccupation with social reward. It is characterized by the tendency to respond, with intensity, to gratifying stimuli, signs of social approval, signs of rewards. Sentimentalism, sensitivity, intimacy, and the dependence on the approval of others all depend on the activity level of this temperamental trait. According to Cloninger, such personality dimensions should be developed more in subjects placed in cluster B of the DSM personality disorders (borderline, antisocial, histrionic, narcissistic), characterized by melodramatic, unpredictable, and emotional behaviour. A low RD characterizes a child who is detached, reserved, cold, and independent, while an elevated RD characterizes a child who is sentimental, open, warm, and appreciative.

Table 14.3 Association among stimuli, emotions, and behaviour according to the Cloninger model

Temperament traits	Neurotransmitter	Environmental stimuli	Early emotions	Automatic behaviour reactions	High scorer manifestation	Low scorer manifestation
NS Novelty Seeking	Dopamine	Novelty	Anger	Activation or initiation of exploratory activity, temper, active avoidance of frustration	Exploratory, Impulsive, Extravagant, Irritable	Reserved, Deliberate, Thrifty, Stoical
HA Harm Avoidance	Serotonine	Danger	Fear	Inhibition or cessation of behaviours, passive avoidant behaviours	Pessimistic, Fearful, Shy, Fatigable	Optimistic, Daring, Outgoing, Energetic
RD Reward Dependence	Noradrenaline	Reward	Attachment	Maintenance or continuation of ongoing behaviours, dependence on approval of others	Sentimental, Open, Warm, Appreciative	Detached, Reserved, Cold, Independent
PS Persistence	Noradrenaline	Reward	Ambition	Maintenance or continuation of behaviours, perseverance despite frustration	Industrious, Determined, Enthusiastic, Perfectionistic	Inert, Spoiled, Underachiever, Pragmatic

Persistence (PS) refers to the maintenance of adaptive behaviour. It is a temperamental trait that can be defined as perseverance in the face of frustration and fatigue, a determination to reach objectives. This dimension, added after the first (RD), identifies the propensity to make effort without reward. It predicts determination, industriousness, perfectionism, and ambition. An elevated level of PS characterizes a child who is industrious, determined, ambitious, and perfectionist (who is inspired by theoretical considerations). A low level of PS characterizes a child who is lazy, passive, disinterested, and pragmatic (who is inspired by practical considerations).

It can be seen that the four temperaments observed by Cloninger are independently heritable and are dimensional. This means that each person can be born with a different combination of traits and that each of the traits can have a low or high expression. This means that 16 natural temperamental configurations are possible (Table 14.4).

Temperament and Transactional Analysis

The 16 temperamental configurations represent the natural temperamental inclination of the child at birth. In Transactional Analysis, there are numerous concepts developed over time that refer to the overall phenomena described by Cloninger as temperament. The concept of temperament can be seen as broadly correspondent to the concepts of Natural Child, Free Child, Somatic Child in Transactional Analysis (Cornell et al., 2016), which refer to Ego states that are free from parental or environmental influence. In other words, they express their own natural tendencies. Schiff and colleagues (1975) describe the third order structure (B_0, A_0, G_0) present from birth, repository of the individual's motivation, where B_0 represents the reactions reflected onto perceptions, such as internal stimuli (for example, hunger and crying) and external stimuli (such as contact with the breast/suction). English (1971) proposes her theory of subsystems of the Child, subdivided in sleepy/lazy, spunky/courageous, and spooky/scared. Holloway (1977) proposes differentiating the Child along the lines of helpless/impotent, helpful/servient, hurtful/offensive. We can observe that while English refers to substructures present naturally in the Natural Child, Holloway refers to three roles of the Adapted Child. The model of Cloninger suggests an expansion of the concept of Child Ego state and considers 16 potential types of B_0 or Natural/Free/Somatic Child, present from birth, free from parental influence, the develop of which depends on the interaction with familiar and social environment. For the sake of simplicity, we will call this innate temperamental disposition, Temperamental Child. To comprehend the natural temperament of the patient allows us to focus on the conflicts that can be verified with the parental figures during development. Furthermore, identifying which of the 16 types of Temperamental Child the patient corresponds to allows attunement with the deepest inclinations and needs of the patient and not to confuse them with adaptations appearing subsequently so as to deal with environmental requests. Indeed, it is possible to confuse a temperamental trait of the Temperamental Child with an adaptation of the Adapted Child, with an injunction or with

Table 14.4 Configurations of temperamental traits within Temperamental Child

Temperamental traits	Types of Temperamental Child															
	1	2	3	4	5	6	7	8	9	10	11	12	13	14	15	16
NS	+	–	+	+	+	–	+	+	–	–	+	–	+	–	–	–
HA	+	+	–	+	+	–	–	+	+	+	–	–	–	+	–	–
RD	+	+	+	–	+	+	–	–	+	–	+	–	–	–	+	–
PS	+	+	+	+	–	+	+	–	–	+	–	+	–	–	–	–

Note: NS = Novelty Seeking. HA = Harm Avoidance. RD = Reward Dependence. PS = Persistence. + = high scorer. – = low scorer. Numbers from 1 to 16 represents 16 types of Temperamental Child, with any given configuration of temperament traits.

a driver. For example, the stoicism of a person with low novelty seeking can be confused with a "be strong" driver; the recognition of and the search for gratification in relationships by a person with elevated reward dependance can be confused with an "please people" driver; the persistence in the absence of gratification in a person with elevated persistence can be confused with a "try hard" driver. At the same time, it is possible to confuse a temperamental trait with an injunction. For example, stoicism and reservedness in a person with low novelty seeking can be confused with a "don't be close" injunction or a "don't feel" injunction.

The genetic and temperamental impasses according to Transactional Analysis

The concept of the impasse in Transactional Analysis indicates a condition of being blocked due to the contraposition of two opposing forces, generally between the need of the Child and the prohibition of the Parent. Goulding and Goulding (1976) have described three degrees of impasse:

1   First-type impasse describes a structural conflict between a parental message introjected in the Parent Ego state (G_3) that is unconsciously followed by the Child of the patient (A_1), even though it does not satisfy a need or a desire present in the Child Ego state (B_1). The conflict is between self and object (Ego–You). Typically, this kind of impasse corresponds to the verbal, introjected counter-injunctions that generate drivers and counterscript, and which are accessible at the verbal, cognitive, conscious, and preconscious level.

2   Second-type impasse describes a structural conflict between a non-verbal prohibition introjected into the Child Ego state (G_1), unconsciously followed by the Child of the patient (A_1) against the need of the Child (B_1). Also in this case, the conflict is between self and object (Ego–You), however, they are more archaic selves and objects, often not completely differentiated one from another, where the fantasies and emotions of the child are confused with the messages that are really sent from the parent. Typically, it is an impasse between non-verbal injunctions that generate script decisions. They are accessible, with greater difficulty, at the verbal, emotional, preconscious, and unconscious level.

3   Third-type impasse describes a functional conflict inside the Adult in the Child (A_1), between the Natural Child (inside A_1) and the Adapted Child (inside A_1). In this situation, the conflict is perceived by different parts of self (Ego–Ego), in as much as it cannot be traced back to an external object, because the injunction was sent before the differentiation between self and object. Typically, it is an impasse between natural dispositions and non-verbal injunctions, which emerge at an affective and a mostly somatic level, a deeply unconscious level.

Mellor (1980) proposes a "structuralist" revision of Goulding and Goulding's "functionalist" model. The impasses are described as conflicts occurring at different evolutionary levels of the child's development. The three degrees of impasse, therefore, can always be conceptualized as conflicts between Child and Parent in different developmental phases. We therefore have a third-degree impasse P_0-C_0 (protocol), second-degree impasse P_1-C_1 (script), and first-degree impasse P_2-C_2 (counter-script).

Mellor's model underlines the intersubjective and relational aspect of impasse which can be understood as the reactivation of a dialogue between needs of the child and the unattuned responses of the social and familial environment, in various developmental moments: therefore, during an impasse there can be a reactivation of the needs of the Child and relative Parent unattuned responses obtained at one year (B_0-G_0), three years (B_1-G_1), or six years (B_2-G_2).

Considering Cloninger's model, we can conceptualize the conflicts that derive from the unsuccessful attunement between the temperamental needs of the child and the nurturing relational environment as an impasse in Transactional Analysis. Therefore, we propose the definition of temperamental impasses as being those third-degree impasses that express the conflict between the genetically determined temperament of the child and the attunement of the nurturing environment with the child's genetic needs. Consideration of which of the 16 temperaments of the Temperamental Child (B_0) best describes a patient favours the attunement with the Child's most archaic needs and avoids involuntary retraumatizing the expression of temperamental needs. The task of the therapist is to identify the needs and provide attuned responses, or in other words, the authorizations, the permissions, and the protection that were missing in the unattuned environmental responses.

There is also a deeper level of impasse, in which the conflict is between different natural temperamental dispositions (Ego–Ego). We can note the difference with the third-degree impasses described by Goulding and Goulding, which while being an Ego–Ego type of impasse, they attribute one of the poles of conflict to the Adapted Child, while in our case both of the poles of conflict belong to the Natural Child. We also note the difference with third-degree conflicts described by Mellor, where the conflict is Ego–You. For this type of conflict, and to differentiate them from the third type of impasse (Ego–Ego, Natural Child/Adapted Child within A_1) or third-degree (Ego–You, G_0/B_0), we propose the definition of genetic impasse, or of fourth-degree impasse (Ego–Ego, Temperamental Child / Temperamental Child). For example, it might be that a person has elevated novelty seeking and elevated harm avoidance. In this case, the child has a natural tendency to be both explorative, impulsive, and irritable, and to be fearful in the face of the stimuli. The tendency to explore can easily conflict with the fear and manifest itself through irritative behaviours. If we add an elevated level of reward dependence, that is, the tendency to depend on attachment, we have the description of a "difficult" child who continually seeks out the parent to explore and to be reassured, and who gets irritated impulsively when their intense needs for exploration, reassurance, and attachment are not sustained. The genetic impasses, in as much as they express the natural disposition of the child, cannot be resolved like a conflict: genetics cannot be modified, but they can be comprehended and integrated rather than denied and split off. Probably, the genetic expression can be modulated through the ample modulatory connections of the semantic system when the various aspects of temperament are comprehended and integrated, while the modulation might be less if the awareness of one's own temperamental aspects remains split and denied. When we are treating a child with this type of temperament, the interventions can help the parents to understand the complex and contrasting temperamental dispositions of the child and to support the development of self-reassurance in order to favour future explorations. If, however, we are treating an adult who has this sort of temperament as a child, then attention should be shifted to recognizing the suffering derived from the lack of attunement. For example, highlighting the difficulty of the parents to recognize their natural dispositions and the pain provoked. When the patients feel their own genetic impasses to be recognized, they tend to feel understood and they develop a better therapeutic alliance thereby improving self-esteem and the sense of identity.

Conclusions

ITAP is an intense therapeutic approach that focuses on impulses, the anxiety that they activate, and consequential defences, in both the relational episodes of the present life of the patient and in the scenic episodes displayed with the therapist, as well as in the archaic episodes in the past life of the patient.

Its strength consists in guiding the clinician and identifying the conflicts that have developed, right from the start of life, between the patients' temperamental dispositions in conflict between themselves (genetic impasses) and with the environment (temperamental impasses), then looking back over the developmental course of the person and identifying the conflicts that have then occurred, leading to defence mechanisms and to the formation of the structure of the personality.

In this chapter, we have indicated which disorders and psychopathological frameworks are suitable for ITAP. We have shown how to integrate the diagnosis of mental disorders (signs and symptoms) with the diagnosis of level of mental functioning and personality type. We have proposed a list of essential basic mental functions necessary for good mental functioning, suggesting that in cases of structural deficit the psychotherapist has to focus first on the structure and then on the analysis of conflicts through the ITAP triangles.

We have provided a summary of the nuclear conflicts underlying the different frameworks of personality proposed by the PDM-2 and how to conceptualize them with the use of the ITAP intrapsychic triangles.

Lastly, we have presented an integration between Transactional Analysis and Cloninger's model that allows the conceptualization of the interaction between relational environment and genetic predispositions as conflicts, and how these interactions influence first temperament and then later personality.

We expect that present and future studies concerning the efficacy of ITAP will validate the diagnostic suggestions reported here and favour the evolution of the intervention techniques, in a virtuous cycle between theory, treatment, and research.

Notes

1 This chapter was written by Enrico Benelli.
2 For a list of CMD consult the site http://apps.who.int/iris/bitstream/10665/254610/1/WHO-MSD-MER-2017.2-eng.pdf
3 To see the systematic reviews on the efficacy of CMD treatment see the Cochrane site: http://cmd.cochrane.org

References

American Psychiatric Association. (2013). *Diagnostic and Statistical Manual of Mental Disorders, Fifth Edition (DSM-5)*. Washington, DC: APA.

Berne, E. (1961). *Transactional Analysis in Psychotherapy: A Systematic Individual and Social Psychiatry*. New York: Grove Press.

Cloninger, C. R., Svrakic, D. M., & Przybeck, T. R. (1993). A psychobiological model of temperament and character. *Archives of General Psychiatry*, 50(12): 975–970. doi:10.1001/archpsyc.1993.01820240059008. PMID 8250684.

Cornell, W. F., de Graaf, A., Newton, T., & Thunnissen, M. (2016). *Into TA: A Comprehensive Textbook on Transactional Analysis*. London: Karnac.

English, F. (1971). The substitution factor: Rackets and real feelings. *Transactional Analysis Journal*, 1(4): 225–230.

Goulding, R., & Goulding, M. (1976). Injunctions, decisions, and redecisions. *Transactional Analysis Journal*, 6(1): 41–48.

Holloway, W. H. (1977). Transactional analysis: An integrative view. In G. Barnes (Ed.), *Transactional Analysis after Berne*. New York: Harper's College Press.

Lingiardi, V., & McWilliams, N. (Eds.) (2017). *Psychodynamic Diagnostic Manual, 2nd Ed. (PDM-2)*. New York: Guilford Press.

McWilliams (1994). *Psychoanalytic Diagnosis: Understanding Personality Structure in the Clinical Process*. New York, London: The Guilford Press.

Mellor, K. (1980). Impasses: A developmental and structural understanding. *Transactional Analysis Journal*, 10(3): 213–222.

OPD Task Force (Eds.) (2008). *Operationalized Psychodynamic Diagnosis OPD-2*. Goettingen: Hogrefe & Huber Publishers.

PDM Task Force (2006). *Psychodynamic Diagnostic Manual (PDM)*. Silver Spring, MD: Alliance of Psychoanalytic Organizations.

Schiff, J. L., Schiff, A. W., Mellor, K., Schiff, E., Schiff, S., Richman, D., Fishman, J., Wolz, L., . . . & Momb, D. (1975). *The Cathexis Reader: Transactional Analysis Treatment of Psychosis*. New York: Harper and Row.

Shedler, J., & Westen, D. (2010). The Shedler-Westen assessment procedure: Making personality diagnosis clinically meaningful. In J. F. Clarkin, P. Fonagy, & G. O. Gabbard (Eds.), *Psychodynamic Psychotherapy for Personality Disorders* (pp. 125–161). Washington, DC: American Psychiatric Publishing.

World Health Organization. (2010). *The ICD-10 Classification of Mental and Behavioural Disorders: Clinical Descriptions and Diagnostic Guidelines*. Geneva: World Health Organization.

Appendix 1
Essential glossary of Transactional Analysis (TA)

Adapted Child: acts under the influence of the parents, as well as models, references, and social rules.

Adult: Ego state that processes data coming from the here-and-now; an autonomous collection of feelings, attitudes, and behavioural models connected and communicating with the present reality (Novellino, 2014).

Adult in the Child (little professor): in structural analysis it is present in the intuitive function, understood as the child's strategy during development in order to examine and comprehend the surrounding reality.

Agitation: passive behaviour that leads the person to utilize the energy to complete repetitive activities without them being useful in modifying or resolving the problematic situation.

Autonomy: ultimate objective of Transactional Analysis treatment. It takes shape through recovery, consolidation, and construction of three fundamental capacities: awareness, spontaneity, and intimacy.

Awareness: one of three foundational elements of autonomy. In line with Berne, we can affirm that we are dealing with the capacity for creating an efficacious distinction between internal and external worlds (Berne, 1964, 1966). For Stewart and Jones (1987), it is the capacity to instigate pure impressions derived from the senses, without interpretation.

Child: Ego state that includes a collection of feelings, thoughts, and behavioural models that originate from our childhood. From a functional point of view, they can be divided into:

- Free: acts in the expression of emotions and desires by manifesting autonomous forms of behaviour, free from the dictates of the Parent and from the rules of society.
- Rebel: acts in opposition (that is, in rebellion) to rules and models, instead of following them.
- Adapted: acts according to the influence of the Parent, as well as according to models of reference and of social rules.

Child in the Child: within the Child (C_2) it is present as a Somatic Child (C_1), and represents all the stored memories of experiences coming from early stages of development (Stuart & Joines, 1987).

Contamination: form of pathology identified by Berne in which content coming from the Child or from the Parent is erroneously considered to come from the Adult, who therefore perceives it as being Ego syntonic (Moiso & Novellino, 1982).

Contract: explicit bilateral agreement between patient and therapist on the objectives, the stages, and the modalities of the therapy (Novellino, 2014; Woollams & Brown, 1978).

Diagnosis: Berne defines it as a judgement formulated by a receiver in relation to a sender, and he identifies four stages (Berne, 1972; Novellino, 2014):

- Behavioural: through direct observation of the subject
- Social: through the Ego state that is stimulated in the interlocutor it is possible to hypothesize which Ego state the send of the communication is in
- Historical: through the memory of events it is possible to recognize the Ego state
- Phenomenological: through the analysis of that which is relived in the here-and-now, it is possible to recognize the Ego state

Discounting: internal psychological mechanism through which a subject minimizes or ignores aspects of themselves, of others, or of the real situation which they have to deal with. In this way, the person maintains and reinforces the script, continuing or starting relationships based on symbiosis. It is possible to discount the very existence of a problem, its importance, the possibility to change the problem itself, or the possibility of reacting differently.

Doing nothing: one of the four passive behaviours in which energy present in the person, rather than being channelled into the resolution of the problem, is utilized in the inhibition of the reactions (Schiff et al., 1975).

Driver: behavioural sequence derived from counter-script messages originating from the Parent of the person, who is convinced that they can only be OK if they obey such messages. The main five drives are: Be perfect, Be strong, Try Hard, Please People, Hurry Up.

Ego state: fundamental concept of Transactional Analysis. Originally derived from studies conducted by Penfield, who managed to demonstrate, in subjects with epilepsy, that memories can be stored as Ego states and that, furthermore, it is possible to demonstrate that two Ego states can be present simultaneously as distinct and separate psychological entities. It was further defined by Weiss who, confirming the findings of Penfield, underlined how Ego states from previous stages remain, potentially, within the personality structure. Furthermore, it was described by Federn who thinks of psychological reality as being based on complete and distinct Ego states (Berne, 1958, 1966; Moiso & Novellino, 1982; Novellino, 2014). We can define it synthetically as being a uniform collection of emotions and experiences directly correlated with a corresponding uniform schema of behaviour.

Excluder (Ego state): pathological mechanism whereby one Ego state holds all of the free energy, while the other two, in that moment, are excluded.

Exclusion (Ego state):   pathological mechanism whereby one or two Ego states are de-energized.

Functional analysis (of the Ego states):   analysis of the processes concerning the dynamics of relational and behavioural expression (Moiso & Novellino, 1982) and the analysis of the modalities of use of the Ego states.

Game (psychological):   unconscious, dysfunctional, relational modality that is based on the exchange of transactions that constitute a process with a predictable course that leads to the maintenance of script through a payoff for both the players (Berne, 1964). They are subdivided according to the degree of intensity (first degree: mild, second degree: moderate, third degree: extreme or dangerous).

Impasse: intrapsychic conflict or point of resistance between Ego states resulting from a script decision (Novellino, 2014).

Incapacitation: one of four passive behaviours in which there are discharges of energy that has been accumulated by the person, in the absence of thoughts, through passivity (for example, headaches, fainting, and so on) (Schiff et al., 1975).

Injunctions: preverbal or non-verbal negative script messages from the Child of the subject, who responds through a script decision (Berne, 1972). There are 11 main injunctions (Goulding, 1979): don't, don't exist, don't be close, don't be important, don't be a child, don't grow, don't make it, don't be you, don't be well, don't be sane, don't belong.

Integrated Adult: Adult who adopts as their own the positive peculiarities originating from the Child and from the Parent. Good integration between Ego states favours good functioning of the person, whose psychic energy "flows" between them.

Intimacy: one of the three foundations of autonomy. It is based on the capacity of the person to remain in a relationship where the expression of emotions, needs, and authentic desires is allowed and favour.

OKness: to be ok, to feel ok. One of Berne's main philosophies by which each human being is born with equal value and dignity.

Overadaptation: one of four passive behaviours in which the person accepts objectives and modalities established by others, without thinking of their value or of their personal meaning, and without being aware of their own objectives and modalities (Schiff et al., 1975).

Parent: Ego state that includes feelings, thoughts, and behavioural models assimilated from parental figures (Novellino, 2014). From the functional point of view there is a division between:

- Affective: that provides protection, affection, it takes care or supports. It can be positive if it is able to give permission, or negative if it becomes overprotective thereby limiting liberty.
- Normative: has characteristics of control regarding models of rules; it can represent a form of channelling or criticism. It can be positive if it is able to give protection, negative if it excessively limits freedom of personal expression or if it is undermining.

Parent in the Child (P1): in the second degree structure, it represents all the fantastical and magic versions of the Child in childhood, as opposed considering the messages received from parental figures (Stuart & Joines, 1987).

Passive behaviour: modality of behaviour that leads to the presence of discounting and that does not lead the individual to really resolve the problem, instead leading to the manipulation of the environment so it can act effectively on the subject's behalf. There are four passive behaviours: doing nothing, overadaptation, agitation, incapacitation or violence.

Passivity: internal or external actions enacted so as to avoid acting autonomously with the aim of fulfilling one's own needs or stimuli, reaching one's own predefined goals (Schiff et al., 1975).

Permissions: positive parental messages emitted from the Child of the parental figure and aimed at the Child of the subject. One of the three Ps, together with protection and potency: a therapeutic instrument through which the professional helps the patient to allow themself to instigate an emotion that was not originally allowed by the parental figure.

Potency: a therapeutic instrument through which the professional opposes the life script of the patient and all their limiting derivatives through strong, determined, stable, coherent, attentive, and efficacious presence.

Protection: a therapeutic instrument through which the professional openly acts for the wellbeing of the patient, through care and interest, conveying a sense of safety in the patient (Woollams & Brown, 1978).

Racket emotions: emotions linked to a script that substitutes a natural emotion that has been repressed and disapproved by the nurturing environment. The emotion can be read as the stereotyped, artificial, and repetition expression of an unauthentic feeling and generate doubts regarding its authenticity in the interlocutor (English, 1976).

Redecision: a process through which it is possible to substitute an early limiting script decision with a new decision that allows the individual to reach a higher level of wellbeing and that takes in consideration the resources present in the environment and all those adult resources of the person.

Script system: a dynamic, self-reinforcing, and distorted mechanism, made up of thoughts, emotions, and behaviours maintained by people linked to their own script.

Spontaneity: one of the three foundations of autonomy. The capacity to freely express emotions, thoughts, and actions in harmony with the here and now.

Structural analysis (of the Ego states): analysis of the contents present within the Ego states.

Structural pathology: see contamination, excluder, and exclusion.

Symbiosis: a relationship in which two or more people behave as if they are psychologically only one person, and in which no one completely energizes all of their own Ego states (Schiff et al., 1975).

Thought disorders: processes that make up part of the mechanism of redefinition (Schiff et al., 1975), which make thoughts ineffective:

* Overdetailing: overload of information that leads to confusion
* Overgeneralization: excessively wide definition of the problem that consequently becomes impossible to deal with and/or impossible to resolve through logic

Transaction: minimal and foundational unit of social communication composed of a transactional stimulus and a response. There can be different typologies of transactions (Berne, 1961, 1972; Novellino, 2014; Stuart & Joines, 1987; Woollams & Brown, 1978):

* Carom: ulterior transaction, the psychological component of which is aimed at a third person (Woollams & Brown, 1978).
* Angular: ulterior transaction that involves three Ego states.
* Complementary: in which the communicative vectors are parallel and the same Ego state that is addressed is the same one that responds.
* Gallows: laugh or smile that accompanies a discounting aimed at the self or another person.
* Redefinition: occurs when a person discounts an aspect of the ongoing communication and shifts the problem. They divide themselves in tangential transactions when the people involved consider different problems or different aspects of the same problem or blocking when the intention is not to deal with the meaning originally contained within the communication.
* Duplicate transactions: communication that involves the four Ego states at the same time.
* Crossed: in which the four communicative vectors are not parallel and the Ego state which the communication is aimed at is not the same as the one that responds.
* Ulterior: a communication composed simultaneously of an explicit message and an implicit message.

Transactional analysis: system of psychotherapy as well as theory of psychological development. It can be subdivided into four principal areas: structural analysis, which studies the intrapsychic processes of the person; analysis of transactions, which looks at the modalities with which human beings enter in relationships with each other; the analysis of psychological Games, which aims to understand the particular modalities of distorted communication that ends up reinforcing the psychopathology of the person; script analysis, which deals with describing how human beings construct and maintain their own convictions regarding themselves, others, and the world, constructing a life plan and an operational plan of action (Moiso & Novellino, 1982).

Violence: one of four passive behaviours in which the person discharges energy accumulated previously through passivity. The subject physically attacks people or things without really acting to resolve the problem, rather they force the environment to resolve the problem for them.

References

Allen J. R., & Allen, B. A. (1991). Concepts of transference: A critique, a tipology, an alternative hypothesis and some proposals. *Transactional Analysis Journal, TAJ*, 21(2): 77–92.

Baruh, L. (2010). Prolegolemi alla diagnosi in Psicoterapia Intensiva Breve Dinamico-Esperienziale (PIBD-E) [Prolegomena to diagnosis in brief dynamic-experiential brief intensive psychotherapy]. *Psyche Nuova*, 2010: 117–121.

Berne, E. (1955). *Intuition and Ego States*. San Francisco: TA Press.

Berne, E. (1961). *Transactional Analysis in Psychotherapy*. New York: Grove Press.

Berne, E. (1964). *Games People Play*. New York: Grow Press.

Berne, E. (1966). *Principles of Group Treatment*. Menlo Park, CA: Shea Books.

Berne, E. (1972). *What Do You Say After You Say Hello?* London: Corgi.

Bollas, C. (1987). *The Shadow of the Object*. London: Free Association Books.

Clarkson, P. (1992). *Transactional Analysis Psychotherapy*. London: Routledge.

Cornell, W. F. (2006). Another perspective on the therapist's stance. *The Script*, 36(3): 4.

English, F. (1976). *Analyse transactionelle et émotions [Transactional Analysis and Emotions]*. Paris: Desclée de Brouwer.

Erskine, R. G. (1991). Transference and transactions: Critique from an intrapsychic and integrative perspective. *Transactional Analysis Journal*, 21(2): 63–76.

Erskine, R. G. (2010). *Life Scripts: A Transactional Analysis of Unconscious Relational Patterns*. London: Karnac.

Erskine, R. G., & Zalcman, M. (1979). The racket system: A model for racket analysis. *Transactional Analysis Journal*, 9(1): 51–59.

Favasuli, M. A. (2010). La rappresentazione – forme e contenuti della mente [Representation – Forms and Contents of the Mind]. *Corpo Narrante*, 2: 1–17.

Goulding, M. M., & Goulding, R. L. (1979). *Changing Lives Through Redecision Therapy*. New York: Grove Press.

Gregoire, J. (2007). *Les orientations récentes de l'analyse transactionelle [The Recent Orientations of Transactional Analysis]*. Lyon: Les Éditions d'Analyse Transactionelle.

Hargaden, H., & Sills, C. (2002). *Transactional Analysis – A Relational Perspective*. London: Psychology Press, Taylor & Francis Group.

Klein, M. (1932). *The Psychoanalysis of Children*. London: Vintage Publishers.

Menninger, K. (1958). *Theory of Psychoanalytic Technique*. New York: Basic Books.

Moiso, C. M. (1985). Ego states and transference. *Transactional Analysis Journal*, 15(3): 194–201.

Moiso, C. M., & Novellino, M. (1982). *Stati dell'Io [Ego States]*. Roma: Astrolabio.

Novellino, M. (2014). *Dizionario Didattico di Analisi Transazionale [Dydactic Dictionary of Transactional Analysis]*. Roma: Astrolabio.

Schiff, J. L., Schiff, A. W., Mellor, K., Schiff, E., Schiff, S., Richman, D., Fishman, J., Wolz, L., Fishman, C., & Momb, D. (1975). *The Cathexis Reader: Transactional Analysis Treatment of Psychosis*. New York: Harper and Row.

Stuart, I., & Joines, V. (1987). *TA Today: A New Introduction to Transactional Analysis* (2nd edn.). Nottingham: Lifespace.

Vygotskij, L. S. (1978). *Mind in Society: Development of Higher Psychological Processes.* Cambridge, MA: Harvard University Press.

Winnicott, D. W. (1953). Transitional objects and transitional phenomena: A study of the first not-me possession. *The International Journal of Psychoanalysis*, 34(2): 89–97.

Winnicott, D. W. (1967). Mirror-role of the mother and family in child development. In P. Lomas (Ed.), *The Predicament of the Family: A Psycho-analytical Symposium*. London: Hogarth Press.

Woollams, S., & Brown, M. (1978). *Transactional Analysis*. Dexter: Huron Valley Institute.

Index

Page numbers in *italic* indicate figures and in **bold** indicate tables on the corresponding pages.